Ohr Nissan Talmud Center, Inc.

Spreading *Torah* Throughout the World!

With the strong support of world-renowned *Torah* leaders, **Ohr Nissan Talmud Center, Inc.** has been devoted to training educators and scholars in the finest tradition of *Sefaradi* Jewry for more than twenty years.

In the words of Rabbi Aharon Feldman שליט״א, dean of Ner Israel Rabbinical College, "Virtually every institution which provides for the spiritual needs of Iranian Jewry in the United States is staffed by former members of **Ohr Nissan Talmud Center, Inc.**"

Ohr Nissan Talmud Center, Inc. provides scholar-ships to more than two dozen highly dedicated *Torah* scho-lars who study full-time with the goal of gaining the know-ledge necessary to strengthen and perpetuate the *Sefaradi* heritage.

We appreciate your generous support. Please help us continue our vital work by sending in your tax deductible contribution today.

Ohr Nissan Talmud Center, Inc.
400 Mount Wilson Lane
Baltimore, MD 21208
(410) 340-4496

בס"ד
ראשית חכמה יראת ה'

הגדה טוב להודות

THE
TOV LEHODOTH
HAGGADAH

Written by
Yehuda Cahn

Illustrated by
Elka Aviva Cahn

VOLUME I

"It is good to give thanks to
Hashem" — Psalms 92:2

Published by:

OHR NISSAN TALMUD CENTER, INC.
400 Mount Wilson Lane
Baltimore, MD 21208

(410) 340-4496

ISBN: 0-9707757-8-4

Printed in the United States of America

לעלוי נשמות

אברהם יהודה בן יוסף ז״ל

עלקא בת בער הירש ז״ל

In loving memory of

LOUIS AND ELLA
ELLISON

By the Ellison Family

תהי נשמתם צרורה בצרור החיים

ACKNOWLEDGMENTS

I would like to thank Rabbi Moshe Heinemann שליט״א, one of the foremost *Torah* scholars of our generation, for taking time from his busy schedule to read my manuscript and give me a detailed critique which I used to produce the final work.

I would also like to thank my wife, Geoula, for editing and correcting the Hebrew instructions and for her continuing support of all my endeavors.

My daughter, Sarah Chaya, proofread the English text and offered constructive comments on it. Shlomo Menchel and Rason Gholian proofread the Hebrew text of the *Haggadah*.

Mrs. Chaya Greenwald, Dr. David Levy, and Sarah Chaya Cahn helped with typing the manuscript.

-- Yehuda Cahn

ABOUT THE AUTHOR

Yehuda Cahn holds a Masters degree from Ner Israel Rabbinical College and degrees from Columbia University and the University of Maryland School of Law. He has rabbinic ordination from Rabbi Moshe Heinemann שליט״א.

Other books by Yehuda Cahn include *Torah from Jerusalem* — translations of the *Aggadoth* of the Jerusalem *Talmud* with commentary; *Wake up to the New Year* — stories and insights for the *Yamim Noraim*; *The Power of Speech: Chassidic Insights into Lashon Hara*; and *An Ancient Tale of Rags and Riches* — a novel for young people set in the time of the Second Temple.

ENDORSEMENT OF
RABBI MOSHE HEINEMANN שליט״א

RABBI MOSHE HEINEMANN
6109 Gist Avenue
Baltimore, MD 21215
Tel. (410) 358-9828
Fax. (410) 358-9838

משה היינעמאן
אב״ד ק״ק אגודת ישראל
באלטימאר
טל. 764-7778 (410)
פקס 764-8878 (410)

בס״ד

באתי בשורות אלו להגיד לאדם ישרו ה״ה ר' יהודה קאן שליט״א המפורסם
בחיבוריו "תורה מירושלים' ב״ח על אגדות הירושלי זרעים ושאר חיבורים וענשו
הניף ידו שנית להוציא לאור הגדה של פסח "טוב להודות" שבו מצאר דיני
הסדר עם פרושיס וביאורים חדשיס על ההגדה ועל עניני גאולה. ההגדה
הוא לפי מנהג האשכנזים וגם כפי מנהג הספרדים בסדר נכון ובהבנה ישרה.
יהי רצון שחפץ ד' בידו יצלח וימצא פרי עמלו חן בעיני כל ישראל הקטנים עס
הגדולים.

ועל זאת באתי עה״ח ביום ... בשבת לסדר ויצא פרח וינץ ציץ ויגמל שקדיס שמונה
ועשרים יום לחדש סיון שנת חמשת אלפים ושבע מאות ושבים ושבע לבריאת עולם.

מצה בהחר ... ברוך גדליה למשפחת היינעמאן החונף ומף באלטימאר

TABLE OF CONTENTS

THE *HAGGADAH*

DIVREI TORAH

PARABLES

APPENDICES

THE SEARCH
FOR LEAVEN

סֵדֶר בְּדִיקַת חָמֵץ

קוֹדֶם שֶׁיַּתְחִיל לִבְדּוֹק יֹאמַר:

בָּרוּךְ אַתָּה יְיָ אֱלֹהֵינוּ מֶלֶךְ הָעוֹלָם אֲשֶׁר קִדְּשָׁנוּ בְּמִצְוֹתָיו וְצִוָּנוּ עַל בִּעוּר חָמֵץ.

כְּשֶׁגּוֹמֵר אֶת הַבְּדִיקָה אוֹמֵר:

כָּל חֲמִירָא וַחֲמִיעָא דְּאִכָּא בִרְשׁוּתִי דְּלָא חֲמִיתֵּיהּ וּדְלָא בְעַרְתֵּהּ וּדְלָא יְדַעְנָא לֵיהּ לִבָּטֵל וְלֶהֱוֵי הֶפְקֵר כְּעַפְרָא דְאַרְעָא.

לְאַחַר שְׂרִיפַת הֶחָמֵץ יֹאמַר:

כָּל חֲמִירָא וַחֲמִיעָא דְּאִכָּא בִרְשׁוּתִי דַּחֲזִתֵּהּ וּדְלָא חֲזִתֵּהּ דְּבִעַרְתֵּהּ וּדְלָא בְעַרְתֵּהּ לִבָּטֵל וְלֶהֱוֵי הֶפְקֵר כְּעַפְרָא דְאַרְעָא.

Before commencing the search, say this:

Blessed are You, *Hashem,* our God, King of the Universe, Who sanctified us with His commandments and commanded us concerning removal of leaven.[1]

After completing the search, say this: (Some repeat it three times.)

All leaven and sourdough which is in my domain which I did not see, or did not remove, or did not know about, should be nullified and ownerless like the dust of the earth.

After destroying the leaven in the morning, one should say the following. (Some repeat it three times.)

All leaven and sourdough which is in my domain which I saw or did not see, which I removed or did not remove, should be nullified and ownerless like the dust of the earth.

---

[1]   Although the leaven is not actually destroyed until the morning of Passover eve, the sages formulated the blessing this way because searching for leaven counts as the beginning of its elimination (*Kaf Hachaim* and *Mishnah Berurah* on *Shulchan Aruch, Orach Chaim* 432:1).

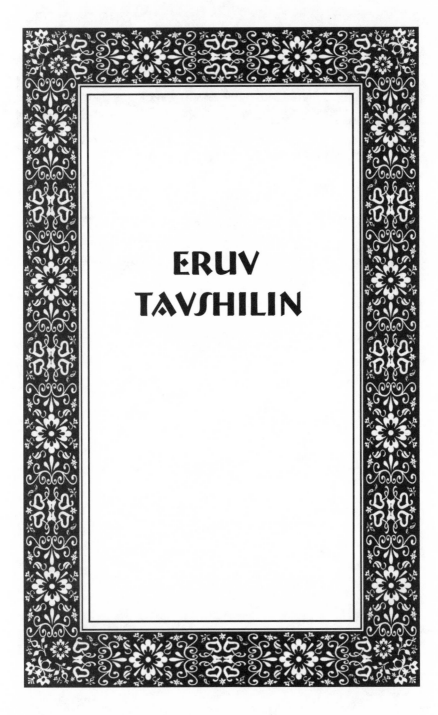

ERUV
TAVSHILIN

סֵדֶר עֵרוּב תַּבְשִׁילִין

אסור לבשל אוכל לשבת ביום טוב שחל בערב שבת אלא אם כן מכינים ערוב תבשילין
בערב יום טוב.   לכן בחוץ לארץ כאשר חל חג הפסח ביום חמישי חייבים להניח ערוב
תבשילין ביום רביעי קודם התחלת החג.   לוקחים מצה יחד עם לפחות כזית של איזה
תבשיל ואומרים:

בָּרוּךְ אַתָּה יְיָ אֱלֹהֵינוּ מֶלֶךְ הָעוֹלָם אֲשֶׁר קִדְּשָׁנוּ בְּמִצְוֹתָיו וְצִוָּנוּ עַל
מִצְוַת עֵרוּב.

בְּדֵין עֵרוּבָא יְהֵא שָׁרֵא לָנָא לְאֲפוּיֵי וּלְבַשּׁוּלֵי וּלְאַטְמוּנֵי וּלְאַדְלוּקֵי
שְׁרָגָא וּלְתַקָּנָא וּלְמֶעְבַּד כָּל צָרְכָנָא מִיּוֹמָא טָבָא לְשַׁבַּתָּא לָנָא וּלְכָל
יִשְׂרָאֵל הַדָּרִים בָּעִיר הַזֹּאת.

When a holiday falls on a Friday, one may not cook food for the Sabbath without first making an *Eruv Tavshilin* before the holiday starts. When Passover falls on a Thursday in places where two days are observed, the *Eruv Tavshilin* should be prepared on Wednesday afternoon. One takes a piece of *Matzah* together with at least an olive's bulk of cooked food — such as a boiled egg, meat, or fish — and recites the following:

Blessed are You, *Hashem*, our God, King of the Universe, Who sanctified us with His commandments and commanded us concerning the commandment of *Eruv*.

With this *Eruv* it should be permitted for us to bake, to cook, to insulate, to light candles, to prepare [for the Sabbath], and to perform any task we need on the holiday for the Sabbath both for ourselves and for any Jews who dwell in this town.

ORGANIZING
THE
SEDER PLATE

There are several different customs for arranging the *Seder* plate. Ideally, each person should follow the custom of his family. Below is an illustration of the arrangement of the *Seder* plate according to the custom of the *Arizal*.

The three *Matzoth* represent the three spiritual worlds of Wisdom, Understanding, and Knowledge. Each item on the *Seder* plate also represents a spiritual world.

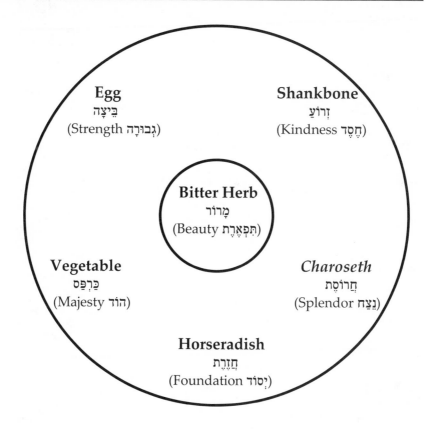

Egg
בֵּיצָה
(Strength גְּבוּרָה)

Shankbone
זְרוֹעַ
(Kindness חֶסֶד)

Bitter Herb
מָרוֹר
(Beauty תִּפְאֶרֶת)

Vegetable
כַּרְפַּס
(Majesty הוֹד)

Charoseth
חֲרוֹסֶת
(Splendor נֶצַח)

Horseradish
חֲזֶרֶת
(Foundation יְסוֹד)

The plate itself represents the tenth spiritual realm — Kingship (מַלְכוּת).[2]

---

[2] *Be'er Heitev* on *Shulchan Aruch, Orach Chaim* 473:4.

This is an illustration of the arrangement of the *Seder* plate according to the custom of the *Vilna Gaon*.

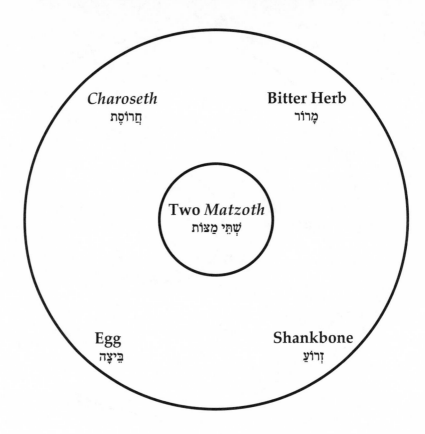

This is an illustration of the arrangement of the *Seder* plate according to the custom of the *Rama*.

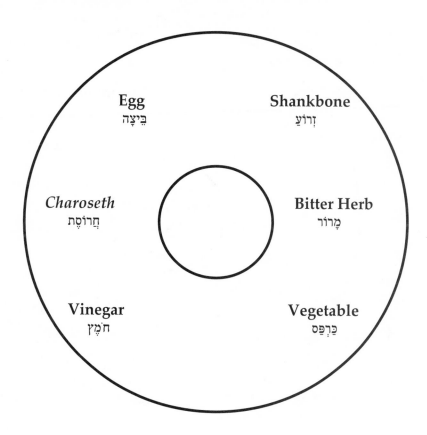

Egg
בֵּיצָה

Shankbone
זְרוֹעַ

Charoseth
חֲרוֹסֶת

Bitter Herb
מָרוֹר

Vinegar
חֹמֶץ

Vegetable
כַּרְפַּס

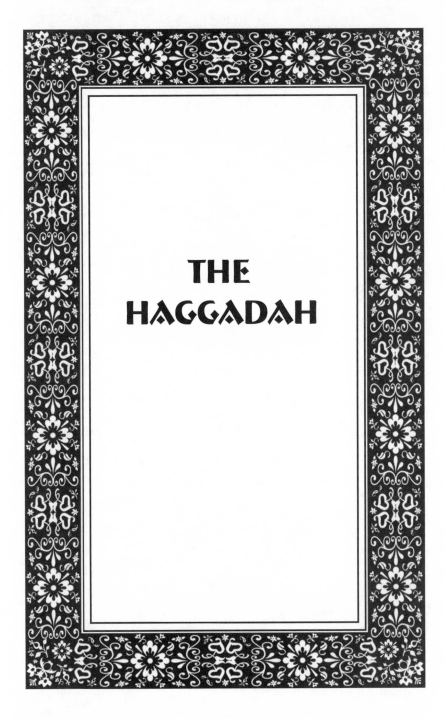

THE
HAGGADAH

מתחילים את סדר ליל פסח באמירת סימני הסדר:

🔲 קַדֵּשׁ

🔲 וּרְחַץ

🔲 כַּרְפַּס

🔲 יַחַץ

🔲 מַגִּיד

🔲 רָחְצָה

🔲 מוֹצִיא

🔲 מַצָּה

🔲 מָרוֹר

🔲 כּוֹרֵךְ

🔲 שֻׁלְחָן עוֹרֵךְ

🔲 צָפוּן

🔲 בָּרֵךְ

🔲 הַלֵּל

🔲 נִרְצָה

One should recite the fifteen elements of the *Seder* service before beginning. This helps orient the participants by reminding them of what they will be doing.[3]

- KIDDUSH
- WASHING
- VEGETABLE
- SPLITTING
- TELLING
- WASHING
- BLESSING FOR BREAD
- MATZAH
- MAROR
- COMBINATION
- SET TABLE
- AFIKOMAN
- GRACE
- HALLEL
- CONCLUSION

---

[3] In addition, the deliberate order of the *Seder* reminds us that the events of Passover were not random. *Hashem* guided them to produce the result He desired (*Chiddushei Harim Al Hatorah*, citing *Maharal*; *Shem Mishmuel*).

⬖ קַדֵּשׁ

ממלאים כוס לכל אחד מן המסובים ויש נוהגים למלאות כוס נוספת הנקרא "כוס של
אליהו" ויש שממתינים למלאות את הכוס של אליהו ב"שְׁפֹךְ חֲמָתְךָ."

בשבת מתחילים כאן:

(בלחש:) וַיְהִי עֶרֶב וַיְהִי בֹקֶר

יוֹם הַשִּׁשִּׁי. וַיְכֻלּוּ הַשָּׁמַיִם וְהָאָרֶץ וְכָל צְבָאָם. וַיְכַל אֱלֹהִים בַּיּוֹם
הַשְּׁבִיעִי מְלַאכְתּוֹ אֲשֶׁר עָשָׂה וַיִּשְׁבֹּת בַּיּוֹם הַשְּׁבִיעִי מִכָּל מְלַאכְתּוֹ
אֲשֶׁר עָשָׂה. וַיְבָרֶךְ אֱלֹהִים אֶת יוֹם הַשְּׁבִיעִי וַיְקַדֵּשׁ אֹתוֹ כִּי בוֹ שָׁבַת
מִכָּל מְלַאכְתּוֹ אֲשֶׁר בָּרָא אֱלֹהִים לַעֲשׂוֹת.

בשאר ימי השבוע מתחילים כאן:

סַבְרִי מָרָנָן וְרַבָּנָן וְרַבּוֹתַי:

בָּרוּךְ אַתָּה יְיָ אֱלֹהֵינוּ מֶלֶךְ הָעוֹלָם בּוֹרֵא פְּרִי הַגָּפֶן.

בשבת מוסיפים את המילים שבסוגריים.

בָּרוּךְ אַתָּה יְיָ אֱלֹהֵינוּ מֶלֶךְ הָעוֹלָם אֲשֶׁר בָּחַר בָּנוּ מִכָּל עָם
וְרוֹמְמָנוּ מִכָּל לָשׁוֹן וְקִדְּשָׁנוּ בְּמִצְוֹתָיו וַתִּתֶּן לָנוּ יְיָ אֱלֹהֵינוּ בְּאַהֲבָה
[שַׁבָּתוֹת לִמְנוּחָה וּ] מוֹעֲדִים לְשִׂמְחָה חַגִּים וּזְמַנִּים לְשָׂשׂוֹן אֶת יוֹם
[הַשַּׁבָּת הַזֶּה וְאֶת יוֹם]

✠ KIDDUSH

One should use a full cup of wine for reciting *Kiddush*, the first of the Four Cups to be drunk during the *Seder*. Some also have the custom to fill the "Cup of Elijah" at this point. Others wait until just before reciting "Pour out Your wrath."

If Passover falls on Friday night, the following paragraph is recited:

[*Recite this phrase in an undertone:* It was evening and it was morning,] the sixth day. The Heaven and Earth were completed with all their multitudes. God completed on the seventh day His labor which He had done and rested on the seventh day from all His labor which He did. God blessed the seventh day and sanctified it because upon it He rested from all His labor which God created to do.[4]

On other nights of the week, start from here:

Attention, gentlemen, rabbis, and masters:

Blessed are You, *Hashem*, our God, King of the Universe, Creator of the fruit of the vine.

On Friday nights, add the words in brackets:

Blessed are You, *Hashem*, our God, King of the Universe, Who chose us from all nations, exalted us from all tongues, sanctified us with His commandments, and gave us, *Hashem*, our God, with love [Sabbaths for rest and] seasons for happiness, festivals and times for joy, this day of [the Sabbath and this day of]

---

[4] Genesis 2:1-3. The expression "which God created to do" suggests that *Hashem* did not finish the Creation, but left something for people "to do." By studying the *Torah* and performing its commandments, Jews fulfill the purpose of Creation and thus complete it (*Peninim Mishulchan Gavohah* by Rabbi Dov Eliach, p.69, quoting the *Beth Halevi*).

חַג הַמַּצּוֹת הַזֶּה זְמַן חֵרוּתֵנוּ [בְּאַהֲבָה] מִקְרָא קֹדֶשׁ זֵכֶר לִיצִיאַת מִצְרָיִם כִּי בָנוּ בָחַרְתָּ וְאוֹתָנוּ קִדַּשְׁתָּ מִכָּל הָעַמִּים [וְשַׁבָּת] וּמוֹעֲדֵי קָדְשֶׁךָ [בְּאַהֲבָה וּבְרָצוֹן] בְּשִׂמְחָה וּבְשָׂשׂוֹן הִנְחַלְתָּנוּ. בָּרוּךְ אַתָּה יְיָ מְקַדֵּשׁ [הַשַּׁבָּת וְ] יִשְׂרָאֵל וְהַזְּמַנִּים.

במוצאי שבת מוסיפים:

בָּרוּךְ אַתָּה יְיָ אֱלֹהֵינוּ מֶלֶךְ הָעוֹלָם בּוֹרֵא מְאוֹרֵי הָאֵשׁ.

בָּרוּךְ אַתָּה יְיָ אֱלֹהֵינוּ מֶלֶךְ הָעוֹלָם הַמַּבְדִּיל בֵּין קֹדֶשׁ לְחוֹל בֵּין אוֹר לְחֹשֶׁךְ בֵּין יִשְׂרָאֵל לָעַמִּים בֵּין יוֹם הַשְּׁבִיעִי לְשֵׁשֶׁת יְמֵי הַמַּעֲשֶׂה בֵּין קְדֻשַּׁת שַׁבָּת לִקְדֻשַּׁת יוֹם טוֹב הִבְדַּלְתָּ וְאֶת יוֹם הַשְּׁבִיעִי מִשֵּׁשֶׁת יְמֵי הַמַּעֲשֶׂה קִדַּשְׁתָּ הִבְדַּלְתָּ וְקִדַּשְׁתָּ אֶת עַמְּךָ יִשְׂרָאֵל בִּקְדֻשָּׁתֶךָ. בָּרוּךְ אַתָּה יְיָ הַמַּבְדִּיל בֵּין קֹדֶשׁ לְקֹדֶשׁ.

בכל ערב ממשיכים:

בָּרוּךְ אַתָּה יְיָ אֱלֹהֵינוּ מֶלֶךְ הָעוֹלָם שֶׁהֶחֱיָנוּ וְקִיְּמָנוּ וְהִגִּיעָנוּ לַזְּמַן הַזֶּה.

שותים את הכוס והזכרים מסיבים על צד שמאל.

וּרְחַץ

בעל הבית או לפי כמה מנהגים כל הנוכחים נוטלים ידים כמו שעושים לפני אכילת לחם אבל לא מברכים.

the festival of *Matzoth*, time of our liberation [with love], a holy gathering, a commemoration of the departure from Egypt, for You chose us and sanctified us from all nations, [and the Sabbath] and Your holy seasons [with love and with willingness,] with happiness and with joy You bequeathed us. Blessed are You God, Who sanctifies [the Sabbath, and] Israel and the festive seasons.

If Passover falls on Saturday night, add:

> **Blessed are You,** *Hashem*, our God, King of the Universe, Creator of the lights of fire.
>
> **Blessed are You,** *Hashem*, our God, King of the Universe, Who distinguishes between holy and profane, between light and darkness, between Israel and the nations, between the seventh day and the six work days; between the holiness of the Sabbath and the holiness of festivals You distinguished, and the seventh day from the six days of Creation you sanctified; You distinguished and sanctified Your people Israel with Your holiness. Blessed are You, *Hashem*, Who distinguishes between holiness and holiness.

On every night, continue:

Blessed are You, *Hashem*, our God, King of the Universe, Who kept us alive, preserved us, and brought us to this season.

Drink the wine. Males should do so while leaning to the left.

 WASHING

The leader of the *Seder*, or according to some customs, all who are present, wash their hands as they would for bread, but do not recite a blessing.

✠ כַּרְפַּס

לוקחים פחות מכזית של כרפס וטובלים אותו במי מלח ומברכים:

בָּרוּךְ אַתָּה יְיָ אֱלֹהֵינוּ מֶלֶךְ הָעוֹלָם בּוֹרֵא פְּרִי הָאֲדָמָה.

✠ יַחַץ

בעל הבית לוקח את המצה האמצעית וחוצה אותה לשתים. את החתיכה הקטנה הוא מחזיר למקומה בין שתי המצות השלמות ואת החתיכה הגדולה הוא מחביא עד סוף הסדר בשביל האפיקומן.

✠ מַגִּיד

בעל הבית מגביה את חתיכת המצה השבורה ואומר את הקטע הבא. ויש נוהגים להסיר את הביצה ואת הזרוע מן הקערה ולגלות את המצה ולהגביה את כל הקערה כשאומרים:

הָא לַחְמָא עַנְיָא דִי אֲכָלוּ אַבְהָתָנָא בְּאַרְעָא דְמִצְרָיִם. כָּל דִכְפִין יֵיתֵי וְיֵכֹל. כָּל

✠ VEGETABLE

Each person present takes a piece of vegetable and dips it in salt water.[5] The quantity taken should be less than an olive's bulk (about 29 milliliters). It may be eaten either sitting or reclining according to one's family custom.

Blessed are You, *Hashem,* our God, King of the Universe, Creator of the fruit of the ground.

✠ SPLITTING

The person conducting the *Seder* takes the middle *Matzah* and breaks it in two.[6] He or she places the smaller piece back between the other two *Matzoth.* The larger piece should be hidden away to be used later as the *Afikoman.*

✠ TELLING

The leader lifts the middle *Matzah* and reads the following paragraph. (According to some customs, the leader removes the egg and shankbone from the *Seder* plate, exposes the *Matzoth,* and lifts the *Seder* plate.)

This is the bread of the poor which our ancestors ate in the Land of Egypt. Let all who are hungry come and eat. Let all who

---

[5] The salt water recalls the tears the Jews shed as slaves. The letters of the word for "vegetable" (כַּרְפַּס) can be rearranged to mean "sixty at labor" (ס' פֶּרֶךְ), referring to the sixty myriads — the six hundred thousand Jewish men — who were slaves (*Mishnah Berurah* on *Shulchan Aruch, Orach Chaim* 473:4).

[6] The *Torah* calls *Matzah* "bread of the poor" (Deuteronomy 16:3). The *Matzah* is split in two at the *Seder* because a poor person may not be able to afford a whole loaf of bread and must make do with a slice. Alternatively, not knowing where his next meal may come from, he breaks his loaf, eating part now and saving part for later (See B.T. *Pesachim* 115B-116A).

דִּצְרִיךְ יֵיתֵי וְיִפְסַח. הָשַׁתָּא הָכָא לְשָׁנָה הַבָּאָה בְּאַרְעָא דְיִשְׂרָאֵל. הָשַׁתָּא עַבְדֵי לְשָׁנָה הַבָּאָה בְּנֵי חוֹרִין.

מחזירים את המצה השבורה למקומה בין שתי השלמות ומכסים את כולם. אלה שנוהגים להסיר את הביצה ואת הזרוע שמים אותם בחזרה על הקערה, מכסים את המצות ושמים את הקערה על השלחן בחזרה. מוזגים כוס שניה וכאן הבן שואל:

מַה נִּשְׁתַּנָּה הַלַּיְלָה הַזֶּה מִכָּל הַלֵּילוֹת?

שֶׁבְּכָל הַלֵּילוֹת אָנוּ אוֹכְלִין חָמֵץ וּמַצָּה, הַלַּיְלָה הַזֶּה כֻּלּוֹ מַצָּה.

שֶׁבְּכָל הַלֵּילוֹת אָנוּ אוֹכְלִין שְׁאָר יְרָקוֹת, הַלַּיְלָה הַזֶּה מָרוֹר.

שֶׁבְּכָל הַלֵּילוֹת אֵין אָנוּ מַטְבִּילִין אֲפִילוּ פַּעַם אֶחָת, הַלַּיְלָה הַזֶּה שְׁתֵּי פְעָמִים.

שֶׁבְּכָל הַלֵּילוֹת אָנוּ אוֹכְלִין בֵּין יוֹשְׁבִין וּבֵין מְסֻבִּין, הַלַּיְלָה הַזֶּה כֻּלָּנוּ מְסֻבִּין.

need come and celebrate Passover. Now we are here. Next year may we be in the Land of Israel. Now we are slaves. Next year may we be free.

> The middle *Matzah* is placed back between the two whole *Matzoth*, and all the *Matzoth* are covered. (Those who removed the egg and shank-bone should place them back on the *Seder* plate, cover the *Matzoth*, and put the plate back on the table.) The second of the Four Cups is poured. The youngest person present then says:

Why is this night different from all other nights? [7]

On all other nights, we eat both leavened grain products and *Matzah*, but on this night only *Matzah*.

On all other nights, we eat other vegetables, but on this night [we make it a point to eat] *Maror*.

On all other nights, we do not dip [our food] even once, but on this night we do so two times.[8]

On all other nights, we eat either sitting or reclining, but on this night we all recline.

---

[7] Although this is the traditional translation, מַה נִּשְׁתַּנָּה is not necessarily a question. Rather, one could understand it as a child's exclamation of surprise: "How different is this night from all other nights!" (*Aruch Hashulchan, Orach Chaim* 473:21).

[8] Of course, people do dip their food on other occasions. The question is why there is an **obligation** to do so now. Alternatively, the child asks why we dip and eat the *Karpas* prior to starting the meal, rather than waiting until the meal begins.

One reason is that it was customary for wealthy, free people to eat a dipped appetizer prior to commencing their meal. Another reason is that tonight we will spend a good deal of time reciting the *Haggadah* before the meal. We take a bite now rather than remain hungry during all that time (*Beth Yosef* on *Tur Shulchan Aruch, Orach Chaim* 473).

מגלים את המצות ואומרים:

עֲבָדִים הָיִינוּ לְפַרְעֹה בְּמִצְרָיִם וַיּוֹצִיאֵנוּ יְיָ אֱלֹהֵינוּ מִשָּׁם בְּיָד חֲזָקָה וּבִזְרוֹעַ נְטוּיָה. וְאִלּוּ לֹא הוֹצִיא הַקָּדוֹשׁ בָּרוּךְ הוּא אֶת אֲבוֹתֵינוּ מִמִּצְרַיִם הֲרֵי אָנוּ וּבָנֵינוּ וּבְנֵי בָנֵינוּ מְשֻׁעְבָּדִים הָיִינוּ לְפַרְעֹה בְּמִצְרָיִם. וַאֲפִילוּ כֻּלָּנוּ חֲכָמִים כֻּלָּנוּ נְבוֹנִים כֻּלָּנוּ זְקֵנִים כֻּלָּנוּ יוֹדְעִים אֶת הַתּוֹרָה, מִצְוָה עָלֵינוּ לְסַפֵּר בִּיצִיאַת מִצְרָיִם. וְכָל הַמַּרְבֶּה לְסַפֵּר בִּיצִיאַת מִצְרַיִם הֲרֵי זֶה מְשֻׁבָּח.

מַעֲשֶׂה בְּרַבִּי אֱלִיעֶזֶר וְרַבִּי יְהוֹשֻׁעַ וְרַבִּי אֶלְעָזָר בֶּן עֲזַרְיָה וְרַבִּי עֲקִיבָא וְרַבִּי טַרְפוֹן שֶׁהָיוּ מְסֻבִּין בִּבְנֵי בְרַק וְהָיוּ מְסַפְּרִים בִּיצִיאַת מִצְרַיִם כָּל אוֹתוֹ הַלַּיְלָה עַד שֶׁבָּאוּ תַלְמִידֵיהֶם וְאָמְרוּ לָהֶם, "רַבּוֹתֵינוּ הִגִּיעַ זְמַן קְרִיאַת שְׁמַע שֶׁל שַׁחֲרִית."

אָמַר רַבִּי אֶלְעָזָר בֶּן עֲזַרְיָה: הֲרֵי אֲנִי כְּבֶן שִׁבְעִים שָׁנָה וְלֹא זָכִיתִי שֶׁתֵּאָמֵר יְצִיאַת מִצְרַיִם בַּלֵּילוֹת עַד שֶׁדְּרָשָׁה בֶּן זוֹמָא שֶׁנֶּאֱמַר, "לְמַעַן תִּזְכֹּר אֶת יוֹם צֵאתְךָ מֵאֶרֶץ מִצְרַיִם כֹּל יְמֵי חַיֶּיךָ." "יְמֵי חַיֶּיךָ"

The *Matzoth* are uncovered.

We *were slaves to Pharaoh in Egypt* and *Hashem*, our God, took us out from there with a strong hand and an outstretched arm.[9] If the Holy One, Blessed be He, had not taken out our ancestors from Egypt, surely we, our children, and our children's children would have been enslaved to Pharaoh in Egypt. Even were all of us sages, all of us intellectuals, all of us elderly scholars, and all of us knowledgeable in the *Torah*, it would nonetheless be a *Mitzvah* for us to speak about the departure from Egypt; and whoever expands upon the departure from Egypt is praiseworthy.[10]

There *was an incident* where Rabbi Eliezer, Rabbi Yehoshua, Rabbi Elazar ben Azariah, Rabbi Akiva, and Rabbi Tarfon were reclining in B'nei Brak, and they were discussing the departure from Egypt all that night until their students came and said to them, "Our Masters, the time for recitation of the morning *Shema* has arrived."

Rabbi Elazar ben Azariah said: Take note that I am about seventy years old, yet I did not merit [to know the source of the rule] that the departure from Egypt should be recited each night until Ben Zoma expounded it, for it is said, "In order that you remember the day of your departure from the Land of Egypt all the days of your life."[11] [The phrase] "days of your life" [refers to]

---

[9] This is a paraphrase of Deuteronomy 6:21

[10] The references to sages, intellectuals, and so forth are not redundant. Rather, they refer to different types of wisdom: a) a flash of inspiration or intuitive insight; b) the logic one uses to develop new ideas through careful analysis of existing information; c) the accumulation of knowledge through the vast experience which accompanies old age; d) the wisdom one gains through Divine assistance when studying the *Torah*, as the *Tanach* says, "The *Torah* of *Hashem* is perfect...making wise the foolish" (Psalms 19:8).

[11] Deuteronomy 16:3.

הַיָּמִים. "כֹּל יְמֵי חַיֶּיךָ" הַלֵּילוֹת. וַחֲכָמִים אוֹמְרִים: "יְמֵי חַיֶּיךָ"
הָעוֹלָם הַזֶּה, "כֹּל יְמֵי חַיֶּיךָ" לְהָבִיא לִימוֹת הַמָּשִׁיחַ.

בָּרוּךְ הַמָּקוֹם, בָּרוּךְ הוּא. בָּרוּךְ שֶׁנָּתַן תּוֹרָה לְעַמּוֹ יִשְׂרָאֵל,
בָּרוּךְ הוּא. כְּנֶגֶד אַרְבָּעָה בָנִים דִּבְּרָה תוֹרָה. אֶחָד חָכָם וְאֶחָד רָשָׁע
וְאֶחָד תָּם וְאֶחָד שֶׁאֵינוֹ יוֹדֵעַ לִשְׁאוֹל.

חָכָם מָה הוּא אוֹמֵר? "מָה הָעֵדֹת וְהַחֻקִּים וְהַמִּשְׁפָּטִים
אֲשֶׁר צִוָּה יְיָ אֱלֹהֵינוּ אֶתְכֶם." וְאַף אַתָּה אֱמָר לוֹ כְּהִלְכוֹת הַפֶּסַח:
אֵין מַפְטִירִין אַחַר הַפֶּסַח אֲפִיקוֹמָן.

רָשָׁע מָה הוּא אוֹמֵר? "מָה הָעֲבֹדָה הַזֹּאת לָכֶם." לָכֶם
וְלֹא לוֹ. וּלְפִי שֶׁהוֹצִיא אֶת עַצְמוֹ מִן הַכְּלָל כָּפַר בְּעִקָּר. וְאַף אַתָּה
הַקְהֵה אֶת שִׁנָּיו וֶאֱמָר לוֹ, "בַּעֲבוּר זֶה עָשָׂה יְיָ לִי בְּצֵאתִי מִמִּצְרָיִם."
לִי וְלֹא לוֹ. אִלּוּ הָיָה שָׁם לֹא הָיָה נִגְאָל.

תָּם מָה הוּא אוֹמֵר? "מַה זֹּאת?"

the days. [The phrase] "all the days of your life" [includes] the nights. The sages say: [the phrase] "days of your life" [refers to] the present, [while the phrase] "all the days of your life" includes the days of the *Mashiach*.

Blessed is the Omnipresent, blessed is He. Blessed is He who gave the *Torah* to His people Israel, blessed is He. Corresponding to Four Sons the *Torah* spoke: One wise, one wicked, one unsophisticated, and one who does not know how to ask.

What does the wise son say? "What are the testimonies, laws, and statutes which *Hashem*, our God, commanded you?"[12]

You should answer him [by explaining] the laws of the Passover sacrifice: We do not eat desert after [consuming] the Passover sacrifice.

What does the wicked son say? "What is this service to you?"[13] [He views the *Seder* as something] "for you," but not for him. Since he excludes himself from the group, he denies a fundamental principle [of the Jewish religion].

You should respond to him bluntly and tell him, "Because of this which *Hashem* did for me during my departure from Egypt,"[14] [emphasizing that it is] "for me," but not for him.[15] If he had been there, he would not have been saved.

What does the unsophisticated son say? "What is this?"[16]

---

[12] Deuteronomy 6:20.

[13] Exodus 12:26.

[14] Exodus 13:8.

[15] The Hebrew for "respond to him bluntly" translates literally as "blunt his teeth." When a person observes others feasting but cannot join them, his teeth are "blunted" because he feels miserable about it. In this case, the father's sharp retort makes the wicked son realize that, unless he mends his ways, he is unworthy of participating in the Passover feast (See *Abudraham*).

[16] Exodus 13:14. Since he is unsophisticated, he cannot articulate a question. When he observes the unusual customs of Passover evening, he simply

וְאָמַרְתָּ אֵלָיו, "בְּחֹזֶק יָד הוֹצִיאָנוּ יְיָ מִמִּצְרַיִם מִבֵּית עֲבָדִים."

וְשֶׁאֵינוֹ יוֹדֵעַ לִשְׁאוֹל אַתְּ פְּתַח לוֹ שֶׁנֶּאֱמַר, "וְהִגַּדְתָּ לְבִנְךָ בַּיּוֹם הַהוּא לֵאמֹר בַּעֲבוּר זֶה עָשָׂה יְיָ לִי בְּצֵאתִי מִמִּצְרָיִם."

יָכוֹל מֵרֹאשׁ חֹדֶשׁ. תַּלְמוּד לוֹמַר, "בַּיּוֹם הַהוּא." אִי "בַּיּוֹם הַהוּא" יָכוֹל מִבְּעוֹד יוֹם. תַּלְמוּד לוֹמַר, "בַּעֲבוּר זֶה." "בַּעֲבוּר זֶה" לֹא אָמַרְתִּי אֶלָּא בְּשָׁעָה שֶׁיֵּשׁ מַצָּה וּמָרוֹר מֻנָּחִים לְפָנֶיךָ.

מִתְּחִלָּה עוֹבְדֵי עֲבוֹדָה זָרָה הָיוּ אֲבוֹתֵינוּ וְעַכְשָׁו קֵרְבָנוּ הַמָּקוֹם לַעֲבוֹדָתוֹ, שֶׁנֶּאֱמַר, "וַיֹּאמֶר יְהוֹשֻׁעַ אֶל כָּל הָעָם כֹּה אָמַר יְיָ אֱלֹהֵי יִשְׂרָאֵל בְּעֵבֶר הַנָּהָר יָשְׁבוּ אֲבוֹתֵיכֶם מֵעוֹלָם תֶּרַח אֲבִי אַבְרָהָם וַאֲבִי נָחוֹר

wonders what is going on.

You shall tell him, "With a strong hand *Hashem* brought us out of Egypt, the place of enslavement."[17]

As for the son who does not know how to ask, you should introduce the subject for him, as it says, "You shall tell your son on that day, saying, 'Because of this, *Hashem* did so for me during my departure from Egypt.'"[18]

It could be [that the obligation to tell one's children about the Exodus commences] from the beginning of the month [of *Nissan*]. The *Torah* says, "on that day" [to clarify that the obligation applies only to the day of Passover itself]. If [the obligation applies] "on that day," it could be [that it applies] while it is still daytime. The *Torah* says, "because of this." I do not understand "because of this" [to mean] other than the time when *Matzah* and *Maror* are placed before you.[19]

At first, our ancestors were idol worshipers, but now the Omnipresent has drawn us close to His service, as it says, "Joshua said to all the people: Thus said *Hashem*, God of Israel, 'Since antiquity your ancestors dwelled on the other side of the river — Terach, father of Abraham and father of Nachor — and they

---

[17] Exodus 13:14.

[18] Exodus 13:8. When God appeared to Moses at the burning bush, He told him that after leaving Egypt, the Jews would "serve God upon this mountain" (Exodus 3:12), indicating that God rescued the Jews because they would later accept the *Torah* on Mount Sinai. The verse, "Because of **this**, *Hashem* did so for me..." refers to the *Torah* which *Hashem* told Moses He would give "upon **this** mountain" (See *Rashi* on Exodus 3:12 and Rabbi Avraham Ibn Ezra on Exodus 13:8).

[19] The phrase "because of this" suggests that the father is pointing to items such as *Matzah* and *Maror* and explaining to his children how they symbolize the departure from Egypt (*Shibalei Haleket*). Since the *Halachah* is clear that one does not consume these foods until Passover night, the story must also be told then and not before.

וַיַּעַבְדוּ אֱלֹהִים אֲחֵרִים. וָאֶקַּח אֶת אֲבִיכֶם אֶת אַבְרָהָם מֵעֵבֶר הַנָּהָר וָאוֹלֵךְ אוֹתוֹ בְּכָל אֶרֶץ כְּנָעַן וָאַרְבֶּה אֶת זַרְעוֹ וָאֶתֶּן לוֹ אֶת יִצְחָק. וָאֶתֵּן לְיִצְחָק אֶת יַעֲקֹב וְאֶת עֵשָׂו וָאֶתֵּן לְעֵשָׂו אֶת הַר שֵׂעִיר לָרֶשֶׁת אוֹתוֹ וְיַעֲקֹב וּבָנָיו יָרְדוּ מִצְרָיִם."

בָּרוּךְ שׁוֹמֵר הַבְטָחָתוֹ לְיִשְׂרָאֵל, בָּרוּךְ הוּא, שֶׁהַקָּדוֹשׁ בָּרוּךְ הוּא חִשַּׁב אֶת הַקֵּץ לַעֲשׂוֹת כְּמָה שֶׁאָמַר לְאַבְרָהָם אָבִינוּ בִּבְרִית בֵּין הַבְּתָרִים, שֶׁנֶּאֱמַר, "וַיֹּאמֶר לְאַבְרָם יָדֹעַ תֵּדַע כִּי גֵר יִהְיֶה זַרְעֲךָ בְּאֶרֶץ לֹא לָהֶם וַעֲבָדוּם וְעִנּוּ אֹתָם אַרְבַּע מֵאוֹת שָׁנָה. וְגַם אֶת הַגּוֹי אֲשֶׁר יַעֲבֹדוּ דָּן אָנֹכִי וְאַחֲרֵי כֵן יֵצְאוּ בִּרְכֻשׁ גָּדוֹל."

מכסים את המצות ומרימים את הכוס ואומרים:

וְהִיא שֶׁעָמְדָה לַאֲבוֹתֵינוּ וְלָנוּ, שֶׁלֹּא אֶחָד בִּלְבָד עָמַד עָלֵינוּ לְכַלּוֹתֵנוּ אֶלָּא שֶׁבְּכָל דּוֹר וָדוֹר עוֹמְדִים עָלֵינוּ לְכַלּוֹתֵנוּ וְהַקָּדוֹשׁ בָּרוּךְ הוּא מַצִּילֵנוּ מִיָּדָם.

served other gods. I took your ancestor, Abraham, from the other side of the river, and walked him through all the Land of Canaan, and increased his offspring, and gave him Isaac. To Isaac I gave Jacob and Esau, and to Esau I gave Mount Seir to inherit, and Jacob and his children descended to Egypt.'"[20]

Blessed is He who keeps His promise to Israel, blessed is He. For the Holy One, Blessed be He, predicted the end [in order] to fulfill that which He said to Abraham, our father, at the covenant between the pieces, as it says, "He said to Abram, 'Know most certainly that your offspring will be strangers in a land not theirs, and they shall enslave them and torment them [for] four hundred years. I shall also judge the nation which they will serve, and afterwards they shall go out with much wealth.'"[21]

The *Matzoth* are covered, and the Second Cup of wine is raised while the following is recited:

It is that [covenant] which maintained our ancestors and us. For not just one [enemy] stood up against us to finish us off.[22] Rather, in each and every generation there are those who stand up against us to finish us off, but the Holy One, Blessed be He, saves us from their hands.[23]

---

[20] Joshua 24:2-4. Why does God say that He "increased the offspring" of Abraham, but then say He gave him one son, Isaac? Perhaps Isaac was so great that he counted as many offspring, just as Abraham's servant Eliezer was so great that he counted as three hundred eighteen men (See B.T. *Nedarim* 32A). Alternatively, *Rashi* explains that the Hebrew word for "increased" (וָאַרְבֶּה) is written defectively in the *Tanach* (וָאַרְבְּ) to suggest "strife" (רִיב). *Hashem* put Abraham through many hardships before giving him offspring worthy of carrying on his mission.

[21] Genesis 15:13-14.

[22] Some interpret the phrase "for not just one" (שֶׁלֹּא אֶחָד בִּלְבָד) as referring to the Unique One. The schemes of our enemies to finish us off all failed because the One God never concurred with them (*Botzinah Dinehura*).

[23] The promise God gave to Abraham that He would eventually save us

צֵא וּלְמַד מַה בִּקֵשׁ לָבָן הָאֲרַמִּי לַעֲשׂוֹת לְיַעֲקֹב אָבִינוּ,
שֶׁפַּרְעֹה לֹא גָזַר אֶלָּא עַל הַזְּכָרִים וְלָבָן בִּקֵשׁ לַעֲקֹר אֶת הַכֹּל,
שֶׁנֶּאֱמַר, "אֲרַמִּי אֹבֵד אָבִי וַיֵּרֶד מִצְרַיְמָה וַיָּגָר שָׁם בִּמְתֵי מְעָט
וַיְהִי שָׁם לְגוֹי גָּדוֹל עָצוּם וָרָב."

"וַיֵּרֶד מִצְרַיְמָה" אָנוּס עַל פִּי הַדִּבּוּר.

"וַיָּגָר שָׁם" מְלַמֵּד שֶׁלֹּא יָרַד יַעֲקֹב אָבִינוּ לְהִשְׁתַּקֵּעַ
בְּמִצְרַיִם אֶלָּא לָגוּר שָׁם שֶׁנֶּאֱמַר, "וַיֹּאמְרוּ אֶל פַּרְעֹה לָגוּר בָּאָרֶץ
בָּאנוּ כִּי אֵין מִרְעֶה לַצֹּאן אֲשֶׁר לַעֲבָדֶיךָ כִּי כָבֵד הָרָעָב בְּאֶרֶץ כְּנַעַן
וְעַתָּה יֵשְׁבוּ נָא עֲבָדֶיךָ בְּאֶרֶץ גֹּשֶׁן."

"בִּמְתֵי מְעָט" כְּמָה שֶׁנֶּאֱמַר, "בְּשִׁבְעִים נֶפֶשׁ יָרְדוּ אֲבֹתֶיךָ
מִצְרָיְמָה וְעַתָּה שָׂמְךָ יְיָ אֱלֹהֶיךָ כְּכוֹכְבֵי הַשָּׁמַיִם לָרֹב."

---

from our enemies applies throughout all generations. Moreover, the *Midrash*
repeatedly states that whatever befell our ancestors is indicative of what will
happen to us (*Breishith Rabbah* 54:5; *Vayikra Rabbah* 29:1).

The wine cup is set back down, and the *Matzoth* are uncovered.

Go and study what Laban the Aramean sought to do to our father Jacob. For Pharaoh did not decree but upon the males, whereas Laban sought to uproot everything, as it says, "An Aramean destroyed my forefather, and he descended to Egypt, and lodged there few in number, and became there a nation, great, strong, and numerous."[24]

The *Haggadah* proceeds to analyze each phrase of this verse.

"descended to Egypt" He was forced by Divine command.

"and lodged there" This teaches that our ancestor Jacob did not descend [in order] to submerge himself in Egypt, but [merely] to lodge there, as it says, "They said to Pharaoh, 'To lodge in the land we have come, for there is no pasture for the flocks of sheep of your servants, for the famine is severe in the Land of Canaan; now let your servants settle in the Land of Goshen.'"[25]

"few in number" as it says, "With seventy souls your ancestors descended to Egypt, and now *Hashem*, your God, has made you as the stars of the Heavens in abundance."[26]

---

[24] Deuteronomy 26:5. Laban would surely have carried out his plan to destroy Jacob had God not intervened. The *Torah* therefore considers it as though Laban fulfilled his evil scheme and declares that "an Aramean **destroyed** my forefather," rather than "**sought** to destroy my forefather" (*Rashi* ad. loc.).

[25] Genesis 47:4. The Hebrew words וַיָּגָר and לָגוּר, translated here as "lodge," are related to the word גֵר, which means "stranger." No matter how long Jacob and his family stayed in Egypt, they regarded themselves as "strangers" rather than as permanent citizens.

[26] Deuteronomy 10:22.

"וַיְהִי שָׁם לְגוֹי", מְלַמֵּד שֶׁהָיוּ יִשְׂרָאֵל מְצֻיָּנִים שָׁם.

"גָּדוֹל עָצוּם" כְּמָה שֶׁנֶּאֱמַר, "וּבְנֵי יִשְׂרָאֵל פָּרוּ וַיִּשְׁרְצוּ
וַיִּרְבּוּ וַיַּעַצְמוּ בִּמְאֹד מְאֹד וַתִּמָּלֵא הָאָרֶץ אֹתָם."

"וָרָב" כְּמָה שֶׁנֶּאֱמַר, "רְבָבָה כְּצֶמַח הַשָּׂדֶה נְתַתִּיךְ וַתִּרְבִּי וַתִּגְדְּלִי
וַתָּבֹאִי בַּעֲדִי עֲדָיִים שָׁדַיִם נָכֹנוּ וּשְׂעָרֵךְ צִמֵּחַ וְאַתְּ עֵרֹם וְעֶרְיָה.
וָאֶעֱבֹר עָלַיִךְ וָאֶרְאֵךְ מִתְבּוֹסֶסֶת בְּדָמָיִךְ וָאֹמַר לָךְ בְּדָמַיִךְ חֲיִי וָאֹמַר
לָךְ בְּדָמַיִךְ חֲיִי."

"וַיָּרֵעוּ אֹתָנוּ הַמִּצְרִים וַיְעַנּוּנוּ וַיִּתְּנוּ עָלֵינוּ עֲבֹדָה קָשָׁה."

"became there a nation" This teaches that Jews were distinguishable there.

"great, strong" as it says, "The Children of Israel flourished, and swarmed, and increased, and grew very, very strong, and the land was full of them."

"and numerous" as it says, "Numerous as the vegetation of the field did I make you;[27] you increased and became great; you came into [the age of donning the] choicest jewelry, and you developed, and your hair sprouted, yet you were unclothed and exposed. I passed upon you, and I saw you wallowing in your blood, and I said to you, 'By your blood shall you live,' and I said to you, 'By your blood shall you live.'"[28]

"The Egyptians wronged us, and afflicted us, and they imposed upon us difficult labor."[29]

The *Haggadah* proceeds to analyze each phrase of this verse.

---

[27] Just as wild vegetation sprouts without any effort, the Jewish slaves experienced a phenomenal increase in population. When one prunes a tree, the cutting of its branches stimulates further growth. Likewise, the Egyptian oppression only caused the Jewish population to swell further, as the *Torah* states, "The more they afflicted [the Jewish nation], the more it increased, and the more it burst forth" (Exodus 1:12) (*Abudraham*).

[28] Ezekiel 16:6-7. The metaphor of this passage is that just as a girl reaches adolescence and is ready to wear jewelry, so the time had arrived for the redemption *Hashem* had promised Abraham.

The emergence of the Jewish nation from Egypt is comparable to a woman giving birth who is soiled with blood. Although childbirth is neither pretty nor pleasant, it is through this very process that life emerges. So, too, it was through the awful suffering in Egypt that the Jewish nation was born.

[29] Deuteronomy 26:6.

"וַיָּרֵעוּ אֹתָנוּ הַמִּצְרִים" כְּמָה שֶׁנֶּאֱמַר, "הָבָה נִתְחַכְּמָה לוֹ פֶּן יִרְבֶּה וְהָיָה כִּי תִקְרֶאנָה מִלְחָמָה וְנוֹסַף גַּם הוּא עַל שֹׂנְאֵינוּ וְנִלְחַם בָּנוּ וְעָלָה מִן הָאָרֶץ."

"וַיְעַנּוּנוּ" כְּמָה שֶׁנֶּאֱמַר, "וַיָּשִׂימוּ עָלָיו שָׂרֵי מִסִּים לְמַעַן עַנֹּתוֹ בְּסִבְלֹתָם וַיִּבֶן עָרֵי מִסְכְּנוֹת לְפַרְעֹה אֶת פִּתֹם וְאֶת רַעַמְסֵס."

"וַיִּתְּנוּ עָלֵינוּ עֲבֹדָה קָשָׁה" כְּמָה שֶׁנֶּאֱמַר, "וַיַּעֲבִדוּ מִצְרַיִם אֶת בְּנֵי יִשְׂרָאֵל בְּפָרֶךְ."

"וַנִּצְעַק אֶל יְיָ אֱלֹהֵי אֲבֹתֵינוּ וַיִּשְׁמַע יְיָ אֶת קֹלֵנוּ וַיַּרְא אֶת עָנְיֵנוּ וְאֶת עֲמָלֵנוּ וְאֶת לַחֲצֵנוּ."

"וַנִּצְעַק אֶל יְיָ אֱלֹהֵי אֲבֹתֵינוּ" כְּמָה שֶׁנֶּאֱמַר, "וַיְהִי בַיָּמִים הָרַבִּים הָהֵם וַיָּמָת מֶלֶךְ מִצְרַיִם וַיֵּאָנְחוּ בְנֵי יִשְׂרָאֵל מִן הָעֲבֹדָה וַיִּזְעָקוּ וַתַּעַל שַׁוְעָתָם אֶל הָאֱלֹהִים מִן הָעֲבֹדָה."

"**The Egyptians wronged us**" as it says, "Come let us deal craftily with [the Jewish nation], lest it increase, and it come about when a war happens [that] it will join together with our enemies and wage war on us and go up from the land."[30]

"**and afflicted us**" as it says, "They placed upon [the Jewish nation] tax collectors in order to afflict it with their burdens; and they built storage cities for Pharaoh, [namely,] Pithom and Raamses."[31]

"**and they imposed upon us difficult labor**" as it says, "Egypt worked the Children of Israel with harshness."[32]

"**We cried to Hashem, God of our ancestors, and Hashem heard our voice and saw our affliction, our toil, and our oppression.**"[33]

The *Haggadah* proceeds to analyze each phrase of this verse.

"**We cried to Hashem, God of our ancestors**" as it says, "It was during those many days that the king of Egypt died, and the Children of Israel groaned from the servitude, and they cried out, and their clamor from the servitude rose to God."[34]

---

[30] Exodus 1:10.

[31] Exodus 1:11. The Hebrew term for "storage cities" (מִסְכְּנוֹת) hints at the eventual downfall of the Egyptians because it is related to the word for "danger" (סַכָּנָה), and suggests that the Egyptians brought danger upon themselves by their behavior towards the Jews. Alternatively, it is similar to the word for "beggar" (מִסְכֵּן) and foreshadows the impoverishment of Egypt after the ex-slaves made off with their masters' wealth (B.T. *Sotah* 11A).

[32] Exodus 1:13.

[33] Deuteronomy 26:7.

[34] Exodus 2:23. According to Rabbi Avraham ibn Ezra, the verse is talking about the time during which Moses fled from Egypt to escape punishment for having killed an Egyptian who attacked a Jew. Pharaoh's death meant

"וַיִּשְׁמַע יְיָ אֶת קֹלֵנוּ" כְּמָה שֶׁנֶּאֱמַר, "וַיִּשְׁמַע אֱלֹהִים אֶת
נַאֲקָתָם וַיִּזְכֹּר אֱלֹהִים אֶת בְּרִיתוֹ אֶת אַבְרָהָם אֶת יִצְחָק וְאֶת יַעֲקֹב."

"וַיַּרְא אֶת עָנְיֵנוּ", זוֹ פְּרִישׁוּת דֶּרֶךְ אֶרֶץ כְּמָה שֶׁנֶּאֱמַר,
"וַיַּרְא אֱלֹהִים אֶת בְּנֵי יִשְׂרָאֵל וַיֵּדַע אֱלֹהִים."

"וְאֶת עֲמָלֵנוּ", אֵלּוּ הַבָּנִים כְּמָה שֶׁנֶּאֱמַר, "כָּל הַבֵּן הַיִּלּוֹד
הַיְאֹרָה תַּשְׁלִיכֻהוּ וְכָל הַבַּת תְּחַיּוּן."

"וְאֶת לַחֲצֵנוּ", זוֹ הַדַּחַק כְּמָה שֶׁנֶּאֱמַר, "וְגַם רָאִיתִי אֶת
הַלַּחַץ אֲשֶׁר מִצְרַיִם לֹחֲצִים אֹתָם."

"וַיּוֹצִאֵנוּ יְיָ מִמִּצְרַיִם בְּיָד חֲזָקָה וּבִזְרֹעַ נְטוּיָה וּבְמֹרָא גָּדֹל
וּבְאֹתוֹת וּבְמֹפְתִים."

"וַיּוֹצִאֵנוּ יְיָ מִמִּצְרַיִם" לֹא עַל יְדֵי מַלְאָךְ וְלֹא עַל יְדֵי שָׂרָף וְלֹא
עַל יְדֵי שָׁלִיחַ אֶלָּא הַקָּדוֹשׁ בָּרוּךְ הוּא בִּכְבוֹדוֹ וּבְעַצְמוֹ שֶׁנֶּאֱמַר,
"וְעָבַרְתִּי בְאֶרֶץ מִצְרַיִם בַּלַּיְלָה הַזֶּה וְהִכֵּיתִי כָל בְּכוֹר בְּאֶרֶץ מִצְרַיִם
מֵאָדָם וְעַד בְּהֵמָה וּבְכָל אֱלֹהֵי מִצְרַיִם אֶעֱשֶׂה שְׁפָטִים אֲנִי

---

that it was now safe for Moses to return.

"and Hashem heard our voice" as it says, "God heard their cry, and God remembered His covenant with Abraham, Isaac, and Jacob."[35]

"and saw our affliction" This refers to hindering of marital relations, as it says, "God saw the Children of Israel, and God knew."[36]

"our toil" These are the sons, as it says, "Every son who is born you shall cast into the river, and every daughter you shall keep alive."[37]

"our oppression" This refers to overcrowding, as it says, "I also saw the oppression with which Egypt oppressed them."[38]

"Hashem took us out of Egypt with a strong hand and an outstretched arm, with great awe, and with signs and wonders."[39]

The *Haggadah* proceeds to analyze each phrase of this verse.

"Hashem took us out of Egypt" Not through a messenger, nor through an angel, nor through an agent, but the Holy One, Blessed be He, in His glory, personally, as it says, "I shall pass through the Land of Egypt on this night and strike down every first-born in the Land of Egypt from man to beast, and I shall execute judgments upon all the gods of Egypt; I am

---

[35] Exodus 2:23-24.

[36] Exodus 2:25.

[37] Exodus 1:22. Toil refers to children because parents labor greatly to support and care for them (*Abudraham*).

[38] Exodus 3:9. The Egyptians forced the Jews to live in cramped conditions, so that the oppression consisted of literally *pressing* the Jews into overcrowded quarters (*Rabbeinu Bachya*).

[39] Deuteronomy 26:8.

‫"יְיָ.‬
‫ד:‬

‫"וְעָבַרְתִּי בְאֶרֶץ מִצְרַיִם בַּלַּיְלָה הַזֶּה" אֲנִי וְלֹא מַלְאָךְ.‬
‫"וְהִכֵּיתִי כָל בְּכוֹר בְּאֶרֶץ מִצְרַיִם" אֲנִי וְלֹא שָׂרָף.   "וּבְכָל אֱלֹהֵי‬
‫מִצְרַיִם אֶעֱשֶׂה שְׁפָטִים" אֲנִי וְלֹא הַשָּׁלִיחַ. "אֲנִי יְיָ" אֲנִי הוּא וְלֹא‬
‫אַחֵר.‬

‫"בְּיָד חֲזָקָה," זוֹ הַדֶּבֶר כְּמָה שֶׁנֶּאֱמַר, "הִנֵּה יַד יְיָ הוֹיָה‬
‫בְּמִקְנְךָ אֲשֶׁר בַּשָּׂדֶה בַּסּוּסִים בַּחֲמֹרִים בַּגְּמַלִּים בַּבָּקָר וּבַצֹּאן דֶּבֶר‬
‫כָּבֵד מְאֹד."‬

‫"וּבִזְרֹעַ נְטוּיָה," זוֹ הַחֶרֶב כְּמָה שֶׁנֶּאֱמַר, "וְחַרְבּוֹ שְׁלוּפָה‬
‫בְּיָדוֹ נְטוּיָה עַל יְרוּשָׁלָיִם [יְרוּשָׁלִַם כתיב]."‬

Hashem."[40]

"I shall pass through the Land of Egypt on this night" — I and not a messenger; "and strike down every first-born in the Land of Egypt" — I and not an angel;[41] "and I shall execute judgments upon all the gods of Egypt" — I and not an agent; "I am *Hashem*" — It is I and not another.[42]

"with a strong hand" This is the pestilence, as it says, "Behold, the hand of *Hashem* is upon your livestock which is in the fields — upon the horses, donkeys, camels, cattle, and sheep — a very severe pestilence."[43]

"and an outstretched arm" This is the sword, as it says, "His sword is unsheathed in his hand, stretched upon Jerusalem."[44]

---

[40] Exodus 12:12. Since any deity other than *Hashem* has no reality, what did He mean by saying that He would execute judgment against the gods of Egypt? The *Midrash* explains that when the Egyptians saw their first-born being stricken, they tried to hide them in their idolatrous temples. To show that their idols were useless, God destroyed them as well. The wooden ones rotted, the stone ones dissolved, and those of silver, gold, or copper melted (*Shemoth Rabbah* 15:15).

[41] The impurity of Egypt was so extreme that angels were too holy to enter it. Although *Hashem's* holiness is even greater, He has no limitations, so He can go where angels cannot (*Zohar* I:117A).

This explains why Moses was reluctant to go to Pharaoh, claiming that he was not sufficiently articulate. He meant that if he entered a place of such great spiritual contamination, his power of prophecy would be impaired (*Yismach Moshe, Parashath Va'era* 134A).

[42] *Hashem* controls childbirth directly, and no angel has charge of it (B.T. *Ta'anith* 2A). Israel's departure from Egypt resembled childbirth because it marked its formation as a nation. Therefore, only God Himself could direct the Exodus (*Yad Mitzrayim*).

[43] Exodus 9:3.

[44] I Chronicles 21:16.

"וּבְמֹרָא גָּדֹל" זוֹ גִּלּוּי שְׁכִינָה כְּמָה שֶׁנֶּאֱמַר, "אוֹ הֲנִסָּה אֱלֹהִים לָבוֹא לָקַחַת לוֹ גוֹי מִקֶּרֶב גּוֹי בְּמַסֹּת בְּאֹתֹת וּבְמוֹפְתִים וּבְמִלְחָמָה וּבְיָד חֲזָקָה וּבִזְרוֹעַ נְטוּיָה וּבְמוֹרָאִים גְּדֹלִים כְּכֹל אֲשֶׁר עָשָׂה לָכֶם יְיָ אֱלֹהֵיכֶם בְּמִצְרַיִם לְעֵינֶיךָ."

"וּבְאֹתוֹת," זֶה הַמַּטֶּה כְּמָה שֶׁנֶּאֱמַר, "וְאֶת הַמַּטֶּה הַזֶּה תִּקַּח בְּיָדֶךָ אֲשֶׁר תַּעֲשֶׂה בּוֹ אֶת הָאֹתֹת."

"וּבְמֹפְתִים," זֶה הַדָּם כְּמָה שֶׁנֶּאֱמַר,

שׁוֹפְכִים טִיפָה מִן הַכּוֹס כְּשֶׁאוֹמְרִים "דָּם" וְכֵן בְּ"וָאֵשׁ" וְכֵן בְּ"וְתִימְרוֹת עָשָׁן":

"וְנָתַתִּי מוֹפְתִים בַּשָּׁמַיִם וּבָאָרֶץ

דָּם
וָאֵשׁ
וְתִימְרוֹת עָשָׁן."

"and with great awe" This is the revelation of the Divine Presence, as it says, "Or has any god tried to come to take for himself a nation from the midst of another nation with miracles, signs, wonders, and warfare, and with a strong hand and an outstretched arm, and with great visions, as all which *Hashem*, your God, did for you in Egypt before your eyes."[45]

"with signs" This is the staff [of Moses], as it says, "Take this staff in your hand so that you may perform signs with it."[46]

"and wonders." This is the blood, as it is written,

> One should spill a drop of wine when mentioning "blood," another when mentioning "fire," and a third when mentioning "and columns of smoke."[47]

"I placed wonders in the Heavens and upon the Earth:

BLOOD,
FIRE
AND COLUMNS OF SMOKE."

---

[45] Deuteronomy 4:34. Although the מוֹרָא usually translates as "awe," from the root ירא, meaning "fear," the *Haggadah* understands it to mean "vision," from the root ראה, meaning "to see." The phrase "before your eyes" at the end of the verse supports this interpretation.

[46] Exodus 4:17. Moses's staff had inscribed upon it the letters דְּצַ"ךְ עֲדַ"שׁ בְּאַחַ"ב which are abbreviations, or signs, for the Ten Plagues (*Shemoth Rabbah* 5:6). When the verse speaks of Moses using the staff to "perform signs," it means that he used it to initiate the plagues represented by those abbreviations.

[47] Some use the index finger to do this to recall how Pharaoh's magicians eventually admitted that the plagues emanated from the "finger of God" (Exodus 8:15) (*Mishnah Berurah* on *Shulchan Aruch, Orach Chaim* 473:7). Others have the custom to use the little finger. The *Arizal*, however, taught that one should not use one's fingers, but spill drops of wine from the cup into a broken dish (*Ta'amei Haminhagim* 538).

דָּבָר אַחֵר, "בְּיָד חֲזָקָה" שְׁתַּיִם, "וּבִזְרֹעַ נְטוּיָה" שְׁתַּיִם, "וּבְמֹרָא גָּדֹל" שְׁתַּיִם, "וּבְאֹתוֹת" שְׁתַּיִם, "וּבְמֹפְתִים" שְׁתַּיִם, אֵלּוּ עֶשֶׂר מַכּוֹת שֶׁהֵבִיא הַקָּדוֹשׁ בָּרוּךְ הוּא עַל הַמִּצְרִים בְּמִצְרַיִם, וְאֵלּוּ הֵן:

עִם אֲמִירַת כָּל אַחַת מִן הַמַּכּוֹת שׁוֹפְכִים טִיפָּה מִן הַכּוֹס:

 דָּם

 צְפַרְדֵּעַ

 כִּנִּים

 עָרוֹב

 דֶּבֶר

 שְׁחִין

 בָּרָד

 אַרְבֶּה

 חֹשֶׁךְ

 מַכַּת בְּכוֹרוֹת

Another interpretation: "with a strong hand" is two; "outstretched arm" is two; "great awe" is two; "signs" is two; "wonders" is two. These are the Ten Plagues which the Holy One, Blessed be He, brought upon the Egyptians in Egypt, and they are:

One should spill a drop of wine from his or her cup at the mention of each of the Ten Plagues.

✠ **BLOOD**

✠ **FROGS**

✠ **LICE**

✠ **WILD ANIMALS**

✠ **PESTILENCE**

✠ **BOILS**

✠ **HAIL**

✠ **LOCUSTS**

✠ **DARKNESS**[48]

✠ **PLAGUE OF THE FIRST-BORN**[49]

---

[48] Unlike ordinary darkness, which is merely the absence of light, this plague consisted of a type of foggy darkness which the Egyptians could feel (*Shemoth Rabbah* 14:3). The Egyptians attributed power to false deities, treating their idols as if they were real beings. Measure for measure, God punished them with a type of darkness which seemed to possess real substance.

[49] *Hashem* never punishes indiscriminately. He only destroyed the wicked first-born. Pharaoh's first-born daughter, Bathya, who had rescued Moses from the Nile River, was spared (*Shemoth Rabbah* 18:3).

רַבִּי יְהוּדָה הָיָה נוֹתֵן בָּהֶם סִמָּנִים:

עם אמירת כל אחת מן הסימנים שופכים טיפה מכוס היין:

 דְּצַ"ךְ

 עֲדַ"שׁ

 בְּאַחַ"ב

יש נוהגים למלאות בחזרה את הכוסות לפני שממשיכים ויש נוהגים להשאיר אותן כמו
שהן עד שתייתן:

רַבִּי יוֹסֵי הַגְּלִילִי אוֹמֵר: מִנַּיִן אַתָּה אוֹמֵר שֶׁלָּקוּ הַמִּצְרִים
בְּמִצְרַיִם עֶשֶׂר מַכּוֹת וְעַל הַיָּם לָקוּ חֲמִשִּׁים מַכּוֹת? בְּמִצְרַיִם מָה
הוּא אוֹמֵר? "וַיֹּאמְרוּ הַחַרְטֻמִּם אֶל פַּרְעֹה אֶצְבַּע אֱלֹהִים הוּא"
וְעַל הַיָּם מָה הוּא אוֹמֵר? "וַיַּרְא יִשְׂרָאֵל אֶת הַיָּד הַגְּדֹלָה אֲשֶׁר עָשָׂה
יְיָ בְּמִצְרַיִם וַיִּירְאוּ הָעָם אֶת יְיָ וַיַּאֲמִינוּ בַּייָ וּבְמֹשֶׁה עַבְדּוֹ." כַּמָּה

Rabbi Yehudah used to give them abbreviations:

> One should spill a drop from his or her cup at the mention of each abbreviation.

✠ DETZACH
✠ ADASH
✠ B'ACHAV[50]

> Some have the custom to refill the wine cups before continuing the *Seder*. Others let them remain as they are until they are drunk.[51]

Rabbi Yossi Hagalili says: From where can you say that the Egyptians were stricken in Egypt with Ten Plagues, and at the sea they were stricken with fifty plagues? In Egypt, what does it say? "The sorcerers said to Pharaoh, 'It is the finger of God.'"[52] At the sea what does it says? "Israel saw [what] the great hand of *Hashem* did to Egypt, and the people feared *Hashem* and believed in *Hashem* and in Moses, His servant."[53] How many times were

---

[50] In the paragraphs which follow, the *Haggadah* will quote the opinions of several rabbis who expand the number of plagues to fifty, two hundred, or two hundred fifty. These three numbers together add up to five hundred, virtually identical to the numerical value of these abbreviations, which comes to five hundred one (*Shibalei Haleket*).

[51] If so much wine has been removed from the cup that it no longer contains the minimum amount required for one of the Four Cups, then one must refill it.

[52] Exodus 8:15. Once the magicians acknowledged that the plague was the "finger of God" and not merely a magic trick, why did Pharaoh continue to resist freeing the Jews?

This shows just how wicked Pharaoh was. He even refused to accept the conclusion of his own advisors. Instead, he reasoned that Moses was simply a more adept sorcerer and that they were mistaken in thinking that *Hashem* had sent the plagues (*Arvei Nachal* on *Parashath Va'era*).

[53] Exodus 14:31.

לָקוּ בְאֶצְבַּע? עֶשֶׂר מַכּוֹת. אֱמוֹר מֵעַתָּה בְּמִצְרַיִם לָקוּ עֶשֶׂר מַכּוֹת וְעַל הַיָּם לָקוּ חֲמִשִּׁים מַכּוֹת.

רַבִּי אֱלִיעֶזֶר אוֹמֵר: מִנַּיִן שֶׁכָּל מַכָּה וּמַכָּה שֶׁהֵבִיא הַקָּדוֹשׁ בָּרוּךְ הוּא עַל הַמִּצְרִים בְּמִצְרַיִם הָיְתָה שֶׁל אַרְבַּע מַכּוֹת? שֶׁנֶּאֱמַר, "יְשַׁלַּח בָּם חֲרוֹן אַפּוֹ עֶבְרָה וָזַעַם וְצָרָה מִשְׁלַחַת מַלְאֲכֵי רָעִים." "עֶבְרָה" אַחַת, "וָזַעַם" שְׁתַּיִם, "וְצָרָה" שָׁלֹשׁ, "מִשְׁלַחַת מַלְאֲכֵי רָעִים" אַרְבַּע. אֱמוֹר מֵעַתָּה בְּמִצְרַיִם לָקוּ אַרְבָּעִים מַכּוֹת וְעַל הַיָּם לָקוּ מָאתַיִם מַכּוֹת.

רַבִּי עֲקִיבָא אוֹמֵר: מִנַּיִן שֶׁכָּל מַכָּה וּמַכָּה שֶׁהֵבִיא הַקָּדוֹשׁ בָּרוּךְ הוּא עַל הַמִּצְרִים בְּמִצְרַיִם הָיְתָה שֶׁל חָמֵשׁ מַכּוֹת? שֶׁנֶּאֱמַר, "יְשַׁלַּח בָּם חֲרוֹן אַפּוֹ עֶבְרָה וָזַעַם וְצָרָה מִשְׁלַחַת מַלְאֲכֵי רָעִים." "חֲרוֹן אַפּוֹ" אַחַת, "עֶבְרָה" שְׁתַּיִם, "וָזַעַם" שָׁלֹשׁ, "וְצָרָה" אַרְבַּע, "מִשְׁלַחַת מַלְאֲכֵי רָעִים" חָמֵשׁ. אֱמוֹר מֵעַתָּה בְּמִצְרַיִם לָקוּ חֲמִשִּׁים

they stricken with a finger? Ten. Conclude from this that in Egypt they were stricken with ten plagues, whereas at the sea they were stricken with fifty plagues.[54]

Rabbi Eliezer says: From where [can you say] that each and every plague which the Holy One, Blessed be He, brought upon the Egyptians in Egypt consisted of four plagues?[55] As it says, "He sent upon them his furious anger, wrath, rage, trouble, [and] a contingent of evil angels."[56] "Wrath" is one, "rage" is two, "trouble" is three, "a contingent of evil angels" is four.[57] Say from this that in Egypt they were stricken with forty plagues, whereas at the sea they were stricken with two hundred plagues.

Rabbi Akiva says: From where [can you say] that each and every plague which the Holy One, Blessed be He, brought upon the Egyptians in Egypt consisted of five plagues? As it says, "He sent upon them His furious anger, wrath, rage, trouble, [and] a contingent of evil angels."[58] "His furious anger" is one, "wrath" is two, "rage" is three, "trouble" is four, "a contingent of evil angels" is five. Say from this that in Egypt they were stricken with fifty

---

[54] *Hashem* sent fifty plagues at the sea as punishment for Pharaoh asking, "Who is *Hashem* that I should listen to His voice?" The Hebrew for "who" (מי) has a numerical value of fifty and when spelled backwards it means "sea" (ים) (*Shemoth Rabbah* 5:14).

[55] Each plague in Egypt included several miraculous aspects. The plague of blood, for example, affected not only the water in rivers and lakes, but also water which the Egyptians had stored in jugs. Even when the Egyptians spat, their spittle turned into blood. Another supernatural aspect of this plague was that water belonging to Jews did not turn into blood. This forced the Egyptians to purchase water from the Jewish slaves whom they detested (*Shemoth Rabbah* 9:10). If one views the miraculous features of each plague independently, then each one counts as several.

[56] Psalms 78:49.

[57] The verse could simply have said, "He sent upon them furious anger," and the meaning would have been clear. The use of all these additional synonyms suggests that each plague had several subdivisions.

[58] Psalms 78:49.

מַכּוֹת וְעַל הַיָּם לָקוּ חֲמִשִּׁים וּמָאתַיִם מַכּוֹת.

כַּמָּה מַעֲלוֹת טוֹבוֹת לַמָּקוֹם עָלֵינוּ:

אִלּוּ הוֹצִיאָנוּ מִמִּצְרַיִם
וְלֹא עָשָׂה בָהֶם שְׁפָטִים   דַּיֵּנוּ !

אִלּוּ עָשָׂה בָהֶם שְׁפָטִים
וְלֹא עָשָׂה בֵאלֹהֵיהֶם   דַּיֵּנוּ !

אִלּוּ עָשָׂה בֵאלֹהֵיהֶם
וְלֹא הָרַג אֶת בְּכוֹרֵיהֶם   דַּיֵּנוּ !

אִלּוּ הָרַג אֶת בְּכוֹרֵיהֶם
וְלֹא נָתַן לָנוּ אֶת מָמוֹנָם   דַּיֵּנוּ !

אִלּוּ נָתַן לָנוּ אֶת מָמוֹנָם
וְלֹא קָרַע לָנוּ אֶת הַיָּם   דַּיֵּנוּ !

אִלּוּ קָרַע לָנוּ אֶת הַיָּם
וְלֹא הֶעֱבִירָנוּ בְתוֹכוֹ בֶּחָרָבָה   דַּיֵּנוּ !

אִלּוּ הֶעֱבִירָנוּ בְתוֹכוֹ בֶּחָרָבָה
וְלֹא שִׁקַּע צָרֵינוּ בְּתוֹכוֹ   דַּיֵּנוּ !

plagues, whereas at the sea they were stricken with two hundred fifty plagues.

How many great benefits has the Omnipresent bestowed upon us?[59]

If He had taken us out of Egypt, but not executed upon them judgments, *it would have been enough!*

If He had executed upon them judgments, but not acted against their idols, *it would have been enough!*

If He had acted against their idols, but not killed their first-born, *it would have been enough!*[60]

If He had killed their first-born, but not given us their money, *it would have been enough!*

If He had given us their money, but not split the sea for us, *it would have been enough!*

If He had split the sea for us, but not brought us through it on dry land, *it would have been enough!*

If He had brought us through it on dry land, but not submerged our enemies in it, *it would have been enough!*

---

[59] Although this translation is correct, the Hebrew text actually appears to say, "How many great benefits belong to the Omnipresent" (לַמָּקוֹם instead of מִמָּקוֹם). This is because, in a manner of speaking, God enjoys bestowing kindness to His creatures (Rabbi Levi Yitzchak of Berditchev).

[60] God dislikes destroying His creatures even when they are wicked, so slaying the first-born was more remarkable than any of the other plagues.

אִלוּ שִׁקַּע צָרֵינוּ בְּתוֹכוֹ

וְלֹא סִפֵּק צָרְכֵּנוּ בַּמִּדְבָּר אַרְבָּעִים שָׁנָה   דַּיֵּנוּ !

אִלוּ סִפֵּק צָרְכֵּנוּ בַּמִּדְבָּר אַרְבָּעִים שָׁנָה

וְלֹא הֶאֱכִילָנוּ אֶת הַמָּן   דַּיֵּנוּ !

אִלוּ הֶאֱכִילָנוּ אֶת הַמָּן

וְלֹא נָתַן לָנוּ אֶת הַשַּׁבָּת   דַּיֵּנוּ !

אִלוּ נָתַן לָנוּ אֶת הַשַּׁבָּת

וְלֹא קֵרְבָנוּ לִפְנֵי הַר סִינַי   דַּיֵּנוּ !

אִלוּ קֵרְבָנוּ לִפְנֵי הַר סִינַי

וְלֹא נָתַן לָנוּ אֶת הַתּוֹרָה   דַּיֵּנוּ !

אִלוּ נָתַן לָנוּ אֶת הַתּוֹרָה

וְלֹא הִכְנִיסָנוּ לְאֶרֶץ יִשְׂרָאֵל   דַּיֵּנוּ !

אִלוּ הִכְנִיסָנוּ לְאֶרֶץ יִשְׂרָאֵל

וְלֹא בָנָה לָנוּ אֶת בֵּית הַבְּחִירָה   דַּיֵּנוּ !

If He had submerged our enemies in it, but not supplied our needs in the desert for forty years, it would have been enough!

If He had supplied our needs in the desert for forty years, but not fed us the Manna, it would have been enough![61]

If He had fed us the Manna, but not give us the Sabbath, it would have been enough![62]

If He had given us the Sabbath, but not brought us before Mount Sinai, it would have been enough!

If He had brought us before Mount Sinai, but not given us the *Torah*, it would have been enough!

If He had given us the *Torah*, but not brought us into the Land of Israel, it would have been enough![63]

If He had brought us into the Land of Israel, but not built us the Temple, it would have been enough!

---

[61] When God sent the Flood in Noah's time, the waters rose fifteen cubits above the highest mountains (Genesis 7:20). The *Talmud* explains that because the Divine attribute of kindness exceeds that of punishment, when the Manna came down, it accumulated to a height of sixty cubits (B.T. *Yoma* 76A). As the *Haggadah* states further on, God's blessings were "doubled and redoubled," and four times fifteen equals sixty.

[62] Although every *Mitzvah* is important, the *Haggadah* singles out the Sabbath because it is considered equivalent to all the rest of the *Mitzvoth* combined (*Ma'aseh Nissim*, citing *Shemoth Rabbah* 25:12).

[63] God could have driven the Egyptians away and given their land to the Jewish people, but the Land of Israel possesses a special holiness, so we are thankful that He gave it to us.

עַל אַחַת כַּמָּה וְכַמָּה טוֹבָה כְפוּלָה וּמְכֻפֶּלֶת לַמָּקוֹם עָלֵינוּ שֶׁהוֹצִיאָנוּ מִמִּצְרַיִם וְעָשָׂה בָהֶם שְׁפָטִים וְעָשָׂה בֵאלֹהֵיהֶם וְהָרַג אֶת בְּכוֹרֵיהֶם וְנָתַן לָנוּ אֶת מָמוֹנָם וְקָרַע לָנוּ אֶת הַיָּם וְהֶעֱבִירָנוּ בְתוֹכוֹ בֶּחָרָבָה וְשִׁקַּע צָרֵינוּ בְּתוֹכוֹ וְסִפֵּק צָרְכֵּנוּ בַּמִּדְבָּר אַרְבָּעִים שָׁנָה וְהֶאֱכִילָנוּ אֶת הַמָּן וְנָתַן לָנוּ אֶת הַשַּׁבָּת וְקֵרְבָנוּ לִפְנֵי הַר סִינַי וְנָתַן לָנוּ אֶת הַתּוֹרָה וְהִכְנִיסָנוּ לְאֶרֶץ יִשְׂרָאֵל וּבָנָה לָנוּ אֶת בֵּית הַבְּחִירָה לְכַפֵּר עַל כָּל עֲוֹנוֹתֵינוּ.

רַבָּן גַּמְלִיאֵל הָיָה אוֹמֵר: כָּל שֶׁלֹּא אָמַר שְׁלֹשָׁה דְבָרִים אֵלּוּ בַּפֶּסַח לֹא יָצָא יְדֵי חוֹבָתוֹ, וְאֵלּוּ הֵן:

פֶּסַח

מַצָּה

וּמָרוֹר

אֵין לְהָרִים אֶת הַזְּרוֹעַ אוֹ לְהַצְבִּיעַ עָלָיו בְּשָׁעָה שֶׁאוֹמֵר אֶת הַקֶּטַע הַבָּא, אֲבָל נָכוֹן לְהִסְתַּכֵּל בּוֹ.

פֶּסַח שֶׁהָיוּ אֲבוֹתֵינוּ אוֹכְלִים בִּזְמַן שֶׁבֵּית הַמִּקְדָּשׁ קַיָּם, עַל שׁוּם מָה?

עַל שׁוּם שֶׁפָּסַח הַקָּדוֹשׁ בָּרוּךְ הוּא עַל בָּתֵּי אֲבוֹתֵינוּ בְּמִצְרַיִם, שֶׁנֶּאֱמַר, "וַאֲמַרְתֶּם זֶבַח פֶּסַח הוּא לַיְיָ אֲשֶׁר פָּסַח עַל בָּתֵּי בְנֵי יִשְׂרָאֵל בְּמִצְרַיִם בְּנָגְפּוֹ אֶת מִצְרַיִם וְאֶת בָּתֵּינוּ הִצִּיל וַיִּקֹּד הָעָם וַיִּשְׁתַּחֲווּ."

How many benefits, doubled and redoubled, has the Omnipresent bestowed upon us! For He took us out of Egypt, executed upon them judgments, acted against their idols, killed their first-born, gave us their money, split the sea for us, brought us through it on dry land, submerged our enemies in it, supplied our needs in the desert for forty years, fed us the Manna, gave us the Sabbath, brought us before Mount Sinai, gave us the *Torah*, brought us into the Land of Israel, and built us the Temple to atone for all our sins!

Rabban Gamliel used to say: Whoever does not discuss these three things on Passover has not discharged his obligation. They are:

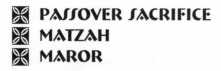

- ✠ **PASSOVER SACRIFICE**
- ✠ **MATZAH**
- ✠ **MAROR**

> One should not hold or point to the meat (זְרוֹעַ) on the *Seder* plate which symbolizes the Passover sacrifice when referring to it because it might appear as though he or she had declared it to have the sanctity of a sacrifice, and sacrifices may not be offered outside the Temple.[64]

The **PASSOVER SACRIFICE** which our ancestors used to eat during the time when the Temple stood, what was it for?

It was because the Holy One, Blessed be He, passed over the houses of our ancestors in Egypt, as it says, "You shall say, 'It is a Passover sacrifice for *Hashem*, Who passed over the houses of the Children of Israel in Egypt when He plagued the Egyptians, but our houses He saved.' And the people bowed and prostrated themselves."[65]

---

[64] *Mishnah Berurah* on *Shulchan Aruch, Orach Chaim* 473:7.

[65] Exodus 12:27. Rabbi Shimshon Raphael Hirsch points out that the word "Pesach" (פֶּסַח) means "to limp" and suggests that God hesitated when He passed over the houses of the Jews, only sparing them thanks to the merit

יקח את חתיכת המצה הפרוסה ויראנה לכל המסובים ויאמר:

מַצָּה זוֹ שֶׁאָנוּ אוֹכְלִים, עַל שׁוּם מָה?

עַל שׁוּם שֶׁלֹּא הִסְפִּיק בְּצֵקָם (נ"א: בְּצֵקָת) שֶׁל אֲבוֹתֵינוּ לְהַחֲמִיץ עַד שֶׁנִּגְלָה עֲלֵיהֶם מֶלֶךְ מַלְכֵי הַמְּלָכִים הַקָּדוֹשׁ בָּרוּךְ הוּא וּגְאָלָם שֶׁנֶּאֱמַר, "וַיֹּאפוּ אֶת הַבָּצֵק אֲשֶׁר הוֹצִיאוּ מִמִּצְרַיִם עֻגֹת מַצּוֹת כִּי לֹא חָמֵץ כִּי גֹרְשׁוּ מִמִּצְרַיִם וְלֹא יָכְלוּ לְהִתְמַהְמֵהַּ וְגַם צֵדָה לֹא עָשׂוּ לָהֶם."

יקח את המרור ויראנה לכל המסובים ויאמר:

מָרוֹר זֶה שֶׁאָנוּ אוֹכְלִים, עַל שׁוּם מָה?

עַל שׁוּם שֶׁמֵּרְרוּ הַמִּצְרִים אֶת חַיֵּי אֲבוֹתֵינוּ בְּמִצְרַיִם, שֶׁנֶּאֱמַר, "וַיְמָרְרוּ אֶת חַיֵּיהֶם בַּעֲבֹדָה קָשָׁה בְּחֹמֶר וּבִלְבֵנִים וּבְכָל עֲבֹדָה בַּשָּׂדֶה אֵת כָּל עֲבֹדָתָם אֲשֶׁר עָבְדוּ בָהֶם בְּפָרֶךְ."

בְּכָל דּוֹר וָדוֹר חַיָּב אָדָם לִרְאוֹת אֶת עַצְמוֹ כְּאִלּוּ הוּא יָצָא מִמִּצְרַיִם, שֶׁנֶּאֱמַר, "וְהִגַּדְתָּ לְבִנְךָ בַּיּוֹם הַהוּא לֵאמֹר בַּעֲבוּר זֶה עָשָׂה יְיָ לִי בְּצֵאתִי מִמִּצְרַיִם." לֹא אֶת אֲבוֹתֵינוּ בִּלְבָד גָּאַל הַקָּדוֹשׁ בָּרוּךְ הוּא אֶלָּא אַף אוֹתָנוּ גָּאַל עִמָּהֶם

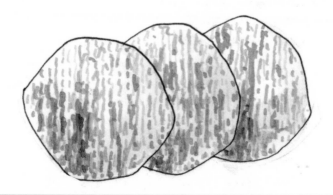

they gained by observing the *Mitzvoth* associated with the Passover holiday (Commentary to Exodus 12:11).

> When discussing the *Matzah*, one should display the broken middle *Matzah* for all to see.

This **MATZAH** which we eat, what is it for?

It is because the dough of our ancestors did not have time to rise before the King of Kings, the Holy One, Blessed be He, revealed Himself to them and redeemed them, as it says, "They baked the dough which they brought out of Egypt [into] unleavened cakes, for it did not rise because they were driven out from Egypt and could not delay; also provisions [for the trip] they did not make for themselves."[66]

> When discussing the *Maror*, one should display it for all to see.

This **MAROR** which we eat, what is it for?

It is because the Egyptians embittered the lives of our ancestors in Egypt, as it says, "They embittered their lives with harsh servitude, with mortar and with bricks, and with all [kinds of] labor in the field; and all their labor which they made them perform was with harshness."[67]

In every generation a person is obliged to view himself as though he exited Egypt, as it says, "You shall tell your son on that day, saying, 'Because of this which *Hashem* did for me during my departure from Egypt.'"[68] Not only did the Holy One, Blessed be He, redeem our ancestors, but He also redeemed us with them, as

---

[66] Exodus 12:39.

[67] Exodus 1:14. Rabbi Shimshon Raphael Hirsch draws a parallel between the Hebrew words for harshness (פֶּרֶךְ) and for the curtain (פָּרֹכֶת) which separated between the Holy of Holies and the rest of the Tabernacle. Before reducing them to slavery, Pharaoh separated the Jews from the rest of the Egyptian population by declaring them foreigners who must contribute money and manpower for building Egyptian storage cities in exchange for the so-called "privilege" of being permitted to reside in Egypt.

[68] Exodus 13:8.

שֶׁנֶּאֱמַר, "וְאוֹתָנוּ הוֹצִיא מִשָּׁם לְמַעַן הָבִיא אֹתָנוּ לָתֶת לָנוּ אֶת
הָאָרֶץ אֲשֶׁר נִשְׁבַּע לַאֲבֹתֵינוּ."

מכסים את המצות ואוחז את הכוס בידו עד ששותה ממנה ויש נוהגים שלא לאחוז את
הכוס כאן אלא בתחילת ברכת "גָּאַל יִשְׂרָאֵל."

לְפִיכָךְ אֲנַחְנוּ חַיָּבִים לְהוֹדוֹת לְהַלֵּל לְשַׁבֵּחַ לְפָאֵר לְרוֹמֵם
לְהַדֵּר לְבָרֵךְ לְעַלֵּה וּלְקַלֵּס לְמִי שֶׁעָשָׂה לַאֲבוֹתֵינוּ וְלָנוּ אֶת כָּל הַנִּסִּים
הָאֵלּוּ. הוֹצִיאָנוּ מֵעַבְדוּת לְחֵרוּת מִיָּגוֹן לְשִׂמְחָה וּמֵאֵבֶל לְיוֹם טוֹב
וּמֵאֲפֵלָה לְאוֹר גָּדוֹל וּמִשִׁעְבּוּד לִגְאֻלָּה וְנֹאמַר (נ"א: וְנֶאֱמַר) לְפָנָיו
שִׁירָה חֲדָשָׁה הַלְלוּיָהּ.

יש נוהגים כאן להניח את הכוס ולכסות את המצות ולהרים את הכוס לפני ברכת "גָּאַל
יִשְׂרָאֵל".

הַלְלוּיָהּ הַלְלוּ עַבְדֵי יְיָ הַלְלוּ אֶת שֵׁם יְיָ. יְהִי שֵׁם יְיָ מְבֹרָךְ
מֵעַתָּה וְעַד עוֹלָם. מִמִּזְרַח שֶׁמֶשׁ עַד מְבוֹאוֹ מְהֻלָּל שֵׁם יְיָ. רָם עַל
כָּל גּוֹיִם יְיָ עַל הַשָּׁמַיִם כְּבוֹדוֹ. מִי כַּיְיָ אֱלֹהֵינוּ הַמַּגְבִּיהִי לָשָׁבֶת.
הַמַּשְׁפִּילִי לִרְאוֹת בַּשָּׁמַיִם וּבָאָרֶץ. מְקִימִי מֵעָפָר דָּל מֵאַשְׁפֹּת יָרִים
אֶבְיוֹן. לְהוֹשִׁיבִי עִם נְדִיבִים עִם נְדִיבֵי

it says, "He took us out of there in order to bring us to give us the land which He swore to our ancestors."[69]

The *Matzoth* are covered, and the cup of wine is raised until the conclusion of the blessing "who redeemed Israel." Some, however, do not raise the cup until reciting the blessing.

Therefore, we are obligated to thank, praise, laud, glorify, exalt, honor, bless, elevate, and extol the One Who performed for our ancestors and for us all these miracles: He took us out from slavery to freedom, from sorrow to joy, from mourning to festivity, from murky darkness to great light, from bondage to redemption. Let us say before Him a new song, "Praise God!"[70]

Some have the custom to put down the wine cup and cover the *Matzoth* at this point. They lift it again further on before the blessing "who redeemed Israel."

Praise God! Praise, servants of *Hashem*, praise the Name of *Hashem*! From where the sun rises until where it sets may the Name of *Hashem* be praised. Lofty above all nations is *Hashem*; above the Heavens is His glory.[71] Who is like *Hashem*, our God, Who exalts Himself to dwell [above all]? He lowers Himself to observe what is in the Heavens and the Earth. He raises the downtrodden from the dust; from the trash heap He raises the destitute. To position them with princes, with princes of His

---

[69] Deuteronomy 6:23.

[70] Although the paragraphs of *Hallel* which follow are very ancient, we can nevertheless consider them a "new song" because, as the *Haggadah* just mentioned, we must always view ourselves as though we personally were saved from spiritual oblivion in Egypt.

[71] Since *Hashem* is omnipotent, there is no question that He is more powerful than any nation or combination of nations. Why, then, does the Psalm praise Him as "above all nations?" Rabbi Avraham Ibn Ezra explains that *Hashem* is above the **praise** of all nations, no amount of which could adequately describe Him.

עַמּוֹ. מוֹשִׁיבִי עֲקֶרֶת הַבַּיִת אֵם הַבָּנִים שְׂמֵחָה הַלְלוּיָהּ.

בְּצֵאת יִשְׂרָאֵל מִמִּצְרָיִם בֵּית יַעֲקֹב מֵעַם לֹעֵז. הָיְתָה יְהוּדָה לְקָדְשׁוֹ יִשְׂרָאֵל מַמְשְׁלוֹתָיו. הַיָּם רָאָה וַיָּנֹס הַיַּרְדֵּן יִסֹּב לְאָחוֹר. הֶהָרִים רָקְדוּ כְאֵילִים גְּבָעוֹת כִּבְנֵי צֹאן. מַה לְּךָ הַיָּם כִּי תָנוּס הַיַּרְדֵּן תִּסֹּב לְאָחוֹר. הֶהָרִים תִּרְקְדוּ כְאֵילִים גְּבָעוֹת כִּבְנֵי צֹאן. מִלִּפְנֵי אָדוֹן חוּלִי אָרֶץ מִלִּפְנֵי אֱלוֹהַּ יַעֲקֹב. הַהֹפְכִי הַצּוּר אֲגַם מָיִם חַלָּמִישׁ לְמַעְיְנוֹ מָיִם.

אלה שלא הרימו את הכוס מלפני "לְפִיכָךְ" או שהניחו את הכוס אחר כך מכסים עכשיו את המצות ומגביהים את הכוס.

בָּרוּךְ אַתָּה יְיָ אֱלֹהֵינוּ מֶלֶךְ הָעוֹלָם אֲשֶׁר גְּאָלָנוּ וְגָאַל אֶת אֲבוֹתֵינוּ מִמִּצְרַיִם וְהִגִּיעָנוּ הַלַּיְלָה הַזֶּה לֶאֱכָל בּוֹ מַצָּה וּמָרוֹר כֵּן יְיָ אֱלֹהֵינוּ וֵאלֹהֵי אֲבוֹתֵינוּ יַגִּיעֵנוּ לְמוֹעֲדִים וְלִרְגָלִים אֲחֵרִים הַבָּאִים לִקְרָאתֵנוּ לְשָׁלוֹם שְׂמֵחִים בְּבִנְיַן עִירֶךָ וְשָׂשִׂים בַּעֲבוֹדָתֶךָ וְנֹאכַל שָׁם מִן הַזְּבָחִים וּמִן הַפְּסָחִים (במוצאי שבת אומרים: מִן הַפְּסָחִים וּמִן הַזְּבָחִים) אֲשֶׁר יַגִּיעַ דָּמָם

people. He positions the barren lady of the home as a joyful mother of children. Praise God![72]

Upon the departure of Israel from Egypt, the House of Jacob from a nation of foreign tongue. Judah was His holy one, Israel His dominion. The sea observed and fled; the Jordan turned backward.[73] The mountains danced like rams, the hills like lambs.[74] What is it with you, sea, that you flee, Jordan that you turn backward? Mountains that you dance like rams, hills like lambs? From before *Hashem* Who formed the Earth, from before the God of Jacob. He turns the rock into a pool of water, flint into a spring of water.[75]

Those who did not raise the wine cup earlier, or who set it down, now cover the *Matzoth* and raise it.

Blessed are You, *Hashem*, our God, King of the Universe, who redeemed us, and redeemed our ancestors from Egypt, and brought us this night to eat *Matzah* and *Maror*. So *Hashem*, our God and God of our ancestors, may You bring us to other seasons and festivals which greet us in peace, rejoicing in the building of Your city and delighting in Your service. May we partake there from the offerings and Passover sacrifices (on Saturday night, say instead: from the Passover sacrifices and the offerings)[76] whose blood

---

[72] Psalms 113:1-9.

[73] Although the Jews crossed the Reed Sea after leaving Egypt, the Psalm mentions the Jordan River because every body of water throughout the world also split (*Rashi*, citing *Midrash Tehillim* 114).

[74] Even the mountains and hills surrounding the Reed Sea shook when it split. Alternatively, the Psalm refers to the subsequent Giving of the *Torah* when "all the mountain trembled greatly" (Exodus 19:18) (*Me'am Lo'ez*).

[75] Psalms 114:1-8.

[76] The offerings refer to the festival sacrifices (חֲגִיגוֹת) which the Jews brought in addition to the Passover sacrifice. The meat of those sacrifices was eaten before consuming the Passover sacrifice so that the latter could be eaten on a full stomach as the *Halachah* requires. When Passover fell on a Sunday, the

עַל קִיר מִזְבַּחֲךָ לְרָצוֹן וְנוֹדֶה לְךָ שִׁיר חָדָשׁ עַל גְּאֻלָּתֵנוּ וְעַל פְּדוּת
נַפְשֵׁנוּ. בָּרוּךְ אַתָּה יְיָ גָּאַל יִשְׂרָאֵל.

הספרדים ובני עדות המזרח מדלגים על הברכה ושותים את הכוס מיד.

בָּרוּךְ אַתָּה יְיָ אֱלֹהֵינוּ מֶלֶךְ הָעוֹלָם בּוֹרֵא פְּרִי הַגָּפֶן.

שותים את הכוס השניה והזכרים עושים כן בהסבה על צדם השמאלי.

רָחְצָה

נוטלים ידים ואומרים:

בָּרוּךְ אַתָּה יְיָ אֱלֹהֵינוּ מֶלֶךְ הָעוֹלָם אֲשֶׁר קִדְּשָׁנוּ בְּמִצְוֹתָיו
וְצִוָּנוּ עַל נְטִילַת יָדַיִם.

מוֹצִיא

העורך את הסדר אוחז את כל שלושת המצות ביחד ומכוון להוציא את כל המסובים
כשהוא מברך:

בָּרוּךְ אַתָּה יְיָ אֱלֹהֵינוּ מֶלֶךְ הָעוֹלָם הַמּוֹצִיא לֶחֶם מִן הָאָרֶץ.

Jews slaughtered the Passover lambs on *Shabbath* afternoon. However, it
was forbidden to slaughter other festival sacrifices on *Shabbath* or at night, so
those had to wait until Sunday morning. The wording of the blessing is
therefore changed on Saturday night because the Passover sacrifice preceded
the festival sacrifices.

reaches the walls of Your altar for good will, and we will thank You with a new song for our redemption and the deliverance of our souls. Blessed are You, God who redeemed Israel.

Sefaradi Jews do ***not*** recite this blessing:

Blessed are You, *Hashem*, our God, King of the Universe, Creator of the fruit of the vine.

The *Seder* participants drink the second cup of wine. Males lean on their left sides.

WASHING

Each person should wash his or her hands and recite the following blessing.

Blessed are You, *Hashem*, our God, King of the Universe, Who has sanctified us with His commandments and commanded us concerning handwashing.

BLESSING FOR BREAD

The leader of the *Seder* lifts all three *Matzoth* and recites the following blessing on his own behalf and on behalf of all who are present.

Blessed are You, *Hashem*, our God, King of the Universe, Who brings forth bread from the Earth.

✠ מַצָּה

מי שעורך את הסדר מניח את המצה התחתונה ואוחז בידיו את המצה העליונה עם
המצה האמצעית ומכוון להוציא את כל המסובים כשהוא מברך:

בָּרוּךְ אַתָּה יְיָ אֱלֹהֵינוּ מֶלֶךְ הָעוֹלָם אֲשֶׁר קִדְּשָׁנוּ
בְּמִצְוֹתָיו וְצִוָּנוּ עַל אֲכִילַת מַצָּה.

כל אחד מן המסובים צריך לקבל חתיכה מן המצה העליונה ומן המצה האמצעית. גם
מוסיפים עוד מצה כדי שכל אחד יאכל לפחות כזית. צריכים לאכול את המצה בלי שום
הפסק והזכרים אוכלים את המצה בהסבה על צדם השמאלי.

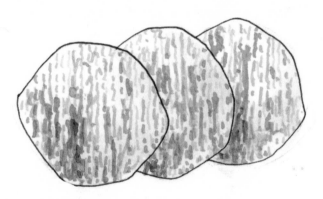

✠ מָרוֹר

יקח כזית מרור ויטביל אותו בחרוסת וינער מעליו את החרוסת ויאמר:

בָּרוּךְ אַתָּה יְיָ אֱלֹהֵינוּ מֶלֶךְ הָעוֹלָם אֲשֶׁר קִדְּשָׁנוּ בְּמִצְוֹתָיו
וְצִוָּנוּ עַל אֲכִילַת מָרוֹר.

אוכלים את המרור בלי הסבה.

MATZAH

The leader of the *Seder* lets go of the bottom *Matzah* and recites the following blessing on the top two *Matzoth* on his own behalf and on behalf of all who are present.

Blessed are You, *Hashem,* our God, King of the Universe, Who has sanctified us with His commandments and commanded us concerning the eating of *Matzah.*

Everyone present should receive a piece from each of the two *Matzoth.* Since each participant must consume at least an olive's bulk of *Matzah,* one should add other *Matzoth* to provide each person with the required amount.[77] The *Matzah* should be eaten without interruption. Males should do so while leaning on their left sides.

MAROR

After eating the *Matzah,* each *Seder* participant takes an olive's bulk of *Maror,* dips it in *Charoseth,* and then shakes off the *Charoseth.* The leader of the *Seder* then recites the following blessing on his own behalf and on behalf of those assembled.

Blessed are You, *Hashem,* our God, King of the Universe, Who has sanctified us with His commandments and commanded us concerning the eating of *Maror.*

One does not recline while eating *Maror.*

---

[77] According to most authorities, an olive's bulk is 29 milliliters, or about one fluid ounce. Some, however, state that this amount should be doubled, and the *Mishnah Berurah* recommends taking this view into account for this *Mitzvah.* One may follow the more lenient view when consuming the combination of *Matzah* and *Maror.*

 **כּוֹרֵךְ**

יקח כזית מן המצה התחתונה וכורך כזית מרור אתו. יש נוהגים להטביל את הכריכה
בחרוסת ולנער אותה לפני שאומרים:

זֵכֶר לְמִקְדָּשׁ כְּהִלֵּל. כֵּן עָשָׂה הִלֵּל בִּזְמַן שֶׁבֵּית הַמִּקְדָּשׁ הָיָה קַיָּם.
הָיָה כּוֹרֵךְ (נ״א פֶּסַח) מַצָּה וּמָרוֹר וְאוֹכֵל בְּיַחַד לְקַיֵּם מַה שֶׁנֶּאֱמַר "עַל
מַצּוֹת וּמְרֹרִים יֹאכְלֻהוּ."

אוכלים את הכריכה והזכרים מסבים על צדם השמאלי.

 שֻׁלְחָן עוֹרֵךְ

אוכלים את הסעודה.

צָפוּן

בסוף הסעודה אוכלים את האפיקומן ושיעורו כזית. אם אין מספיק בחתיכת האפיקומן
כדי לתת לכל אחד מן המסובים כזית אז חייבים להוסיף עליו ממצות אחרות. הזכרים
אוכלים את האפיקומן בהסבה.

COMBINATION

Next, the *Seder* participants combine an olive's bulk of *Matzah* with an olive's bulk of *Maror*. It is preferable to let each person have part of the bottom *Matzah* for this purpose, but other *Matzah* may be added to produce the required quantity. Some have the custom to dip the combination in *Charoseth* and shake it off before reciting the following.

A *memorial* for the Temple according to [the practice of] Hillel. So Hillel did in the time when the Temple stood. He would wrap (*some say*: the Passover sacrifice) *Matzah* and *Maror* and eat them together to fulfill that which it says, "Upon unleavened bread and bitter herbs they shall eat it."[78]

The participants eat the combination. Males should recline to the left when doing so.

SET TABLE

The festive meal is served.

EATING THE AFIKOMAN

At the end of the meal, the *Matzah* which was set aside for the *Afikoman* is brought out. Each participant at the *Seder* should receive a piece of *Afikoman* sufficient to make up an olive's bulk. If not enough *Afikoman* is available to provide an olive's bulk for each participant, one should add other *Matzoth* to reach the required amount. Males should eat the *Afikoman* while reclining to the left.

[78] Numbers 9:11.

✡ בָּרֵךְ

ממלאים את הכוס השלישית. נוסח ברכת המזון לפי מנהג הספרדים ובני עדות המזרח נמצא בעמוד 325.

שִׁיר הַמַּעֲלוֹת בְּשׁוּב יְיָ אֶת שִׁיבַת צִיּוֹן הָיִינוּ כְּחֹלְמִים. אָז יִמָּלֵא שְׂחוֹק פִּינוּ וּלְשׁוֹנֵנוּ רִנָּה אָז יֹאמְרוּ בַגּוֹיִם הִגְדִּיל יְיָ לַעֲשׂוֹת עִם אֵלֶּה. הִגְדִּיל יְיָ לַעֲשׂוֹת עִמָּנוּ הָיִינוּ שְׂמֵחִים. שׁוּבָה יְיָ אֶת שְׁבִיתֵנוּ כַּאֲפִיקִים בַּנֶּגֶב. הַזֹּרְעִים בְּדִמְעָה בְּרִנָּה יִקְצֹרוּ. הָלוֹךְ יֵלֵךְ וּבָכֹה נֹשֵׂא מֶשֶׁךְ הַזָּרַע בֹּא יָבוֹא בְרִנָּה נֹשֵׂא אֲלֻמֹּתָיו.

ויש מוסיפים:

תְּהִלַּת יְיָ יְדַבֶּר פִּי וִיבָרֵךְ כָּל בָּשָׂר שֵׁם קָדְשׁוֹ לְעוֹלָם וָעֶד. וַאֲנַחְנוּ נְבָרֵךְ יָהּ מֵעַתָּה וְעַד עוֹלָם הַלְלוּיָהּ. הוֹדוּ לַיְיָ כִּי טוֹב כִּי לְעוֹלָם חַסְדּוֹ. מִי יְמַלֵּל גְּבוּרוֹת יְיָ יַשְׁמִיעַ כָּל תְּהִלָּתוֹ.

 GRACE

Before reciting Grace, a Third Cup of wine should be poured. **(The** *Sefaradi* **version of Grace may be found on page 326.)**

Psalm 126 is recited before Grace:

A *song of* Ascents: When *Hashem* returns the captivity of Zion, we shall be like dreamers.[79] Then shall laughter fill our mouths and song our tongues; then shall the nations say, "*Hashem* has dealt grandly with these."[80] *Hashem* has dealt grandly with us; we have rejoiced. Return, *Hashem*, our captives as brooks in the Negev [Desert]. Those who plow with tears shall reap with song. He who travels along weeping shall, after time, carry produce; he shall surely come with song, bearing his produce.

Some add:

My mouth shall utter praise of *Hashem*, and all flesh shall bless His holy Name forever and ever.[81] We shall bless God from now until eternity; Praise God![82] Acknowledge *Hashem* for He is good, for His kindness is forever.[83] Who can articulate the mighty deeds of *Hashem*, [and who can] announce all His praise?[84]

---

[79] So great will be the joy of the redemption that prior tribulations will seem like nothing more than a fleeting dream.

[80] The future redemption of the Jews will be so complete and miraculous that even peoples who do not believe in God will be forced to acknowledge that it did not occur through happenstance, but by Divine intervention (*Metzudoth David* on Psalms 126:2). This will resemble what occurred when Israel left Egypt, and Pharaoh finally acknowledged *Hashem's* dominion (Exodus 12:31-32).

[81] Psalms 145:21.

[82] Psalms 115:18.

[83] Psalms 118:1.

[84] Psalms 106:2, according to *Metzudoth David*.

כשיש מזומן המברך אומר:

רַבּוֹתַי נְבָרֵךְ. [או ביידיש:) רַבּוֹתַי מִיר וֶועלִין בֶּענְטְשִׁין.]

השומעים עונים:

יְהִי שֵׁם יְיָ מְבֹרָךְ מֵעַתָּה וְעַד עוֹלָם.

המברך ממשיך:

יְהִי שֵׁם יְיָ מְבֹרָךְ מֵעַתָּה וְעַד עוֹלָם.

בִּרְשׁוּת מָרָנָן וְרַבָּנָן וְרַבּוֹתַי נְבָרֵךְ [במנין: אֱלֹהֵינוּ] שֶׁאָכַלְנוּ מִשֶּׁלּוֹ

השומעים עונים:

בָּרוּךְ [במנין: אֱלֹהֵינוּ] שֶׁאָכַלְנוּ מִשֶּׁלּוֹ וּבְטוּבוֹ חָיִינוּ.

המברך חוזר ואומר:

בָּרוּךְ [במנין: אֱלֹהֵינוּ] שֶׁאָכַלְנוּ מִשֶּׁלּוֹ וּבְטוּבוֹ חָיִינוּ.

בָּרוּךְ הוּא וּבָרוּךְ שְׁמוֹ

When at least three Jewish males over *Bar Mitzvah* age are present, one of them should lead the recitation of Grace. The leader says:

Gentlemen, let us bless:

Everyone else responds:

May the Name of Hashem be blessed from now until eternity.[85]

The leader then repeats:

May the Name of Hashem be blessed from now until eternity.

The leader then says the following, substituting the words "our God" for "Him" if more than ten Jewish males over *Bar Mitzvah* age are present:

With your permission, masters, rabbis, and gentlemen, let us bless Him [our God] from Whom we have eaten.

Everyone else responds, substituting the words "our God" for "He" if more than ten Jewish males over *Bar Mitzvah* age are present:

Blessed is He [our God] from Whom we have eaten and by Whose goodness we live.

The leader recites:

Blessed is He [our God] from Whom we have eaten and by Whose goodness we live.

Blessed is He and blessed is His Name.

---

[85] Psalms 113:2.

בָּרוּךְ אַתָּה יְיָ אֱלֹהֵינוּ מֶלֶךְ הָעוֹלָם הַזָּן אֶת הָעוֹלָם כֻּלּוֹ
בְּטוּבוֹ בְּחֵן בְּחֶסֶד וּבְרַחֲמִים הוּא נֹתֵן לֶחֶם לְכָל בָּשָׂר כִּי לְעוֹלָם
חַסְדּוֹ וּבְטוּבוֹ הַגָּדוֹל תָּמִיד לֹא חָסַר לָנוּ וְאַל יֶחְסַר לָנוּ מָזוֹן לְעוֹלָם
וָעֶד בַּעֲבוּר שְׁמוֹ הַגָּדוֹל כִּי הוּא אֵל זָן וּמְפַרְנֵס לַכֹּל וּמֵטִיב לַכֹּל
וּמֵכִין מָזוֹן לְכָל בְּרִיּוֹתָיו אֲשֶׁר בָּרָא (כָּאָמוּר, "פּוֹתֵחַ אֶת יָדֶךָ וּמַשְׂבִּיעַ
לְכָל חַי רָצוֹן.") בָּרוּךְ אַתָּה יְיָ הַזָּן אֶת הַכֹּל.

נוֹדֶה לְךָ יְיָ אֱלֹהֵינוּ עַל שֶׁהִנְחַלְתָּ לַאֲבוֹתֵינוּ אֶרֶץ חֶמְדָּה
טוֹבָה וּרְחָבָה וְעַל שֶׁהוֹצֵאתָנוּ יְיָ אֱלֹהֵינוּ מֵאֶרֶץ מִצְרַיִם וּפְדִיתָנוּ
מִבֵּית עֲבָדִים וְעַל בְּרִיתְךָ שֶׁחָתַמְתָּ בִּבְשָׂרֵנוּ וְעַל תּוֹרָתְךָ שֶׁלִּמַּדְתָּנוּ
וְעַל חֻקֶּיךָ שֶׁהוֹדַעְתָּנוּ וְעַל חַיִּים חֵן וָחֶסֶד שֶׁחוֹנַנְתָּנוּ וְעַל אֲכִילַת
מָזוֹן שָׁאַתָּה זָן וּמְפַרְנֵס אוֹתָנוּ תָּמִיד בְּכָל יוֹם וּבְכָל עֵת וּבְכָל שָׁעָה.

וְעַל הַכֹּל יְיָ אֱלֹהֵינוּ אֲנַחְנוּ מוֹדִים לָךְ וּמְבָרְכִים אוֹתָךְ
יִתְבָּרַךְ שִׁמְךָ בְּפִי כָל חַי תָּמִיד לְעוֹלָם וָעֶד כַּכָּתוּב, "וְאָכַלְתָּ וְשָׂבָעְתָּ
וּבֵרַכְתָּ אֶת יְיָ אֱלֹהֶיךָ עַל הָאָרֶץ הַטֹּבָה אֲשֶׁר נָתַן לָךְ." בָּרוּךְ אַתָּה יְיָ
עַל הָאָרֶץ וְעַל הַמָּזוֹן.

רַחֶם נָא יְיָ אֱלֹהֵינוּ עַל יִשְׂרָאֵל עַמֶּךָ וְעַל יְרוּשָׁלַיִם עִירֶךָ וְעַל
צִיּוֹן מִשְׁכַּן כְּבוֹדֶךָ וְעַל מַלְכוּת בֵּית דָּוִד מְשִׁיחֶךָ וְעַל הַבַּיִת הַגָּדוֹל
וְהַקָּדוֹשׁ שֶׁנִּקְרָא שִׁמְךָ עָלָיו. אֱלֹהֵינוּ אָבִינוּ רְעֵנוּ זוֹנֵנוּ פַּרְנְסֵנוּ
וְכַלְכְּלֵנוּ

Blessed are You, *Hashem* our God, King of the Universe, Who sustains the entire world with goodness, grace, kindness, and mercy. He gives bread to all flesh, for His kindness is eternal, and in His great goodness we have never lacked — nor shall we ever lack — food to all eternity, for the sake of His great Name, for He is a God who sustains and provides for all, and bestows good to all, and prepares food for all His creatures whom He has created. (*Some add*: As it says, "You open Your hand and satisfy the desires of all the living."[86]) Blessed are You, *Hashem*, Sustainer of all.

We thank you, *Hashem* our God, because You bequeathed to our ancestors a desirable, good, and spacious land, and because You took us out, *Hashem* our God, from the Land of Egypt, redeemed us from the place of servitude, sealed Your covenant in our flesh, taught us Your *Torah*, informed us of Your laws, granted us life, grace, and kindness, and because of the food with which You sustain and provide us continually, every day, at all times, and at every moment.

For everything, *Hashem,* our God, we thank You and bless You. May Your Name be blessed by the mouth of all the living continually for all eternity, as it is written, "You shall eat and be satisfied and bless *Hashem,* your God, for the good land which He gave you."[87] Blessed are You, *Hashem,* for the Land and for the sustenance.

Have mercy, *Hashem,* our God, upon Israel Your people, upon Jerusalem Your city, upon Zion the seat of Your glory, upon the kingdom of the House of David, Your anointed one, and upon the great and holy House upon which Your Name is called. Our God, our Father, shepherd us, nourish us, sustain us, provide for

---

[86] Psalms 145:16.
[87] Deuteronomy 8:10.

וְהַרְוִיחֵנוּ וְהַרְוַח לָנוּ יְיָ אֱלֹהֵינוּ מְהֵרָה מִכָּל צָרוֹתֵנוּ וְנָא אַל תַּצְרִיכֵנוּ
יְיָ אֱלֹהֵינוּ לֹא לִידֵי מַתְּנַת בָּשָׂר וָדָם וְלֹא לִידֵי הַלְוָאָתָם כִּי אִם לְיָדְךָ
הַמְּלֵאָה הַפְּתוּחָה הַקְּדוֹשָׁה וְהָרְחָבָה שֶׁלֹּא נֵבוֹשׁ וְלֹא נִכָּלֵם לְעוֹלָם
וָעֶד.

[בשבת מוסיפים:]   רְצֵה וְהַחֲלִיצֵנוּ יְיָ אֱלֹהֵינוּ בְּמִצְוֹתֶיךָ וּבְמִצְוַת יוֹם
הַשְּׁבִיעִי הַשַּׁבָּת הַגָּדוֹל וְהַקָּדוֹשׁ הַזֶּה כִּי יוֹם זֶה גָּדוֹל וְקָדוֹשׁ הוּא
לְפָנֶיךָ לִשְׁבָּת בּוֹ וְלָנוּחַ בּוֹ בְּאַהֲבָה כְּמִצְוַת רְצוֹנֶךָ וּבִרְצוֹנְךָ הָנִיחַ לָנוּ
יְיָ אֱלֹהֵינוּ שֶׁלֹּא תְהֵא צָרָה וְיָגוֹן וַאֲנָחָה בְּיוֹם מְנוּחָתֵנוּ וְהַרְאֵנוּ יְיָ
אֱלֹהֵינוּ בְּנֶחָמַת צִיּוֹן עִירֶךָ וּבְבִנְיַן יְרוּשָׁלַיִם עִיר קָדְשֶׁךָ כִּי אַתָּה הוּא
בַּעַל הַיְשׁוּעוֹת וּבַעַל הַנֶּחָמוֹת.

אֱלֹהֵינוּ וֵאלֹהֵי אֲבוֹתֵינוּ יַעֲלֶה וְיָבֹא וְיַגִּיעַ וְיֵרָאֶה וְיֵרָצֶה
וְיִשָּׁמַע וְיִפָּקֵד וְיִזָּכֵר זִכְרוֹנֵנוּ וּפִקְדוֹנֵנוּ וְזִכְרוֹן אֲבוֹתֵינוּ וְזִכְרוֹן מָשִׁיחַ
בֶּן דָּוִד עַבְדֶּךָ וְזִכְרוֹן יְרוּשָׁלַיִם עִיר קָדְשֶׁךָ וְזִכְרוֹן כָּל עַמְּךָ בֵּית
יִשְׂרָאֵל לְפָנֶיךָ לִפְלֵיטָה לְטוֹבָה לְחֵן וּלְחֶסֶד וּלְרַחֲמִים לְחַיִּים
וּלְשָׁלוֹם בְּיוֹם חַג הַמַּצּוֹת הַזֶּה זָכְרֵנוּ יְיָ אֱלֹהֵינוּ בּוֹ לְטוֹבָה וּפָקְדֵנוּ
בּוֹ לִבְרָכָה וְהוֹשִׁיעֵנוּ בּוֹ לְחַיִּים (טוֹבִים) וּבִדְבַר יְשׁוּעָה וְרַחֲמִים חוּס
וְחָנֵּנוּ וְרַחֵם עָלֵינוּ וְהוֹשִׁיעֵנוּ כִּי אֵלֶיךָ עֵינֵינוּ כִּי אֵל (מֶלֶךְ) חַנּוּן
וְרַחוּם אָתָּה.

וּבְנֵה יְרוּשָׁלַיִם עִיר הַקֹּדֶשׁ בִּמְהֵרָה בְיָמֵינוּ.   בָּרוּךְ אַתָּה יְיָ
בּוֹנֵה (בְּרַחֲמָיו) יְרוּשָׁלָיִם.   אָמֵן.

us, cause us to prosper and grant us relief, *Hashem* our God, speedily, from all our troubles, and please do not cause us, *Hashem* our God, to rely upon gifts from flesh and blood, or their loans, but rather Your full, open, holy, and generous hand so that we not be shamed or humiliated ever.

[*On the Sabbath add the following*:] Take pleasure and grant us relief, *Hashem*, our God, through Your commandments and the commandment of the seventh day, this great and holy Sabbath; for this day is great and holy before You, to cease work on it and to rest on it with love according to the dictate of Your will; and may it be Your will, *Hashem*, our God, to grant us that there be no trouble, grief, nor lamenting on the day of our rest. Show us, *Hashem*, our God, the consolation of Zion, Your city, and the restoration of Jerusalem, Your holy city, for You are the Master of salvation and consolation.

Our God and God of our ancestors, may it rise, come, reach, be seen, pleasing, heard, recalled, and memorialized our remembrance and our account, and the remembrance of our ancestors, the remembrance of the *Mashiach*, son of David, Your servant, the remembrance of Jerusalem, Your holy city, and the remembrance of all Your people, the House of Israel, for deliverance, for good, for grace, for kindness, for mercy, for life, and for peace on this day, a festival of *Matzoth*. Remember us upon it, *Hashem*, our God, for good, and recall us upon it for blessing, and deliver us upon it for (*some add*: "good") life, and with a word of salvation and mercy; take pity and be gracious to us, and be merciful to us, and save us, for our eyes are upon You, for You are a merciful and gracious God (*some add*: "and King").

Rebuild Jerusalem, the holy city, speedily in our days. Blessed are You, *Hashem*, Who rebuilds Jerusalem (*some add*: "in His mercy"). *Amen.*

בָּרוּךְ אַתָּה יְיָ אֱלֹהֵינוּ מֶלֶךְ הָעוֹלָם הָאֵל אָבִינוּ מַלְכֵּנוּ
אַדִּירֵנוּ בּוֹרְאֵנוּ גּוֹאֲלֵנוּ יוֹצְרֵנוּ קְדוֹשֵׁנוּ קְדוֹשׁ יַעֲקֹב רוֹעֵנוּ רוֹעֵה
יִשְׂרָאֵל הַמֶּלֶךְ הַטּוֹב וְהַמֵּטִיב לַכֹּל שֶׁבְּכָל יוֹם וָיוֹם הוּא הֵטִיב הוּא
מֵטִיב הוּא יֵיטִיב לָנוּ הוּא גְמָלָנוּ הוּא גוֹמְלֵנוּ הוּא יִגְמְלֵנוּ לָעַד לְחֵן
וּלְחֶסֶד וּלְרַחֲמִים וּלְרֶוַח הַצָּלָה וְהַצְלָחָה בְּרָכָה וִישׁוּעָה נֶחָמָה
פַּרְנָסָה וְכַלְכָּלָה וְרַחֲמִים וְחַיִּים וְשָׁלוֹם וְכָל טוֹב וּמִכָּל טוּב לְעוֹלָם
אַל יְחַסְּרֵנוּ.

הָרַחֲמָן הוּא יִמְלוֹךְ עָלֵינוּ לְעוֹלָם וָעֶד.

הָרַחֲמָן הוּא יִתְבָּרַךְ בַּשָּׁמַיִם וּבָאָרֶץ.

הָרַחֲמָן הוּא יִשְׁתַּבַּח לְדוֹר דּוֹרִים וְיִתְפָּאַר בָּנוּ לָעַד וּלְנֵצַח
נְצָחִים וְיִתְהַדַּר בָּנוּ לָעַד וּלְעוֹלְמֵי עוֹלָמִים.

הָרַחֲמָן הוּא יְפַרְנְסֵנוּ בְּכָבוֹד.

הָרַחֲמָן הוּא יִשְׁבּוֹר עֻלֵּנוּ מֵעַל צַוָּארֵנוּ וְהוּא יוֹלִיכֵנוּ
קוֹמְמִיּוּת לְאַרְצֵנוּ.

הָרַחֲמָן הוּא יִשְׁלַח לָנוּ בְּרָכָה מְרֻבָּה בַּבַּיִת הַזֶּה וְעַל שֻׁלְחָן
זֶה שֶׁאָכַלְנוּ עָלָיו.

הָרַחֲמָן הוּא יִשְׁלַח לָנוּ אֶת אֵלִיָּהוּ הַנָּבִיא זָכוּר לַטּוֹב וִיבַשֶּׂר
לָנוּ בְּשׂוֹרוֹת טוֹבוֹת יְשׁוּעוֹת וְנֶחָמוֹת.

האוכל אצל הוריו אומר:

Blessed are You, *Hashem*, our God, King of the Universe, the God who is our Father, our King, our Champion, our Creator, our Redeemer, our Originator, our Holy One, the Holy One of Jacob, our Shepherd, the Shepherd of Israel, the good King, the One who does good to all; for each and every day He has done good, does good, and will do good for us. He has benefited us, benefits us, and will benefit us forever with grace, kindness, mercy, relief, saving, success, blessing, salvation, consolation, livelihood, sustenance, mercy, life, peace, and all good; and He shall never cause us to lack any good thing.

May the Merciful One reign over us.

May the Merciful One be blessed in Heaven and on Earth.

May the Merciful One be blessed for all generations and glory in us forever and to all eternity and take pride in us forever and to all eternity.

May the Merciful One provide for us with honor.

May the Merciful One break the yoke from upon our necks and cause us to walk upright to our land.

May the Merciful One send us plentiful blessing in this house and upon this table where we have eaten.

May the Merciful One send us Elijah the Prophet, of blessed memory, and may he announce to us good news, salvation, and consolation.

One should adapt the following blessing to suit his or her personal situation. If one is eating with one's parents, he or she should say:

הָרַחֲמָן הוּא יְבָרֵךְ אֶת אָבִי מוֹרִי בַּעַל הַבַּיִת הַזֶּה וְאֶת אִמִּי מוֹרָתִי בַּעֲלַת הַבַּיִת הַזֶּה אוֹתָם וְאֶת בֵּיתָם וְאֶת זַרְעָם וְאֶת כָּל אֲשֶׁר לָהֶם...

אנשים או נשים נשואים אומרים:

הָרַחֲמָן הוּא יְבָרֵךְ אוֹתִי וְאֶת אִשְׁתִּי [אוֹ וְאֶת בַּעְלִי] וְאֶת זַרְעִי וְאֶת כָּל אֲשֶׁר לִי...

אורחים אומרים:

הָרַחֲמָן הוּא יְבָרֵךְ אֶת מוֹרִי בַּעַל הַבַּיִת הַזֶּה וְאֶת מוֹרָתִי בַּעֲלַת הַבַּיִת הַזֶּה אוֹתָם וְאֶת בֵּיתָם וְאֶת זַרְעָם וְאֶת כָּל אֲשֶׁר לָהֶם...

ובכל מקרה מסיימים:

...[וְאֶת כָּל הַמְסֻבִּים כַּאן] אוֹתָנוּ וְאֶת כָּל אֲשֶׁר לָנוּ כְּמוֹ שֶׁנִּתְבָּרְכוּ אֲבוֹתֵינוּ אַבְרָהָם יִצְחָק וְיַעֲקֹב בַּכֹּל מִכֹּל כֹּל כֵּן יְבָרֵךְ אוֹתָנוּ כֻּלָּנוּ יַחַד בִּבְרָכָה שְׁלֵמָה וְנֹאמַר אָמֵן.

בַּמָּרוֹם יְלַמְּדוּ עֲלֵיהֶם וְעָלֵינוּ זְכוּת שֶׁתְּהֵא לְמִשְׁמֶרֶת שָׁלוֹם וְנִשָּׂא בְרָכָה מֵאֵת יְיָ וּצְדָקָה מֵאֱלֹהֵי יִשְׁעֵנוּ וְנִמְצָא חֵן וְשֵׂכֶל טוֹב בְּעֵינֵי אֱלֹהִים וְאָדָם.

[בשבת מוסיפים:] הָרַחֲמָן הוּא יַנְחִילֵנוּ יוֹם שֶׁכֻּלּוֹ שַׁבָּת וּמְנוּחָה לְחַיֵּי הָעוֹלָמִים.

May the Merciful One bless my father and teacher, proprietor of this house, and my mother and teacher, proprietress of this house, them, their home, their offspring, and all which is theirs...

Alternatively, one who is married and eating with his or her family should say:

May the Merciful One bless me, my wife [*or* husband], my offspring, and all which is mine...

A guest in another person's home should say:

May the Merciful One bless the proprietor of this house and the proprietress of this house, them, their home, their offspring, and all which is theirs...

In every case, the blessing then concludes:

...[*if applicable, add*: and all who dine here] us, and all which is ours, just as our ancestors Abraham, Isaac, and Jacob were blessed "with all," "from all," and "all,"[88] so should He bless all of us together with a complete blessing, and let us say *Amen*.

May they find merit for them and for us on High that will serve as a bulwark of peace, and may we bear a blessing from *Hashem*, and charity from the God of our salvation, and may we find favor and great success in the eyes of God and humanity.

[*On the Sabbath add*:] May the Merciful One bequeath us a day which is completely Sabbath and rest for eternal life.

---

88   The *Torah* tells how God blessed each of the Patriarchs with "all." "*Hashem* blessed Abraham *with all*" (Genesis 24:1). Isaac told Esau that, "I ate *from all*" (Genesis 27:33). Jacob urged Esau to take the generous gifts he presented him "because I possess *all*" (Genesis 33:11).

הָרַחֲמָן הוּא יַנְחִילֵנוּ יוֹם שֶׁכֻּלוֹ טוֹב.

הָרַחֲמָן הוּא יְזַכֵּנוּ לִימוֹת הַמָּשִׁיחַ וּלְחַיֵּי הָעוֹלָם הַבָּא. מִגְדּוֹל יְשׁוּעוֹת מַלְכּוֹ וְעֹשֶׂה חֶסֶד לִמְשִׁיחוֹ לְדָוִד וּלְזַרְעוֹ עַד עוֹלָם. עֹשֶׂה שָׁלוֹם בִּמְרוֹמָיו הוּא יַעֲשֶׂה שָׁלוֹם עָלֵינוּ וְעַל כָּל יִשְׂרָאֵל וְאִמְרוּ אָמֵן.

יְראוּ אֶת יְיָ קְדֹשָׁיו כִּי אֵין מַחְסוֹר לִירֵאָיו. כְּפִירִים רָשׁוּ וְרָעֵבוּ וְדֹרְשֵׁי יְיָ לֹא יַחְסְרוּ כָל טוֹב. הוֹדוּ לַיְיָ כִּי טוֹב כִּי לְעוֹלָם חַסְדּוֹ. פּוֹתֵחַ אֶת יָדֶךָ וּמַשְׂבִּיעַ לְכָל חַי רָצוֹן. בָּרוּךְ הַגֶּבֶר אֲשֶׁר יִבְטַח בַּיְיָ וְהָיָה יְיָ מִבְטַחוֹ. נַעַר הָיִיתִי גַם זָקַנְתִּי וְלֹא רָאִיתִי צַדִּיק נֶעֱזָב וְזַרְעוֹ מְבַקֶּשׁ לָחֶם. יְיָ עֹז לְעַמּוֹ יִתֵּן יְיָ יְבָרֵךְ אֶת עַמּוֹ בַשָּׁלוֹם.

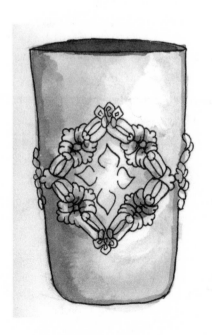

May the Merciful One bequeath us a day which is completely good.

May the Merciful One cause us to merit the days of *Mashiach* and life in the world to come. "[God is] a great worker of salvations for His [earthly] king and does kindness for His anointed one, for David and his offspring forever."[89] May He Who makes peace in His heights make peace for us and for all Israel, and let us say *Amen*.[90]

"Fear Hashem, His holy ones, for there is no want among those who fear Him. Young lions crave and hunger, but those who seek *Hashem* do not lack any good."[91] "Acknowledge *Hashem* for He is good, for His kindness is eternal."[92] "You open Your hand and satisfy the desires of all the living."[93] "Blessed is the man who trusts in *Hashem*; *Hashem* shall be his shelter."[94] "I was a youth and also grew old, yet I never saw a righteous person abandoned nor his offspring scrounging for bread."[95] "May *Hashem* give strength to His people; may *Hashem* bless His people with peace."[96]

---

[89] Psalms 22:51.

[90] Although there are many opposing spiritual forces in Heaven, God's Presence is readily manifest to them. Since they are aware that they all emanate from Him, rather than fighting, they work together to serve their Creator. When the *Mashiach* arrives and God's Presence is revealed on Earth, people, too, will recognize their true Source and all conflict will disappear.

[91] Psalms 34:10-11.

[92] Psalms 136:1.

[93] Psalms 145:16.

[94] Jeremiah 17:7.

[95] Psalms 37:25.

[96] Psalms 29:11.

מברכים על הכוס השלישית:

בָּרוּךְ אַתָּה יְיָ אֱלֹהֵינוּ מֶלֶךְ הָעוֹלָם בּוֹרֵא פְּרִי הַגָּפֶן.

שׁוֹתִים אֶת הַכּוֹס וְהַזְכָרִים מְסִבִּים עַל צַד שְׂמֹאל. אֵלֶּה שֶׁלֹּא מִלְאוּ אֶת הַכּוֹס שֶׁל אֵלִיָּהוּ
בְּקִדּוּשׁ מְמַלְּאִים אוֹתָהּ עַכְשָׁיו וְאַחֲרֵי כֵן פּוֹתְחִים אֶת הַדֶּלֶת וְאוֹמְרִים:

שְׁפֹךְ חֲמָתְךָ אֶל הַגּוֹיִם אֲשֶׁר לֹא יְדָעוּךָ וְעַל מַמְלָכוֹת אֲשֶׁר
בְּשִׁמְךָ לֹא קָרָאוּ. כִּי אָכַל אֶת יַעֲקֹב וְאֶת נָוֵהוּ הֵשַׁמּוּ. שְׁפָךְ עֲלֵיהֶם
זַעְמֶךָ וַחֲרוֹן אַפְּךָ יַשִּׂיגֵם. תִּרְדֹּף בְּאַף וְתַשְׁמִידֵם מִתַּחַת שְׁמֵי יְיָ.

סוֹגְרִים אֶת הַדֶּלֶת וּמְמַלְּאִים אֶת הַכּוֹס הָרְבִיעִית וּמַמְשִׁיכִים:

 הַלֵּל

לֹא לָנוּ יְיָ לֹא לָנוּ כִּי לְשִׁמְךָ תֵּן כָּבוֹד עַל חַסְדְּךָ עַל אֲמִתֶּךָ.
לָמָּה יֹאמְרוּ הַגּוֹיִם אַיֵּה נָא אֱלֹהֵיהֶם. וֵאלֹהֵינוּ בַשָּׁמָיִם כֹּל אֲשֶׁר
חָפֵץ עָשָׂה. עֲצַבֵּיהֶם כֶּסֶף וְזָהָב מַעֲשֵׂה יְדֵי אָדָם. פֶּה לָהֶם וְלֹא
יְדַבֵּרוּ עֵינַיִם לָהֶם וְלֹא יִרְאוּ. אָזְנַיִם לָהֶם וְלֹא יִשְׁמָעוּ אַף לָהֶם וְלֹא
יְרִיחוּן. יְדֵיהֶם וְלֹא יְמִישׁוּן רַגְלֵיהֶם וְלֹא יְהַלֵּכוּ לֹא יֶהְגּוּ בִּגְרוֹנָם.
כְּמוֹהֶם יִהְיוּ עֹשֵׂיהֶם כֹּל אֲשֶׁר בֹּטֵחַ בָּהֶם.

The blessing is recited on the Third Cup which is then drunk. Males should lean to the left when drinking.

Blessed are You, *Hashem,* our God, King of the Universe, Creator of the fruit of the vine.

Those who have not yet poured the Cup of Elijah should do so now. The door is opened and the following recited:

"Pour out Your wrath upon the nations that do not know You and upon the kingdoms which do not call upon Your Name. For they have consumed Jacob and his habitation they have made desolate."[97] "Pour upon them Your fury, and may Your intense anger overtake them."[98] "Pursue them with anger, and destroy them from beneath the heavens of *Hashem.*"[99]

The door is shut, the Fourth Cup poured, and the *Seder* service continues with the recitation of the rest of *Hallel.*

✕ HALLEL

Not for us, *Hashem,* not for us, but for Your Name give honor, because of Your kindness and Your truth. Why should the nations say, "Where is their God?" Our God is in Heaven; whatever He wishes, He does. Their idols are silver and gold, the work of human hands. They have a mouth, but do not speak; they have eyes, but do not see. They have ears, but do not hear; they have a nose, but cannot smell. They have hands, but do not feel; legs, but do not walk; they utter nothing with their throats. Those who make them shall become like them, all who trust in them.

---

[97] Psalms 79:6-7.

[98] Psalms 69:25.

[99] Lamentations 3:66. Just as the Egyptians recognized the "finger of God," but rebelliously refused to obey Him, these verses call upon *Hashem* to punish those nations which deliberately reject Him and persecute Jews.

יִשְׂרָאֵל בְּטַח בַּיְיָ עֶזְרָם וּמָגִנָּם הוּא. בֵּית אַהֲרֹן בִּטְחוּ בַיְיָ עֶזְרָם וּמָגִנָּם הוּא. יִרְאֵי יְיָ בִּטְחוּ בַיְיָ עֶזְרָם וּמָגִנָּם הוּא.

יְיָ זְכָרָנוּ יְבָרֵךְ יְבָרֵךְ אֶת בֵּית יִשְׂרָאֵל יְבָרֵךְ אֶת בֵּית אַהֲרֹן. יְבָרֵךְ יִרְאֵי יְיָ הַקְּטַנִּים עִם הַגְּדֹלִים. יֹסֵף יְיָ עֲלֵיכֶם וְעַל בְּנֵיכֶם. בְּרוּכִים אַתֶּם לַיְיָ עֹשֵׂה שָׁמַיִם וָאָרֶץ. הַשָּׁמַיִם שָׁמַיִם לַיְיָ וְהָאָרֶץ נָתַן לִבְנֵי אָדָם. לֹא הַמֵּתִים יְהַלְלוּ יָהּ וְלֹא כָּל יֹרְדֵי דוּמָה. וַאֲנַחְנוּ נְבָרֵךְ יָהּ מֵעַתָּה וְעַד עוֹלָם הַלְלוּיָהּ.

אָהַבְתִּי כִּי יִשְׁמַע יְיָ אֶת קוֹלִי תַּחֲנוּנָי. כִּי הִטָּה אָזְנוֹ לִי וּבְיָמַי אֶקְרָא. אֲפָפוּנִי חֶבְלֵי מָוֶת וּמְצָרֵי שְׁאוֹל מְצָאוּנִי צָרָה וְיָגוֹן אֶמְצָא. וּבְשֵׁם יְיָ אֶקְרָא אָנָּה יְיָ מַלְּטָה נַפְשִׁי. חַנּוּן יְיָ וְצַדִּיק וֵאלֹהֵינוּ מְרַחֵם. שֹׁמֵר פְּתָאִים יְיָ דַּלּוֹתִי וְלִי יְהוֹשִׁיעַ. שׁוּבִי נַפְשִׁי לִמְנוּחָיְכִי כִּי יְיָ גָּמַל עָלָיְכִי. כִּי חִלַּצְתָּ נַפְשִׁי מִמָּוֶת אֶת עֵינִי מִן דִּמְעָה אֶת רַגְלִי מִדֶּחִי. אֶתְהַלֵּךְ לִפְנֵי יְיָ בְּאַרְצוֹת הַחַיִּים. הֶאֱמַנְתִּי כִּי אֲדַבֵּר אֲנִי עָנִיתִי מְאֹד. אֲנִי אָמַרְתִּי בְחָפְזִי כָּל הָאָדָם כֹּזֵב.

Trust in *Hashem*, Israel; He is your help and shield.   Trust in *Hashem*, House of Aaron; He is your help and shield.   Trust in *Hashem*, those who fear *Hashem*; He is your help and shield.[100]

Hashem, who has always remembered us, shall bless; He shall bless the House of Israel; He shall bless the House of Aaron. He shall bless those who fear *Hashem*, the lesser ones with the greater ones. May *Hashem* increase you — you and your children. Blessed are you to *Hashem*, Maker of Heaven and Earth.   The Heaven is the Heaven of *Hashem*, but the Earth He gave to humankind.[101] The dead do not praise God, nor any who descend to the grave.   But we will bless God from now to eternity; Praise God![102]

I *love Hashem* because He listens to my voice and to my supplications. For He inclines His ear to me, and throughout my days I call [to Him].   Travails of death surrounded me, and the troubles of the grave found me; trouble and grief I found. I called upon the Name of *Hashem*:   "Please, *Hashem*, save my soul! Gracious and righteous is *Hashem*, and our God shows mercy. *Hashem* guards the simple; I am downtrodden but He will save me."[103] Rest easy, my soul, for *Hashem* has granted you good. For You have rescued my soul from death, my eye from tears, my foot from straying. I shall walk before *Hashem* in the land of the living. I believed even when I said, "I am greatly afflicted."   [Even when] I declared in my haste, "All humanity is treacherous!"[104]

---

[100] Psalms 115:1-11.

[101] God directs all that happens everywhere. He has given some control to people over what happens on Earth, however, because He lets people's deeds determine how He will conduct worldly matters (*Malbim* on Psalms 115:16).

[102] Psalms 115:12-18.

[103] King David, the author of this Psalm, obviously possessed great intellect. He nevertheless regarded himself as "simple" because even the cleverest person cannot succeed without Divine assistance (*Radak* on Psalms 116:6).

[104] Psalms 116:1-11.

מָה אָשִׁיב לַיְיָ כָּל תַּגְמוּלוֹהִי עָלָי. כּוֹס יְשׁוּעוֹת אֶשָּׂא וּבְשֵׁם
יְיָ אֶקְרָא. נְדָרַי לַיְיָ אֲשַׁלֵּם נֶגְדָה נָּא לְכָל עַמּוֹ. יָקָר בְּעֵינֵי יְיָ הַמָּוְתָה
לַחֲסִידָיו. אָנָּה יְיָ כִּי אֲנִי עַבְדֶּךָ אֲנִי עַבְדְּךָ בֶּן אֲמָתֶךָ פִּתַּחְתָּ לְמוֹסֵרָי.
לְךָ אֶזְבַּח זֶבַח תּוֹדָה וּבְשֵׁם יְיָ אֶקְרָא. נְדָרַי לַיְיָ אֲשַׁלֵּם נֶגְדָה נָּא לְכָל
עַמּוֹ. בְּחַצְרוֹת בֵּית יְיָ בְּתוֹכֵכִי יְרוּשָׁלָם הַלְלוּיָהּ.

הַלְלוּ אֶת יְיָ כָּל גּוֹיִם שַׁבְּחוּהוּ כָּל הָאֻמִּים. כִּי גָבַר עָלֵינוּ
חַסְדּוֹ וֶאֱמֶת יְיָ לְעוֹלָם הַלְלוּיָהּ.

כאשר יש לפחות שלושה אנשים נוכחים מי שעורך את הסדר אומר, "הודו לה' כי טוב
וכו'" והאחרים עונים לו כמו שעושים בבית הכנסת.

הוֹדוּ לַיְיָ כִּי טוֹב כִּי לְעוֹלָם חַסְדּוֹ.

יֹאמַר נָא יִשְׂרָאֵל כִּי לְעוֹלָם חַסְדּוֹ.

יֹאמְרוּ נָא בֵית אַהֲרֹן כִּי לְעוֹלָם חַסְדּוֹ.

יֹאמְרוּ נָא יִרְאֵי יְיָ כִּי לְעוֹלָם חַסְדּוֹ.

What can I repay *Hashem* for all the good You have granted me? A cup of salvation I shall lift, and I shall call upon the Name of *Hashem*. My vows to *Hashem* I shall fulfill before all His people. Precious in the eyes of *Hashem* is the death of His pious ones. I acknowledge, *Hashem*, that I am Your servant; I am Your servant, the son of Your maidservant; You have released my bonds.[105] To You I will sacrifice a thank-offering and I will call upon the Name of *Hashem*. My vows to *Hashem* I shall fulfill before all His people. In the courtyards of the House of *Hashem*, in the midst of Jerusalem; Praise God![106]

Praise *Hashem* all nations, laud Him all peoples. For His mercy has overtaken us, and *Hashem* is true forever; Praise God![107]

When at least three people are present, the individual leading the *Seder* says, "Acknowledge *Hashem* for He is good..." and the others answer, just as is done in the synagogue during *Hallel*.

Acknowledge *Hashem* for He is good, for His kindness is eternal.

Say please, Israel, that His kindness is eternal.

Say please, House of Aaron, that His kindness is eternal.

Say please, those who fear *Hashem*, that His kindness is eternal.[108]

---

[105] Those who do not have the *Torah* are bound by the limitations of the physical world. Servants of *Hashem*, however, become connected to that which transcends the physical, so they are truly free. Alternatively, we are bound to serve *Hashem* because He released us from Egyptian bondage.

[106] Psalms 116:12-19.

[107] Psalms 117:1-2.

[108] Psalms 118:1-4.

מִן הַמֵּצַר קָרָאתִי יָהּ עָנָנִי בַמֶּרְחָב יָהּ. יְיָ לִי לֹא אִירָא מַה
יַּעֲשֶׂה לִי אָדָם. יְיָ לִי בְּעֹזְרָי וַאֲנִי אֶרְאֶה בְשֹׂנְאָי. טוֹב לַחֲסוֹת בַּיְיָ
מִבְּטֹחַ בָּאָדָם. טוֹב לַחֲסוֹת בַּיְיָ מִבְּטֹחַ בִּנְדִיבִים. כָּל גּוֹיִם סְבָבוּנִי
בְּשֵׁם יְיָ כִּי אֲמִילַם. סַבּוּנִי גַם סְבָבוּנִי בְּשֵׁם יְיָ כִּי אֲמִילַם. סַבּוּנִי
כִדְבוֹרִים דֹּעֲכוּ כְּאֵשׁ קוֹצִים בְּשֵׁם יְיָ כִּי אֲמִילַם. דָּחֹה דְחִיתַנִי לִנְפֹּל
וַיְיָ עֲזָרָנִי. עָזִּי וְזִמְרָת יָהּ וַיְהִי לִי לִישׁוּעָה. קוֹל רִנָּה וִישׁוּעָה בְּאָהֳלֵי
צַדִּיקִים יְמִין יְיָ עֹשָׂה חָיִל. יְמִין יְיָ רוֹמֵמָה יְמִין יְיָ עֹשָׂה חָיִל. לֹא
אָמוּת כִּי אֶחְיֶה וַאֲסַפֵּר מַעֲשֵׂי יָהּ. יַסֹּר יִסְּרַנִּי יָּהּ וְלַמָּוֶת לֹא נְתָנָנִי.
פִּתְחוּ לִי שַׁעֲרֵי צֶדֶק אָבֹא בָם אוֹדֶה יָהּ. זֶה הַשַּׁעַר לַיְיָ צַדִּיקִים
יָבֹאוּ בוֹ.

אוֹדְךָ כִּי עֲנִיתָנִי וַתְּהִי לִי לִישׁוּעָה.
אוֹדְךָ כִּי עֲנִיתָנִי וַתְּהִי לִי לִישׁוּעָה.

אֶבֶן מָאֲסוּ הַבּוֹנִים הָיְתָה לְרֹאשׁ פִּנָּה.
אֶבֶן מָאֲסוּ הַבּוֹנִים הָיְתָה לְרֹאשׁ פִּנָּה.

From distress I called God; He answered me with deliverance. *Hashem* is for me, I shall not fear; what can a person do to me? *Hashem* is for me as a benefactor; I shall see [the downfall of] my enemies. It is better to take refuge in *Hashem* than to trust in humanity. It is better to take refuge in *Hashem* than to trust in princes. [When] all the nations surround me, in the Name of *Hashem*, I shall cut them off. They may surround me again and again, but in the Name of *Hashem*, I shall cut them off. They may surround me like bees, spring like fire upon thorns, but in the Name of *Hashem*, I shall cut them off. You [enemies] repeatedly pushed me to fall, but *Hashem* helped me. Powerful and [worthy of] song is God, and He was my salvation. A sound of song and salvation is in the tents of the righteous; the right hand of *Hashem* does valiantly. The right hand of *Hashem* is uplifted; the right hand of *Hashem* does valiantly. I will not die, but live and tell the works of God. God surely chastised me, but He did not give me over to death. Open for me the gates of righteousness, and I will enter them to thank God. This is the gate of *Hashem*; the righteous enter through it.[109]

I acknowledge You, for You answered me and were a salvation for me.

I acknowledge You, for You answered me and were a salvation for me.

The stone which the builders rejected became the chief cornerstone.

The stone which the builders rejected became the chief cornerstone.[110]

---

[109] Psalms 118:5-20. The phrase, "This is the gate of *Hashem*," refers back to the previous verse. When a person begs *Hashem* to "open for me the gates of righteousness," recognizing how little he or she has achieved spiritually, that itself is the "gate of *Hashem*," the key to rising higher (*Botzina Dinehura*).

[110] This verse held a special meaning for King David. As a youth, he was considered unfit to serve in King Saul's army, yet he later slew Goliath (*Rashi* on B.T. *Pesachim* 119A). As a descendant of Ruth the Moabitess, some

מֵאֵת יְיָ הָיְתָה זֹאת הִיא נִפְלָאת בְּעֵינֵינוּ.
מֵאֵת יְיָ הָיְתָה זֹאת הִיא נִפְלָאת בְּעֵינֵינוּ.

זֶה הַיּוֹם עָשָׂה יְיָ נָגִילָה וְנִשְׂמְחָה בוֹ.
זֶה הַיּוֹם עָשָׂה יְיָ נָגִילָה וְנִשְׂמְחָה בוֹ.

כאשר יש לפחות שלושה אנשים נוכחים מי שעורך את הסדר אומר, "אָנָּא ה' וכו'"
והאחרים עונים לו כמו שעושים בבית הכנסת.

אָנָּא יְיָ הוֹשִׁיעָה נָּא.
אָנָּא יְיָ הוֹשִׁיעָה נָּא.

אָנָּא יְיָ הַצְלִיחָה נָּא.
אָנָּא יְיָ הַצְלִיחָה נָּא.

בָּרוּךְ הַבָּא בְּשֵׁם יְיָ בֵּרַכְנוּכֶם מִבֵּית יְיָ.
בָּרוּךְ הַבָּא בְּשֵׁם יְיָ בֵּרַכְנוּכֶם מִבֵּית יְיָ.

אֵל יְיָ וַיָּאֶר לָנוּ אִסְרוּ חַג בַּעֲבֹתִים עַד קַרְנוֹת הַמִּזְבֵּחַ.
אֵל יְיָ וַיָּאֶר לָנוּ אִסְרוּ חַג בַּעֲבֹתִים עַד קַרְנוֹת הַמִּזְבֵּחַ.

---

questioned whether he could marry another Jew, let alone assume the throne. Even so, the despised and rejected David rose to the greatest heights (*Maharsha* on B.T. *Pesachim* 119A).

The Jewish people found themselves in a similar situation when leaving Egypt. The angels questioned whether they should be saved, not to mention whether they should receive the *Torah* and become *Hashem's* chosen nation, yet they also rose to greatness.

This was from Hashem; it is a marvel in our eyes.

This was from *Hashem*; it is a marvel in our eyes.

This is the day which Hashem made; we shall gladden and rejoice upon it.

This is the day which *Hashem* made; we shall gladden and rejoice upon it.[111]

> When at least three people are present, the individual leading the *Seder* recites, "Please, *Hashem*..." and the others answer, just as is done in the synagogue during *Hallel*.

Please, Hashem, please save!
Please, Hashem, please save!

Please, Hashem, please grant success!
Please, Hashem, please grant success![112]

Blessed be he who comes in the Name of Hashem; we bless you from the house of Hashem!

Blessed be he who comes in the Name of *Hashem*; we bless you from the house of *Hashem*!

Hashem is powerful and illuminates [darkness] for us; bind the festival sacrifice with thick chords until [it is brought to] the protrusions of the altar.

Hashem is powerful and illuminates [darkness] for us; bind the festival sacrifice with think chords until [it is brought to] the protrusions of the altar.[113]

---

[111] Psalms 118:21-24.

[112] Psalms 118:25.

[113] Once an animal was inspected for blemishes and found fit for sacrifice, the owner would tie it up until the time arrived to offer it (*Rashi* on Psalms

אֵלִי אַתָּה וְאוֹדֶךָּ אֱלֹהַי אֲרוֹמְמֶךָּ.

אֵלִי אַתָּה וְאוֹדֶךָּ אֱלֹהַי אֲרוֹמְמֶךָּ.

הוֹדוּ לַיְיָ כִּי טוֹב כִּי לְעוֹלָם חַסְדּוֹ.

הוֹדוּ לַיְיָ כִּי טוֹב כִּי לְעוֹלָם חַסְדּוֹ.

יְהַלְלוּךָ יְיָ אֱלֹהֵנוּ כָּל מַעֲשֶׂיךָ וַחֲסִדֶיךָ צַדִּיקִים עוֹשֵׂי רְצוֹנֶךָ
וְכָל עַמְּךָ בֵּית יִשְׂרָאֵל בְּרִנָּה יוֹדוּ וִיבָרְכוּ וִישַׁבְּחוּ וִיפָאֲרוּ וִירוֹמְמוּ
וְיַעֲרִיצוּ וְיַקְדִּישׁוּ וְיַמְלִיכוּ אֶת שִׁמְךָ מַלְכֵּנוּ כִּי לְךָ טוֹב לְהוֹדוֹת
וּלְשִׁמְךָ נָאֶה לְזַמֵּר כִּי מֵעוֹלָם וְעַד עוֹלָם אַתָּה אֵל.

כִּי לְעוֹלָם חַסְדּוֹ.	הוֹדוּ לַיְיָ כִּי טוֹב
כִּי לְעוֹלָם חַסְדּוֹ.	הוֹדוּ לֵאלֹהֵי הָאֱלֹהִים
כִּי לְעוֹלָם חַסְדּוֹ.	הוֹדוּ לַאֲדֹנֵי הָאֲדֹנִים
כִּי לְעוֹלָם חַסְדּוֹ.	לְעֹשֵׂה נִפְלָאוֹת גְּדֹלוֹת לְבַדּוֹ
כִּי לְעוֹלָם חַסְדּוֹ.	לְעֹשֵׂה הַשָּׁמַיִם בִּתְבוּנָה
כִּי לְעוֹלָם חַסְדּוֹ.	לְרֹקַע הָאָרֶץ עַל הַמָּיִם
כִּי לְעוֹלָם חַסְדּוֹ.	לְעֹשֵׂה אוֹרִים גְּדֹלִים

118:27). The corners of the altar had projections, or protrusions, which rose
one cubit above its top surface (*Midoth* 3:1).

You are my God and I acknowledge You; my God and I exalt You.

You are my God and I acknowledge You; my God and I exalt You.

Acknowledge Hashem for He is good, for His kindness is eternal.

Acknowledge *Hashem* for He is good, for His kindness is eternal.[114]

May all Your works praise You, *Hashem* our God, and Your pious and righteous ones, who perform Your will, and all Your people, the House of Israel, with song shall thank, praise, glorify, exalt, admire, sanctify, and acknowledge the sovereignty of Your Name, our King, for it is fitting to thank You, and it is proper to sing to Your Name because from eternity to eternity You are God.

Acknowledge Hashem for He is good, for His kindness is eternal.

Acknowledge the Power of Powers, for His kindness is eternal.

Acknowledge the Lord of Lords, for His kindness is eternal.

To the One who makes great miracles alone, for His kindness is eternal.

To the One who makes the Heavens with understanding, for His kindness is eternal.

To the One who lays out the Earth upon the water, for His kindness is eternal.

To the One who makes great lights, for His kindness is eternal.

---

[114] Psalms 118:26-29.

אֶת הַשֶּׁמֶשׁ לְמֶמְשֶׁלֶת בַּיּוֹם   כִּי לְעוֹלָם חַסְדּוֹ.

אֶת הַיָּרֵחַ וְכוֹכָבִים לְמֶמְשְׁלוֹת בַּלָּיְלָה   כִּי לְעוֹלָם חַסְדּוֹ.

לְמַכֵּה מִצְרַיִם בִּבְכוֹרֵיהֶם   כִּי לְעוֹלָם חַסְדּוֹ.

וַיּוֹצֵא יִשְׂרָאֵל מִתּוֹכָם   כִּי לְעוֹלָם חַסְדּוֹ.

בְּיָד חֲזָקָה וּבִזְרוֹעַ נְטוּיָה   כִּי לְעוֹלָם חַסְדּוֹ.

לְגֹזֵר יַם סוּף לִגְזָרִים   כִּי לְעוֹלָם חַסְדּוֹ.

וְהֶעֱבִיר יִשְׂרָאֵל בְּתוֹכוֹ   כִּי לְעוֹלָם חַסְדּוֹ.

וְנִעֵר פַּרְעֹה וְחֵילוֹ בְיַם סוּף   כִּי לְעוֹלָם חַסְדּוֹ.

לְמוֹלִיךְ עַמּוֹ בַּמִּדְבָּר   כִּי לְעוֹלָם חַסְדּוֹ.

לְמַכֵּה מְלָכִים גְּדֹלִים   כִּי לְעוֹלָם חַסְדּוֹ.

וַיַּהֲרֹג מְלָכִים אַדִּירִים   כִּי לְעוֹלָם חַסְדּוֹ.

לְסִיחוֹן מֶלֶךְ הָאֱמֹרִי   כִּי לְעוֹלָם חַסְדּוֹ.

The sun for dominion during the day, for His kindness is eternal.

The moon and stars for dominion at night, for His kindness is eternal.

To the One who struck Egypt's first-born, for His kindness is eternal.

And took Israel out from their midst, for His kindness is eternal.

With a strong hand and an outstretched arm, for His kindness is eternal.

To the One who split the Reed Sea into strips, for His kindness is eternal.[115]

And caused Israel to pass through its midst, for His kindness is eternal.

And stirred Pharaoh and his army in the Reed Sea, for His kindness is eternal.

To the One who transported His people through the desert, for His kindness is eternal.

To the One who struck down great kings, for His kindness is eternal.

And slew mighty kings, for His kindness is eternal.

Sihon, king of the Amorites, for His kindness is eternal.

---

[115] The *Midrash* explains that *Hashem* did not merely split the Reed Sea in two. He made twelve lanes — one for each Tribe (*Tanchuma, Beshalach* 10).

כִּי לְעוֹלָם חַסְדּוֹ.	וּלְעוֹג מֶלֶךְ הַבָּשָׁן
כִּי לְעוֹלָם חַסְדּוֹ.	וְנָתַן אַרְצָם לְנַחֲלָה
כִּי לְעוֹלָם חַסְדּוֹ.	נַחֲלָה לְיִשְׂרָאֵל עַבְדּוֹ
כִּי לְעוֹלָם חַסְדּוֹ.	שֶׁבְּשִׁפְלֵנוּ זָכַר לָנוּ
כִּי לְעוֹלָם חַסְדּוֹ.	וַיִּפְרְקֵנוּ מִצָּרֵינוּ
כִּי לְעוֹלָם חַסְדּוֹ.	נֹתֵן לֶחֶם לְכָל בָּשָׂר
כִּי לְעוֹלָם חַסְדּוֹ.	הוֹדוּ לְאֵל הַשָּׁמָיִם

נוסח ״נשמת כל חי״ עד נרצה לפי מנהג הספרדים ובני עדות המזרח נמצא בעמוד 339.

נִשְׁמַת כָּל חַי תְּבָרֵךְ אֶת שִׁמְךָ יְיָ אֱלֹהֵינוּ וְרוּחַ כָּל בָּשָׂר תְּפָאֵר וּתְרוֹמֵם זִכְרְךָ מַלְכֵּנוּ תָּמִיד. מִן הָעוֹלָם וְעַד הָעוֹלָם אַתָּה אֵל וּמִבַּלְעָדֶיךָ אֵין לָנוּ מֶלֶךְ גּוֹאֵל וּמוֹשִׁיעַ פּוֹדֶה וּמַצִּיל וּמְפַרְנֵס וּמְרַחֵם בְּכָל עֵת צָרָה וְצוּקָה אֵין לָנוּ מֶלֶךְ אֶלָּא אָתָּה אֱלֹהֵי הָרִאשׁוֹנִים וְהָאַחֲרוֹנִים אֱלוֹהַּ כָּל בְּרִיּוֹת אֲדוֹן כָּל תּוֹלָדוֹת

Og, king of Bashan, for His kindness is eternal.

And gave their land for an inheritance, for His kindness is eternal.

An inheritance to Israel, His servant, for His kindness is eternal.

That in our lowliness, He remembered us, for His kindness is eternal.

And released us from our trouble, for His kindness is eternal.

He gives bread to all flesh, for His kindness is eternal.

Acknowledge the God of Heaven, for His kindness is eternal.[116]

The *Sefaradi* version of "May the soul of every living creature..." through the Conclusion of the *Seder* is found on page 340.

May the soul of every living creature bless Your Name, *Hashem*, our God, and the spirit of all flesh glorify and exalt Your memory, our King, constantly. From eternity to eternity, You are God, and except for You, we have no King who redeems, rescues, delivers, saves, supports, and shows mercy at all times of trouble and adversity.[117] We have no King but You! God of the first ones and the last ones, God of all creatures, Master of all history,

---

[116] Psalm 136. The Psalm repeats the phrase "for His kindness is eternal" twenty-six times corresponding to the twenty-six generations from the time God created the world until the Giving of the *Torah*. Since the universe only exists in the merit of the *Torah*, the fact that *Hashem* sustained it during this period was an act of pure kindness (B.T. *Pesachim* 118A).

[117] The expression מִן הָעוֹלָם וְעַד הָעוֹלָם translated here as "from eternity to eternity," can also mean "from universe to universe," alluding to the fact that nothing exists in any realm — spiritual or physical — which *Hashem* does not control.

הַמְהֻלָּל בְּרֹב הַתִּשְׁבָּחוֹת הַמְנַהֵג עוֹלָמוֹ בְּחֶסֶד וּבְרִיּוֹתָיו בְּרַחֲמִים. וַיְיָ לֹא יָנוּם וְלֹא יִישָׁן. הַמְעוֹרֵר יְשֵׁנִים וְהַמֵּקִיץ נִרְדָּמִים וְהַמֵּשִׂיחַ אִלְּמִים וְהַמַּתִּיר אֲסוּרִים וְהַסּוֹמֵךְ נוֹפְלִים וְהַזּוֹקֵף כְּפוּפִים. לְךָ לְבַדְּךָ אֲנַחְנוּ מוֹדִים. אִלּוּ פִינוּ מָלֵא שִׁירָה כַּיָּם וּלְשׁוֹנֵנוּ רִנָּה כַּהֲמוֹן גַּלָּיו וְשִׂפְתוֹתֵינוּ שֶׁבַח כְּמֶרְחֲבֵי רָקִיעַ וְעֵינֵינוּ מְאִירוֹת כַּשֶּׁמֶשׁ וְכַיָּרֵחַ וְיָדֵינוּ פְרוּשׂוֹת כְּנִשְׁרֵי שָׁמָיִם וְרַגְלֵינוּ קַלּוֹת כָּאַיָּלוֹת אֵין אֲנַחְנוּ מַסְפִּיקִים לְהוֹדוֹת לְךָ יְיָ אֱלֹהֵינוּ וֵאלֹהֵי אֲבוֹתֵינוּ וּלְבָרֵךְ אֶת שְׁמֶךָ עַל אַחַת מֵאֶלֶף אֶלֶף אַלְפֵי אֲלָפִים וְרִבֵּי רְבָבוֹת פְּעָמִים הַטּוֹבוֹת שֶׁעָשִׂיתָ עִם אֲבוֹתֵינוּ וְעִמָּנוּ. מִמִּצְרַיִם גְּאַלְתָּנוּ יְיָ אֱלֹהֵינוּ וּמִבֵּית עֲבָדִים פְּדִיתָנוּ. בְּרָעָב זַנְתָּנוּ וּבְשָׂבָע כִּלְכַּלְתָּנוּ מֵחֶרֶב הִצַּלְתָּנוּ וּמִדֶּבֶר מִלַּטְתָּנוּ וּמֵחֳלָיִם רָעִים וְנֶאֱמָנִים דִּלִּיתָנוּ. עַד הֵנָּה עֲזָרוּנוּ רַחֲמֶיךָ וְלֹא עֲזָבוּנוּ חֲסָדֶיךָ וְאַל תִּטְּשֵׁנוּ יְיָ אֱלֹהֵינוּ לָנֶצַח.

עַל כֵּן אֵבָרִים שֶׁפִּלַּגְתָּ בָּנוּ וְרוּחַ וּנְשָׁמָה שֶׁנָּפַחְתָּ בְּאַפֵּנוּ וְלָשׁוֹן אֲשֶׁר שַׂמְתָּ בְּפִינוּ הֵן הֵם יוֹדוּ וִיבָרְכוּ וִישַׁבְּחוּ וִיפָאֲרוּ וִירוֹמְמוּ וְיַעֲרִיצוּ וְיַקְדִּישׁוּ וְיַמְלִיכוּ אֶת שִׁמְךָ מַלְכֵּנוּ. כִּי כָל פֶּה לְךָ יוֹדֶה וְכָל לָשׁוֹן לְךָ תִשָּׁבַע וְכָל בֶּרֶךְ לְךָ תִכְרַע וְכָל קוֹמָה לְפָנֶיךָ תִשְׁתַּחֲוֶה וְכָל לְבָבוֹת יִירָאוּךָ וְכָל קֶרֶב וּכְלָיוֹת יְזַמְּרוּ לִשְׁמֶךָ כַּדָּבָר שֶׁכָּתוּב, "כָּל עַצְמֹתַי תֹּאמַרְנָה יְיָ מִי כָמוֹךָ מַצִּיל עָנִי מֵחָזָק מִמֶּנּוּ וְעָנִי וְאֶבְיוֹן מִגֹּזְלוֹ."

praised with many acclamations, Who directs his universe with kindness and His creatures with mercy. *Hashem* neither slumbers nor sleeps. He arouses the sleeping and awakens the slumbering, gives speech to the mute, releases the bound, supports the fallen, and makes upright those who are bent over. You alone do we thank. If our mouths were full of song as the sea, and our tongues [full] of chant as the multitude of waves, our lips [full] of praise as the broad heavens, our eyes glowing as the sun and moon, our hands spread as the eagles of the heavens, and our feet light as harts, we could not sufficiently thank You, *Hashem*, our God, and God of our ancestors, and bless Your Name for one millionth of the numerous millions upon millions of favors You performed for our ancestors and for us. You redeemed us from Egypt, *Hashem*, our God, and from the place of servitude You delivered us. In famine You sustained us, and in plenty You provided for us. From the sword You saved us, from pestilence You rescued us, and from severe and unyielding illnesses You lifted us. Until now Your mercy helped us, and Your kindness did not abandon us. Do not forsake us, *Hashem* our God, ever!

Therefore, the limbs which You have fixed in us, the spirit and soul which You have blown into our nostrils, and the tongue which You have placed in our mouths, behold, they shall thank, bless, praise, glorify, exalt, adore, sanctify, and give sovereignty to Your Name, our King. For every mouth will acknowledge You, every tongue will swear by You, every knee will bend to You, every upright being will prostrate itself before You, all hearts will fear You, and all vital organs will sing to Your Name, according to the word that is written, "All my bones shall say, 'Who is like You, *Hashem*, Who saves the afflicted from one stronger than him and the poor and the destitute from one who would rob him?'"[118]

---

[118] Psalms 35:10. Although people cannot physically perceive God now, when the dead are resurrected in the future, the human body will become refined in a way which will enable it to appreciate holiness (See *Ramban* in

מִי יִדְמֶה לָּךְ וּמִי יִשְׁוֶה לָּךְ וּמִי יַעֲרָךְ לָךְ הָאֵל הַגָּדוֹל הַגִּבּוֹר וְהַנּוֹרָא
אֵל עֶלְיוֹן קֹנֵה שָׁמַיִם וָאָרֶץ. נְהַלֶּלְךָ וּנְשַׁבֵּחֲךָ וּנְפָאֶרְךָ וּנְבָרֵךְ אֶת שֵׁם
קָדְשֶׁךָ כָּאָמוּר, "לְדָוִד, בָּרְכִי נַפְשִׁי אֶת יְיָ וְכָל קְרָבַי אֶת שֵׁם קָדְשׁוֹ."

הָאֵל בְּתַעֲצֻמוֹת עֻזֶּךָ הַגָּדוֹל בִּכְבוֹד שְׁמֶךָ הַגִּבּוֹר לָנֶצַח וְהַנּוֹרָא
בְּנוֹרְאוֹתֶיךָ. הַמֶּלֶךְ הַיּוֹשֵׁב עַל כִּסֵּא רָם וְנִשָּׂא.

שׁוֹכֵן עַד מָרוֹם וְקָדוֹשׁ שְׁמוֹ וְכָתוּב, "רַנְּנוּ צַדִּיקִים בַּיְיָ לַיְשָׁרִים
נָאוָה תְהִלָּה."

בְּפִי יְשָׁרִים תִּתְהַלָּל

וּבְדִבְרֵי צַדִּיקִים תִּתְבָּרַךְ

וּבִלְשׁוֹן חֲסִידִים תִּתְרוֹמָם

וּבְקֶרֶב קְדוֹשִׁים תִּתְקַדָּשׁ

וּבְמַקְהֲלוֹת רִבְבוֹת עַמְּךָ בֵּית יִשְׂרָאֵל בְּרִנָּה יִתְפָּאַר שִׁמְךָ
מַלְכֵּנוּ בְּכָל דּוֹר וָדוֹר שֶׁכֵּן חוֹבַת כָּל הַיְצוּרִים לְפָנֶיךָ יְיָ אֱלֹהֵינוּ
וֵאלֹהֵי אֲבוֹתֵינוּ לְהוֹדוֹת לְהַלֵּל לְשַׁבֵּחַ לְפָאֵר לְרוֹמֵם לְהַדֵּר לְבָרֵךְ
לְעַלֵּה וּלְקַלֵּס עַל כָּל דִּבְרֵי שִׁירוֹת וְתִשְׁבָּחוֹת דָּוִד בֶּן יִשַׁי עַבְדְּךָ
מְשִׁיחֶךָ.

יִשְׁתַּבַּח שִׁמְךָ לָעַד מַלְכֵּנוּ הָאֵל הַמֶּלֶךְ הַגָּדוֹל וְהַקָּדוֹשׁ
בַּשָּׁמַיִם וּבָאָרֶץ כִּי לְךָ נָאֶה יְיָ אֱלֹהֵינוּ וֵאלֹהֵי אֲבוֹתֵינוּ שִׁיר וּשְׁבָחָה
הַלֵּל וְזִמְרָה עֹז וּמֶמְשָׁלָה נֶצַח גְּדֻלָּה וּגְבוּרָה תְּהִלָּה וְתִפְאֶרֶת קְדֻשָּׁה
וּמַלְכוּת

Sha'ar Hagemul). Even a person's physical bones and organs will praise God.

Who resembles You? Who matches You? Who approximates You, the God who is great, mighty and awesome, Supreme Power Who owns Heaven and Earth? We shall praise You, we shall acclaim You, we shall glorify You, and we shall bless Your Holy Name, as it is said, "By David: Bless *Hashem*, my soul, and all my organs His holy Name."[119]

"The God" — Your strength is [displayed] in mighty deeds. "The great" — in the glory of Your Name. "The mighty" — unto eternity. "And the awesome" — through Your awesome deeds. The King who sits upon a lofty and uplifted throne.

Dwelling forever, lofty and holy is His Name, and it is written, "Sing, righteous ones, among [those who praise] *Hashem*; for the upright, praise is desirable."[120] In the mouth of the upright may You be praised, in the words of the righteous may You be blessed, by the tongue of the pious may You be exalted, and among holy ones may You be sanctified.

Among the myriad congregations of Your people, the House of Israel, may Your Name be glorified with song, our King, in each and every generation; for such is the obligation of all creatures before You, *Hashem*, our God, and God of our ancestors, to thank, praise, acclaim, glorify, exalt, adulate, bless, uplift, and venerate with all the words of song and praise of David, son of Jesse, Your anointed servant.

May Your Name be praised forever, our King, the God who is a great and holy King in Heaven and Earth; for to You is fitting, *Hashem*, our God, and God of our ancestors, song and praise, acclaim and hymn, strength and dominion, victory, great-ness and might, adulation and glory, holiness and sovereignty,

---

[119] Psalms 103:1.
[120] Psalms 33:1.

בְּרָכוֹת וְהוֹדָאוֹת מֵעַתָּה וְעַד עוֹלָם.   בָּרוּךְ אַתָּה יְיָ אֵל מֶלֶךְ גָּדוֹל
בַּתִּשְׁבָּחוֹת אֵל הַהוֹדָאוֹת אֲדוֹן הַנִּפְלָאוֹת הַבּוֹחֵר בְּשִׁירֵי זִמְרָה מֶלֶךְ
אֵל חֵי הָעוֹלָמִים.

מברכים ושותים את הכוס הרביעית והזכרים מסיבים על צד שמאל.   ספרדים ובני עדות
המזרח לא אומרים את הברכה הזאת לפני ששותים את הכוס.

בָּרוּךְ אַתָּה יְיָ אֱלֹהֵינוּ מֶלֶךְ הָעוֹלָם בּוֹרֵא פְּרִי הַגָּפֶן.

אחרי שתיית היין אומרים את הברכה הזאת:

בָּרוּךְ אַתָּה יְיָ אֱלֹהֵינוּ מֶלֶךְ הָעוֹלָם עַל הַגֶּפֶן וְעַל פְּרִי הַגֶּפֶן
וְעַל תְּנוּבַת הַשָּׂדֶה וְעַל אֶרֶץ חֶמְדָּה טוֹבָה וּרְחָבָה שֶׁרָצִיתָ וְהִנְחַלְתָּ
לַאֲבוֹתֵינוּ לֶאֱכוֹל מִפִּרְיָהּ וְלִשְׂבּוֹעַ מִטּוּבָהּ.   רַחֵם נָא יְיָ אֱלֹהֵינוּ עַל
יִשְׂרָאֵל עַמֶּךְ וְעַל יְרוּשָׁלַיִם עִירֶךְ וְעַל צִיּוֹן מִשְׁכַּן כְּבוֹדֶךְ וְעַל מִזְבְּחֶךְ
וְעַל הֵיכָלֶךְ.   וּבְנֵה יְרוּשָׁלַיִם עִיר הַקֹּדֶשׁ בִּמְהֵרָה בְיָמֵינוּ וְהַעֲלֵנוּ
לְתוֹכָהּ וְשַׂמְּחֵנוּ בְּבִנְיָנָהּ וְנֹאכַל מִפִּרְיָהּ וְנִשְׂבַּע מִטּוּבָהּ וּנְבָרֶכְךָ עָלֶיהָ
בִּקְדֻשָּׁה וּבְטָהֳרָה [בשבת: וּרְצֵה וְהַחֲלִיצֵנוּ בְּיוֹם הַשַּׁבָּת הַזֶּה] וְשַׂמְּחֵנוּ בְּיוֹם חַג
הַמַּצּוֹת הַזֶּה כִּי אַתָּה יְיָ טוֹב וּמֵטִיב לַכֹּל וְנוֹדֶה לְּךָ עַל הָאָרֶץ וְעַל
פְּרִי הַגָּפֶן.   בָּרוּךְ אַתָּה יְיָ עַל הָאָרֶץ וְעַל פְּרִי הַגָּפֶן. [וְעַל יֵין מֵאֶרֶץ יִשְׂרָאֵל
מְסַיְּמִים "גַּפְנָהּ" בִּמְקוֹם "הַגָּפֶן"]

blessings and thanks from now until eternity. Blessed are You, *Hashem*, kingly God, Who is great in praises, God worthy of thanks, Master of wonders, Who chooses songs of devotion, King, eternal living God.

> Recite the following blessing and then drink the Fourth Cup.   Males should recline on their left side when doing so.   *Sefaradi* Jews drink without reciting this blessing.

Blessed are You, *Hashem*, our God, King of the Universe, Creator of the fruit of the vine.

> After finishing the wine, say the following:

Blessed are You, *Hashem*, our God, King of the Universe, for the vine, for the fruit of the vine, for the produce of the field, and for the desirable, good, and spacious land which You found desirable and bequeathed to our ancestors to eat from its fruit and to be satisfied from its goodness. Have mercy, please, *Hashem*, our God, on Israel Your people, on Jerusalem Your city, on Zion, the habitation of Your glory, on Your altar, and on Your sanctuary. Rebuild the holy city of Jerusalem speedily in our days, bring us up to it, gladden us with its restoration, let us eat of its fruits and be satisfied from its goodness, and we will bless You upon it in holiness and purity; [*On the Sabbath add*: Take pleasure and grant us relief on this Sabbath day] gladden us on this festival of unleavened bread, for You, *Hashem*, are good and do good to all, and we thank You for the Land and for the fruit of the vine. Blessed are You, *Hashem*, for the Land and for the fruit of the vine. [For wine from the Land of Israel, substitute "the fruit of its vine" for "the fruit of the vine."]

✦ נִרְצָה

חֲסַל סִדּוּר פֶּסַח כְּהִלְכָתוֹ כְּכָל מִשְׁפָּטוֹ וְחֻקָּתוֹ. כַּאֲשֶׁר זָכִינוּ לְסַדֵּר אוֹתוֹ כֵּן נִזְכֶּה לַעֲשׂוֹתוֹ. זָךְ שׁוֹכֵן מְעוֹנָה קוֹמֵם קְהַל עֲדַת מִי מָנָה. בְּקָרוֹב נַהֵל נִטְעֵי כַנָּה פְּדוּיִם לְצִיּוֹן בְּרִנָּה.

לְשָׁנָה הַבָּאָה בִּירוּשָׁלָיִם.

✠ CONCLUSION

The Passover Seder has been completed according to its laws, rules, and regulations. Just as we merited to arrange it [this year], so may we merit to do it [in the future]. Pure One, Who dwells in Heaven, raise up the assembly of the countless congregation! Guide soon the well-planted seedlings, redeemed, to Zion with song!

NEXT YEAR IN JERUSALEM!

בחוץ לארץ בלילה הראשון של פסח אומרים "וּבְכֵן וַיְהִי בַּחֲצִי הַלַּיְלָה" וּבליל שני
אומרים "וּבְכֵן וַאֲמַרְתֶּם זֶבַח פֶּסַח" הנמצא בדף 127.

וּבְכֵן וַיְהִי בַּחֲצִי הַלַּיְלָה:

אָז רוֹב נִסִּים הִפְלֵאתָ בַּלַּיְלָה.
בְּרֹאשׁ אַשְׁמוֹרֶת זֶה הַלַּיְלָה.
גֵּר צֶדֶק נִצַּחְתּוֹ כְּנֶחֱלַק לוֹ לַיְלָה.
וַיְהִי בַּחֲצִי הַלַּיְלָה.

דַּנְתָּ מֶלֶךְ גְּרָר בַּחֲלוֹם הַלַּיְלָה.
הִפְחַדְתָּ אֲרַמִּי בְּאֶמֶשׁ לַיְלָה.
וַיָּשַׂר יִשְׂרָאֵל לְמַלְאָךְ וַיּוּכַל לוֹ לַיְלָה.
וַיְהִי בַּחֲצִי הַלַּיְלָה.

זֶרַע בְּכוֹרֵי פַתְרוֹס מָחַצְתָּ בַּחֲצִי הַלַּיְלָה.
חֵילָם לֹא מָצְאוּ בְּקוּמָם בַּלַּיְלָה.

Outside the Land of Israel, "It was in the middle of the night" is recited on the first night of Passover. On the second night, skip to , "You shall say, 'It is the Passover sacrifice,'" on page 128.

Hence, *"It was in the middle of the night"* [121]

א Then You distinguished this night with many miracles.

ב At the chief watch of this night

ג You granted victory to the righteous convert as You divided the night for him. [122]

"It was in the middle of the night"

ד You judged the king of Gerar in the middle of the night. [123]

ה You frightened an Aramean with "last night." [124]

ו Israel strove with an angel and overcame him at night. [125]

"It was in the middle of the night"

ז The first-born offspring of Pathros You crushed in the middle of the night. [126]

ח They did not find their strength when they arose at night. [127]

---

[121] Exodus 12:29.

[122] The righteous convert is Abraham, who abandoned idolatry and became the first Jew. When he went to war to save his nephew, Lot, the *Torah* says, "He and his servants divided [into fighting units] against them at night" (Genesis 14:15). *Hashem* divided that special night, using part for Abraham and saving part for the Exodus from Egypt (*Rashi* ad. loc., citing *Breishith Rabbah* 43:3).

[123] When Abimelech, king of Gerar, seized Sarah, God appeared to him in a dream and said, "Behold you shall die because of the woman you have taken" (Genesis 20:3).

[124] When Laban, the Aramean, pursued Jacob, *Hashem* appeared to him in a dream and cautioned, "Watch yourself lest you speak with Jacob whether for good or for evil!" (Genesis 31:24). Laban told Jacob that he indeed would have harmed him had God not warned him against doing so (Genesis 31:29).

[125] Jacob fought the guardian angel of Esau at night (Genesis 32:24-32).

[126] Pathros is synonymous with Egypt (Genesis 10:14; Jeremiah 44:15; Ezekiel 29:14).

[127] The shock of discovering the dead first-born left the Egyptians feeling powerless. Alternatively, their strength may refer to their wealth, which

טִיסַת נְגִיד חֲרוֹשֶׁת סִלִּיתָ בְּכוֹכְבֵי לַיְלָה.

וַיְהִי בַּחֲצִי הַלַּיְלָה.

יָעַץ מְחָרֵף לְנוֹפֵף אִוּוּי הוֹבַשְׁתָ פְּגָרָיו בַּלַּיְלָה.

כָּרַע בֵּל וּמַצָּבוֹ בְּאִישׁוֹן לַיְלָה.

לְאִישׁ חֲמוּדוֹת נִגְלָה רָז חֲזוֹת לַיְלָה.

וַיְהִי בַּחֲצִי הַלַּיְלָה.

מִשְׁתַּכֵּר בִּכְלֵי קֹדֶשׁ נֶהֱרַג בּוֹ בַּלַּיְלָה.

נוֹשַׁע מִבּוֹר אֲרָיוֹת פּוֹתֵר בְּעֲתוּתֵי לַיְלָה.

שִׂנְאָה נָטַר אֲגָגִי וְכָתַב סְפָרִים בַּלַּיְלָה.

they had given away to the Jews, as the *Torah* says, "And [the Jews] des-
poiled Egypt" (Exodus 12:36). (*Onkelos* on Deuteronomy 8:17 translates
"strength" (חֵיל) as "property.")

ಡ The flight of the prince of Harosheth You marked with the stars of the night.[128]

"It was in the middle of the night"

ಲ The blasphemer took counsel to flaunt his desire.   You dried his corpses at night. [129]

ಸ Bel and his pedestal toppled in the darkness of night.[130]

ಳ To the "man of delights" a secret was revealed in the visions of the night.[131]

"It was in the middle of the night"

ಬ He who became drunk with the holy vessels was killed at night.[132]

ಷ Saved from the lions' den was the one who deciphered frightful dreams of the night.[133]

ಶ An Agagite nurtured enmity and wrote epistles at night.[134]

---

[128]   The Canaanite general Sisra lived in *Harosheth Hagoyim*, literally "the stronghold of the nations" (Judges 4:2).   When Deborah and Barak battled against him, the *Tanach* says that, "From heaven the stars waged war; from their paths they waged war with Sisra" (Judges 5:20).

[129]   The Assyrian king Sennacherib sent messengers to King Hezekiah, blasphemously proclaiming that God could not save Jerusalem (II Kings 18:35).   *Hashem* sent an angel that same night to destroy the Assyrian army, leaving behind 185,000 corpses (II Kings 19:35).

[130]   When enemies laid siege to Babylonia, its idol, Bel, was toppled (Isaiah 46:1; Jeremiah 50:2).   The *Tanach* does not say that this happened at night. However, Israel's rescue on Passover night set a pattern for all future salvations, so it is proper to refer to them as happening at night.

[131]   The *Tanach* calls Daniel a "man of delights," meaning a man possessed of qualities which delighted God (Daniel 10:11 and 10:19).   *Hashem* revealed secrets to him in visions of the night (Daniel 2:19).

[132]   Belshazzar, the grandson of Nebuchadnezzar, defiled the vessels of the Temple by using them as serving pieces at a feast (Daniel 5:1-3).   That same night he was killed (Daniel 5:30).

[133]   When the Babylonian monarchs had nightmares or beheld ghastly omens, they called upon Daniel, who had been saved from the lions' den, to interpret them (Daniel 2:26-48; 4:1-24; 5:5-28; 6:17-23).

[134]   Haman descended from the Amalekite king, Agag.   He clung to the ancient hatred which his family bore toward the Jewish people and sent out letters with instructions to exterminate the Jews (Esther 3:1 and 3:13).

וַיְהִי בַּחֲצִי הַלַּיְלָה.

עוֹרַרְתָּ נִצְחֲךָ עָלָיו בְּנֶדֶד שְׁנַת לַיְלָה.
פּוּרָה תִדְרֹךְ לְשׁוֹמֵר מַה מִּלַּיְלָה.
צָרַח כַּשּׁוֹמֵר וְשָׂח אָתָא בֹקֶר וְגַם לַיְלָה.
וַיְהִי בַּחֲצִי הַלַּיְלָה.

קָרֵב יוֹם אֲשֶׁר הוּא לֹא יוֹם וְלֹא לַיְלָה.
רָם הוֹדַע כִּי לְךָ הַיּוֹם אַף לְךָ הַלַּיְלָה.
שׁוֹמְרִים הַפְקֵד לְעִירְךָ כָּל הַיּוֹם וְכָל הַלַּיְלָה.
תָּאִיר כְּאוֹר יוֹם חֶשְׁכַּת לַיְלָה.
וַיְהִי בַּחֲצִי הַלַּיְלָה.

בחוץ לארץ בליל שני של פסח אומרים "וּבְכֵן וַאֲמַרְתֶּם זֶבַח פֶּסַח" ובלילה הראשון
אומרים "וּבְכֵן וַיְהִי בַּחֲצִי הַלַּיְלָה" לעיל דף 123.

וּבְכֵן וַאֲמַרְתֶּם זֶבַח פֶּסַח:

"It was in the middle of the night"

ע You brought about Your victory over him by making wander the sleep of night.[135]

פ A wine vat You tread, [and people will ask], "Guard, what shall emanate from night?

צ He shall cry out as a guard and say, "Morning comes and also night."[136]

"It was in the middle of the night"

ק A day draws near which is neither day nor night.[137]

ר Make known, Exalted One, that to You belong the day and also the night.[138]

ש Appoint guards for Your city for all the day and all the night.[139]

ת May the darkness of the night be made bright as the light of day.

"It was in the middle of the night"

Outside the Land of Israel, "You shall say, 'It is the Passover sacrifice'" is recited on the second night of Passover. On the first night, "It was in the middle of the night," on page 124, is recited instead.

Hence, "You shall say, 'It is the Passover sacrifice'"[140]

---

[135] God commenced Haman's downfall by disturbing King Ahasuerus's sleep. Troubled by the thought that someone may have done him a favor which he had neglected to repay, the king ordered that his chronicles be read before him. He then found that he had not repaid Mordecai for saving him from a treasonous plot (Esther 6:1-3).

[136] This is based on Isaiah 21:12 and 63:1-3. When Jews see the harsh exile, which is compared to the crushing of grapes, they ask the Guardian of Israel, "What will become of this night?" He responds that ultimately there will be "morning" for the righteous, but "night" for the wicked (J.T. *Ta'anith* 1:1).

[137] This refers to the arrival of the *Mashiach* (Zachariah 14:7).

[138] Based on Psalms 74:16. When God reveals Himself in the future, it will become evident that both day and night — both good and evil — are integral to His Divine plan.

[139] Based on the verse, "Upon your walls, Jerusalem, I have appointed guards for all the day and all the night" (Isaiah 62:6).

[140] Exodus 12:27.

אֹמֶץ גְּבוּרוֹתֶיךָ הִפְלֵאתָ בַּפֶּסַח.
בְּרֹאשׁ כָּל מוֹעֲדוֹת נִשֵּׂאתָ פֶּסַח.
גִּלִּיתָ לְאֶזְרָחִי חֲצוֹת לֵיל פֶּסַח.
וַאֲמַרְתֶּם זֶבַח פֶּסַח.

דְּלָתָיו דָּפַקְתָּ כְּחֹם הַיּוֹם בַּפֶּסַח.
הִסְעִיד נוֹצְצִים עֻגוֹת מַצּוֹת בַּפֶּסַח.
וְאֶל הַבָּקָר רָץ זֵכֶר לְשׁוֹר עֵרֶךְ פֶּסַח.
וַאֲמַרְתֶּם זֶבַח פֶּסַח.

זֹעֲמוּ סְדוֹמִים וְלוֹהֲטוּ בָּאֵשׁ בַּפֶּסַח.
חֻלַּץ לוֹט מֵהֶם וּמַצּוֹת אָפָה בְּקֵץ פֶּסַח.
טִאטֵאתָ אַדְמַת מוֹף וְנוֹף בְּעָבְרְךָ בַּפֶּסַח.
וַאֲמַרְתֶּם זֶבַח פֶּסַח.

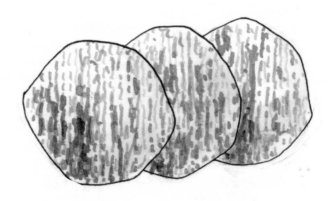

א The power of Your mighty deeds You distinguished on Passover.

ב You elevated Passover to be the head of all the holidays.[141]

ג You revealed Yourself to the one from the east on the midnight of Passover."[142]

"You shall say, 'It is the Passover sacrifice'"

ד At his doors You knocked during the heat of the day on Passover.[143]

ה He fed the sparkling angels cakes of *Matzah* on Passover.[144]

ו To the cattle he ran, reminiscent of the ox which was offered with the Passover sacrifice.[145]

"You shall say, 'It is the Passover sacrifice'"

ז The Sodomites infuriated [God] and were consumed in flame on Passover.

ח Lot was rescued from them and baked *Matzoth* at the end of Passover.

ט You swept the land of Mof and Nof when You crossed [Egypt] on Passover.[146]

"You shall say, 'It is the Passover sacrifice'"

---

[141]   When enumerating the holidays, the *Torah* counts *Nissan* as the first month because Passover falls at that time and marks the beginning of the Jewish nation.

[142]   Abraham is called "the one from the east," presumably because he migrated to the Land of Israel from Ur, which lies to the east in Mesopotamia (See B.T. *Baba Bathra* 15A).

[143]   God visited Abraham during Passover when the latter was recovering from his circumcision (Genesis 18:1).

[144]   Three angels also visited Abraham at that time (Genesis 18:2).   The Prophet Ezekiel described angels as "sparkling" (Ezekiel 1:7).

[145]   Abraham ran to slaughter cattle to feed his angelic guests, who appeared as humans (Genesis 18:7).   In Temple times, Jews brought oxen as festival offerings (חֲגִיגוֹת) together with the Passover sacrifice.

[146]   Mof and Nof refer to the Egyptian city of Memphis (*Targum Yonathan* on Jeremiah 2:16 and Hosea 9:6).   At one time, Memphis was Egypt's capital. Just as Rome denoted the entire Roman Empire even though it was only the capital city, perhaps Memphis denoted the entire Egyptian kingdom.

יָהּ רֹאשׁ כָּל אוֹן מָחַצְתָּ בְּלֵיל שִׁמּוּר פֶּסַח.

כַּבִּיר עַל בֵּן בְּכוֹר פָּסַחְתָּ בְּדַם פֶּסַח.

לְבִלְתִּי תֵּת מַשְׁחִית לָבוֹא בִּפְתָחַי בַּפֶּסַח.

וַאֲמַרְתֶּם זֶבַח פֶּסַח.

מְסֻגֶּרֶת סֻגָּרָה בְּעִתּוֹתֵי פֶּסַח.

נִשְׁמְדָה מִדְיָן בִּצְלִיל שְׂעוֹרֵי עֹמֶר פֶּסַח.

שֹׂרְפוּ מִשְׁמַנֵּי פּוּל וְלוּד בִּיקַד יְקוֹד פֶּסַח.

וַאֲמַרְתֶּם זֶבַח פֶּסַח.

עוֹד הַיּוֹם בְּנוֹב לַעֲמוֹד עַד גָּעָה עוֹנַת פֶּסַח.

' God, You crushed the chief of all the first-born on the guarded night of Passover.[147]

כ Mighty One, You skipped over the first-born son [Israel] by virtue of the blood of the Passover sacrifice.

ל Not permitting the destroyer to come through my doors on Passover.

"You shall say, 'It is the Passover sacrifice'"

מ [Jericho,] which was doubly fortified, was delivered [to Israel] at the time of Passover.[148]

נ Midian was destroyed by a roasted *Omer's* worth of barley on Passover.[149]

ש The prosperous Pul and Lud were burned in a flaming fire on Passover.[150]

"You shall say, 'It is the Passover sacrifice'"

ע [Sennacherib sped and] arrived "yet today to stand in Nob" on the eve of Passover.[151]

---

[147] Pharaoh was also a first-born (*Peskita Rabbethai* 17). Although he did not die, crushing the chief alludes to him (Psalms 110:6, according to *Rashi*).

[148] Joshua 5:10 and 6:1.

[149] Prior to engaging Midian in battle, *Hashem* instructed Gideon and his assistant to approach the enemy camp secretly. There, Gideon overheard one soldier tell another that he had dreamed that a roasted barley bread rolled through their camp and overturned a tent. The soldier's comrade correctly understood the dream as predicting the defeat of Midian (Judges 7:9-14). This took place on Passover when the Jews waved an *Omer's* worth of barley flour in front of the altar, an *"Omer"* (עוֹמֶר) having a volume of about two and half liters. The soldier's dream hinted that God destroyed Midian in the merit of this *Mitzvah* (*Rashi* ad. loc. and on Judges 6:19).

[150] Pul and Lud were generals of the Assyrian army (Rabbi Yitzchak Abrabanel, citing II Kings 15:19). Alternatively, they were states allied with Assyria (Isaiah 66:19). The Prophet Isaiah foretold that Assyria would be burned, a metaphor for the severe defeat they would suffer at the hands of the Jews (Isaiah 10:16-17 according to Rabbi Yitzchak Abrabanel).

[151] King Sennacherib's astrologers predicted that he would defeat the Jews, but only if he did battle that very day. He raced with his army towards Jerusalem, completing what would ordinarily have been a ten day journey in just one day. When he arrived within view of the city on Passover eve, he

פַּס יָד כָּתְבָה לְקַעֲקֵעַ צוּל בַּפֶּסַח.

צָפֹה הַצָּפִית עָרוֹךְ הַשֻּׁלְחָן בַּפֶּסַח.

וַאֲמַרְתֶּם זֶבַח פֶּסַח.

קָהָל כִּנְּסָה הֲדַסָּה צוֹם לְשַׁלֵּשׁ בַּפֶּסַח.

רֹאשׁ מִבֵּית רָשָׁע מָחַצְתָּ בְּעֵץ חֲמִשִּׁים בַּפֶּסַח.

שְׁתֵּי אֵלֶּה רֶגַע תָּבִיא לְעוּצִית בַּפֶּסַח.

תָּעֹז יָדְךָ וְתָרוּם יְמִינְךָ כְּלֵיל הִתְקַדֶּשׁ חַג פֶּסַח.

וַאֲמַרְתֶּם זֶבַח פֶּסַח.

כִּי לוֹ נָאֶה. כִּי לוֹ יָאֶה.

אַדִּיר בִּמְלוּכָה. בָּחוּר כַּהֲלָכָה. גְּדוּדָיו יֹאמְרוּ לוֹ לְךָ וּלְךָ. לְךָ כִּי לְךָ.
לְךָ אַף לְךָ. לְךָ יְיָ הַמַּמְלָכָה.

_____

decided that it was weak and that he could easily capture it the next day, so
he made camp. That night, an angel destroyed his entire army (B.T. *Sanhe-*
drin 95A, citing Isaiah 10:32 and II Kings 19:35).

פ The palm of a hand wrote to exterminate a Babylonian on Passover.[152]

צ Sentries were posted during the banquet at Passover.[153]
"You shall say, 'It is the Passover sacrifice'"

ק Hadassah gathered an assembly on Passover to fast for three days.[154]

ר The head of the wicked house You crushed with a wooden post of fifty [cubits] on Passover.[155]

ש These two may You bring momentarily upon the Uzzites on Passover.[156]

ת May Your hand be strong, and may You raise Your right arm as upon the night when the Passover sacrifice was offered.
"You shall say, 'It is the Passover sacrifice'"

For Him it is fitting, for Him it is becoming.

א Mighty in kingship, perfectly outstanding, His troops say to him, "To You and to You, to You for to You, to You also to You, to You, *Hashem*, is sovereignty."[157]

---

152 This refers to Nebuchadnezzar's grandson, Belshazzar, who made a feast at which he used the vessels of the Temple as serving pieces. A hand appeared and wrote a cryptic message which portended his death (Daniel 5:1-5). The Hebrew צוּל, meaning "swamp," refers to Babylonia, which was low-lying and swampy (See Isaiah 44:27).

153 The Prophet Isaiah predicted that the Babylonians would post lookouts while feasting to warn them of impending attack and that their banquet would be interrupted by the onslaught of the Persians and Medes (Isaiah 21:5).

154 When Mordecai informed Esther (Hadassah) of Haman's plot to exterminate Israel, she instructed him to gather the Jews together to pray and fast for three days (Esther 4:16).

155 Haman was hanged on a gallows fifty cubits tall (Esther 7:9-10).

156 This hymn concludes with a request that God end the present exile and visit retribution upon those who caused it. The *Tanach* refers to the Edomite forebears of the Romans as coming from the land of Uz (עוּץ) (Lamentations 4:21). The expression "these two" alludes to the verse, "These two shall come upon you...bereavement and widowhood" (Isaiah 47:9).

157 The repeated expressions of "To You" refer to Biblical verses which praise

כִּי לוֹ נָאֶה. כִּי לוֹ יָאֶה.

דָּגוּל בִּמְלוּכָה. הָדוּר כַּהֲלָכָה. וָתִיקָיו יֹאמְרוּ לוֹ לְךָ וּלְךָ. לְךָ כִּי לְךָ. לְךָ אַף לְךָ. לְךָ יְיָ הַמַּמְלָכָה.
כִּי לוֹ נָאֶה. כִּי לוֹ יָאֶה.

זַכַּאי בִּמְלוּכָה. חָסִין כַּהֲלָכָה. טַפְסְרָיו יֹאמְרוּ לוֹ לְךָ וּלְךָ. לְךָ כִּי לְךָ. לְךָ אַף לְךָ. לְךָ יְיָ הַמַּמְלָכָה.
כִּי לוֹ נָאֶה. כִּי לוֹ יָאֶה.

יָחִיד בִּמְלוּכָה. כַּבִּיר כַּהֲלָכָה. לִמּוּדָיו יֹאמְרוּ לוֹ לְךָ וּלְךָ. לְךָ כִּי לְךָ. לְךָ אַף לְךָ. לְךָ יְיָ הַמַּמְלָכָה.
כִּי לוֹ נָאֶה. כִּי לוֹ יָאֶה.

מוֹשֵׁל בִּמְלוּכָה. נוֹרָא כַּהֲלָכָה. סְבִיבָיו יֹאמְרוּ לוֹ לְךָ וּלְךָ. לְךָ כִּי לְךָ. לְךָ אַף לְךָ. לְךָ יְיָ הַמַּמְלָכָה.
כִּי לוֹ נָאֶה. כִּי לוֹ יָאֶה.

עָנָו בִּמְלוּכָה. פּוֹדֶה כַּהֲלָכָה. צַדִּיקָיו יֹאמְרוּ לוֹ לְךָ וּלְךָ. לְךָ כִּי לְךָ. לְךָ אַף לְךָ. לְךָ יְיָ הַמַּמְלָכָה.
כִּי לוֹ נָאֶה. כִּי לוֹ יָאֶה.

קָדוֹשׁ בִּמְלוּכָה. רַחוּם כַּהֲלָכָה. שִׁנְאַנָּיו יֹאמְרוּ לוֹ לְךָ וּלְךָ. לְךָ כִּי לְךָ. לְךָ אַף לְךָ. לְךָ יְיָ הַמַּמְלָכָה.
כִּי לוֹ נָאֶה. כִּי לוֹ יָאֶה.

תַּקִּיף בִּמְלוּכָה. תּוֹמֵךְ כַּהֲלָכָה. תְּמִימָיו יֹאמְרוּ לוֹ לְךָ וּלְךָ. לְךָ כִּי לְךָ. לְךָ אַף לְךָ. לְךָ יְיָ הַמַּמְלָכָה.
כִּי לוֹ נָאֶה. כִּי לוֹ יָאֶה.

God: "**To You**, *Hashem*, is the greatness" (I Chronicles 29:11); "**To You**, *Hashem*, is sovereignty" (Ibid.); "Who does not fear You, King of the nations, for **to You** it is fitting" (Jeremiah 10:7); "**To You** is dominion with might" (Psalms 89:14); "**To You** is day; also **to You** is night" (Psalms 74:16); "**To You** is Heaven; also **to You** is Earth" (Psalms 89:12). (Rabbi Yitzchak Abrabanel).

For Him it is fitting, for Him it is becoming.

ד Distinguished in kingship, perfectly majestic, His pious ones say to Him, "To You and to You, to You for to You, to You also to You, to You, *Hashem*, is sovereignty."
For Him it is fitting, for Him it is becoming.

ז Righteously kingly, perfectly strong, His leading angels say to Him, "To You and to You, to You for to You, to You also to You, to You, *Hashem*, is sovereignty."
For Him it is fitting, for Him it is becoming.

י Unique in kingship, perfectly mighty, His learned ones say to Him, "To You and to You, to You for to You, to You also to You, to You, *Hashem*, is sovereignty."
For Him it is fitting, for Him it is becoming.

מ Ruling in kingliness, perfectly awesome, those who surround Him say to Him, "To You and to You, to You for to You, to You also to You, to You, *Hashem*, is sovereignty."
For Him it is fitting, for Him it is becoming.

ע Modest in kingliness, redeeming perfectly, His righteous ones say to Him, "To You and to You, to You for to You, to You also to You, to You, *Hashem*, is sovereignty."
For Him it is fitting, for Him it is becoming.

ק Sanctified in kingliness, perfectly merciful, His angels say to Him, "To You and to You, to You for to You, to You also to You, to You, *Hashem*, is sovereignty."
For Him it is fitting, for Him it is becoming.

ת Forceful in kingliness, perfectly sustaining, His pure ones say to Him, "To You and to You, to You for to You, to You also to You, to You, *Hashem*, is sovereignty."
For Him it is fitting, for Him it is becoming.

אַדִּיר הוּא יִבְנֶה בֵיתוֹ בְּקָרוֹב

בִּמְהֵרָה בִּמְהֵרָה בְּיָמֵינוּ בְּקָרוֹב — אֵל בְּנֵה, אֵל בְּנֵה, בְּנֵה בֵיתְךָ בְּקָרוֹב.

בָּחוּר הוּא גָּדוֹל הוּא דָּגוּל הוּא

יִבְנֶה בֵיתוֹ בְּקָרוֹב.

בִּמְהֵרָה בִּמְהֵרָה בְּיָמֵינוּ בְּקָרוֹב — אֵל בְּנֵה, אֵל בְּנֵה, בְּנֵה בֵיתְךָ בְּקָרוֹב.

הָדוּר הוּא וָתִיק הוּא זַכַּאי הוּא

חָסִיד הוּא יִבְנֶה בֵיתוֹ בְּקָרוֹב.

בִּמְהֵרָה בִּמְהֵרָה בְּיָמֵינוּ בְּקָרוֹב — אֵל בְּנֵה, אֵל בְּנֵה, בְּנֵה בֵיתְךָ בְּקָרוֹב.

טָהוֹר הוּא יָחִיד הוּא כַּבִּיר הוּא לָמוּד הוּא מֶלֶךְ הוּא נוֹרָא הוּא

סַגִּיב הוּא עִזּוּז הוּא פּוֹדֶה הוּא צַדִּיק הוּא יִבְנֶה בֵיתוֹ בְּקָרוֹב.

בִּמְהֵרָה בִּמְהֵרָה בְּיָמֵינוּ בְּקָרוֹב — אֵל בְּנֵה, אֵל בְּנֵה. בְּנֵה בֵיתְךָ בְּקָרוֹב.

קָדוֹשׁ הוּא רַחוּם הוּא שַׁדַּי הוּא

תַּקִּיף הוּא יִבְנֶה בֵיתוֹ בְּקָרוֹב.

בִּמְהֵרָה בִּמְהֵרָה בְּיָמֵינוּ בְּקָרוֹב אֵל בְּנֵה אֵל בְּנֵה. בְּנֵה בֵיתְךָ בְּקָרוֹב.

אֶחָד מִי יוֹדֵעַ?

אֶחָד אֲנִי יוֹדֵעַ אֶחָד. אֶחָד אֱלֹהֵינוּ שֶׁבַּשָּׁמַיִם וּבָאָרֶץ.

שְׁנַיִם מִי יוֹדֵעַ?

שְׁנַיִם אֲנִי יוֹדֵעַ. שְׁנֵי לוּחוֹת הַבְּרִית. אֶחָד אֱלֹהֵינוּ שֶׁבַּשָּׁמַיִם וּבָאָרֶץ.

שְׁלֹשָׁה מִי יוֹדֵעַ?

שְׁלֹשָׁה אֲנִי יוֹדֵעַ. שְׁלֹשָׁה אָבוֹת. שְׁנֵי לוּחוֹת הַבְּרִית. אֶחָד אֱלֹהֵינוּ שֶׁבַּשָּׁמַיִם וּבָאָרֶץ.

אַרְבַּע מִי יוֹדֵעַ?

אַרְבַּע אֲנִי יוֹדֵעַ. אַרְבַּע אִמָּהוֹת. שְׁלֹשָׁה אָבוֹת. שְׁנֵי לוּחוֹת הַבְּרִית. אֶחָד אֱלֹהֵינוּ שֶׁבַּשָּׁמַיִם וּבָאָרֶץ.

א Mighty is He! May He build His house soon!
Speedily, speedily, in our days, soon. God build, God build Your house soon!

ב Outstanding is He! Great is He! Distinguished is He! May He build His house soon!
Speedily, speedily, in our days, soon. God build, God build Your house soon!

ה Majestic is He! Ancient is He! Righteous is He! Pious is He! May He build His house soon!
Speedily, speedily, in our days, soon. God build, God build Your house soon!

ט Pure is He! Unique is He! Mighty is He! Wise is He! King is He! Awesome is He! Exalted is He! Powerful is He! Redeemer is He! Righteous is He! May He build His house soon!
Speedily, speedily, in our days, soon. God build, God build Your house soon!

ק Holy is He! Merciful is He! Almighty is He! Forceful is He! May He build His house soon!
Speedily, speedily, in our days, soon. God build, God build Your house soon!

Who knows one?
I know one: One is our God who is in Heaven and Earth.

Who knows two?
I know two: Two tablets of the covenant; one is our God who is in Heaven and Earth.

Who knows three?
I know three: Three Patriarchs; two tablets of the covenant; one is our God who is in Heaven and Earth.

Who knows four?
I know four: Four Matriarchs; three Patriarchs; two tablets of the covenant; one is our God who is in Heaven and Earth.

חֲמִשָּׁה מִי יוֹדֵעַ?

חֲמִשָּׁה אֲנִי יוֹדֵעַ. חֲמִשָּׁה חֻמְשֵׁי תוֹרָה. אַרְבַּע אִמָּהוֹת. שְׁלֹשָׁה אָבוֹת. שְׁנֵי לוּחוֹת הַבְּרִית. אֶחָד אֱלֹהֵינוּ שֶׁבַּשָּׁמַיִם וּבָאָרֶץ.

שִׁשָּׁה מִי יוֹדֵעַ?

שִׁשָּׁה אֲנִי יוֹדֵעַ. שִׁשָּׁה סִדְרֵי מִשְׁנָה. חֲמִשָּׁה חֻמְשֵׁי תוֹרָה. אַרְבַּע אִמָּהוֹת. שְׁלֹשָׁה אָבוֹת. שְׁנֵי לוּחוֹת הַבְּרִית. אֶחָד אֱלֹהֵינוּ שֶׁבַּשָּׁמַיִם וּבָאָרֶץ.

שִׁבְעָה מִי יוֹדֵעַ?

שִׁבְעָה אֲנִי יוֹדֵעַ. שִׁבְעָה יְמֵי שַׁבַּתָּא. שִׁשָּׁה סִדְרֵי מִשְׁנָה. חֲמִשָּׁה חֻמְשֵׁי תוֹרָה. אַרְבַּע אִמָּהוֹת. שְׁלֹשָׁה אָבוֹת. שְׁנֵי לוּחוֹת הַבְּרִית. אֶחָד אֱלֹהֵינוּ שֶׁבַּשָּׁמַיִם וּבָאָרֶץ.

שְׁמוֹנָה מִי יוֹדֵעַ?

שְׁמוֹנָה אֲנִי יוֹדֵעַ. שְׁמוֹנָה יְמֵי מִילָה. שִׁבְעָה יְמֵי שַׁבַּתָּא. שִׁשָּׁה סִדְרֵי מִשְׁנָה. חֲמִשָּׁה חֻמְשֵׁי תוֹרָה. אַרְבַּע אִמָּהוֹת. שְׁלֹשָׁה אָבוֹת. שְׁנֵי לוּחוֹת הַבְּרִית. אֶחָד אֱלֹהֵינוּ שֶׁבַּשָּׁמַיִם וּבָאָרֶץ.

תִּשְׁעָה מִי יוֹדֵעַ?

תִּשְׁעָה אֲנִי יוֹדֵעַ. תִּשְׁעָה יַרְחֵי לֵדָה. שְׁמוֹנָה יְמֵי מִילָה. שִׁבְעָה יְמֵי שַׁבַּתָּא. שִׁשָּׁה סִדְרֵי מִשְׁנָה. חֲמִשָּׁה חֻמְשֵׁי תוֹרָה. אַרְבַּע אִמָּהוֹת. שְׁלֹשָׁה אָבוֹת. שְׁנֵי לוּחוֹת הַבְּרִית. אֶחָד אֱלֹהֵינוּ שֶׁבַּשָּׁמַיִם וּבָאָרֶץ.

עֲשָׂרָה מִי יוֹדֵעַ?

עֲשָׂרָה אֲנִי יוֹדֵעַ. עֲשָׂרָה דִּבְּרַיָּא. תִּשְׁעָה יַרְחֵי לֵדָה. שְׁמוֹנָה יְמֵי מִילָה. שִׁבְעָה יְמֵי שַׁבַּתָּא. שִׁשָּׁה סִדְרֵי מִשְׁנָה. חֲמִשָּׁה חֻמְשֵׁי תוֹרָה. אַרְבַּע אִמָּהוֹת. שְׁלֹשָׁה אָבוֹת. שְׁנֵי לוּחוֹת הַבְּרִית. אֶחָד אֱלֹהֵינוּ שֶׁבַּשָּׁמַיִם וּבָאָרֶץ.

Who knows five?

I know five: Five books of the *Torah*; four Matriarchs; three Patriarchs; two tablets of the covenant; one is our God who is in Heaven and Earth.

Who knows six?

I know six: Six orders of the *Mishnah*; five books of the *Torah*; four Matriarchs; three Patriarchs; two tablets of the covenant; one is our God who is in Heaven and Earth.

Who knows seven?

I know seven: Seven days of the week; six orders of the *Mishnah*; five books of the *Torah*; four Matriarchs; three Patriarchs; two tablets of the covenant; one is our God who is in Heaven and Earth.

Who knows eight?

I know eight: Eight days [until] circumcision; seven days of the week; six orders of the *Mishnah*; five books of the *Torah*; four Matriarchs; three Patriarchs; two tablets of the covenant; one is our God who is in Heaven and Earth.

Who knows nine?

I know nine: Nine months of gestation; eight days [until] circumcision; seven days of the week; six orders of the *Mishnah*; five books of the *Torah*; four Matriarchs; three Patriarchs; two tablets of the covenant; one is our God who is in Heaven and Earth.

Who knows ten?

I know ten: Ten Commandments; nine months of gestation; eight days [until] circumcision; seven days of the week; six orders of the *Mishnah*; five books of the *Torah*; four Matriarchs; three Patriarchs; two tablets of the covenant; one is our God who is in Heaven and Earth.

אַחַד עָשָׂר מִי יוֹדֵעַ ?

אַחַד עָשָׂר אֲנִי יוֹדֵעַ. אַחַד עָשָׂר כּוֹכְבַיָּא. עֲשָׂרָה דִבְּרַיָּא. תִּשְׁעָה יַרְחֵי לֵדָה. שְׁמוֹנָה יְמֵי מִילָה. שִׁבְעָה יְמֵי שַׁבַּתָּא. שִׁשָּׁה סִדְרֵי מִשְׁנָה. חֲמִשָּׁה חֻמְשֵׁי תוֹרָה. אַרְבַּע אִמָּהוֹת. שְׁלֹשָׁה אָבוֹת. שְׁנֵי לוּחוֹת הַבְּרִית. אֶחָד אֱלֹהֵינוּ שֶׁבַּשָּׁמַיִם וּבָאָרֶץ.

שְׁנֵים עָשָׂר מִי יוֹדֵעַ ?

שְׁנֵים עָשָׂר אֲנִי יוֹדֵעַ. שְׁנֵים עָשָׂר שִׁבְטַיָּא. אַחַד עָשָׂר כּוֹכְבַיָּא. עֲשָׂרָה דִבְּרַיָּא. תִּשְׁעָה יַרְחֵי לֵדָה. שְׁמוֹנָה יְמֵי מִילָה. שִׁבְעָה יְמֵי שַׁבַּתָּא. שִׁשָּׁה סִדְרֵי מִשְׁנָה. חֲמִשָּׁה חֻמְשֵׁי תוֹרָה. אַרְבַּע אִמָּהוֹת. שְׁלֹשָׁה אָבוֹת. שְׁנֵי לוּחוֹת הַבְּרִית. אֶחָד אֱלֹהֵינוּ שֶׁבַּשָּׁמַיִם וּבָאָרֶץ.

שְׁלֹשָׁה עָשָׂר מִי יוֹדֵעַ ?

שְׁלֹשָׁה עָשָׂר אֲנִי יוֹדֵעַ. שְׁלֹשָׁה עָשָׂר מִדַּיָּא. שְׁנֵים עָשָׂר שִׁבְטַיָּא. אַחַד עָשָׂר כּוֹכְבַיָּא. עֲשָׂרָה דִבְּרַיָּא. תִּשְׁעָה יַרְחֵי לֵדָה. שְׁמוֹנָה יְמֵי מִילָה. שִׁבְעָה יְמֵי שַׁבַּתָּא. שִׁשָּׁה סִדְרֵי מִשְׁנָה. חֲמִשָּׁה חֻמְשֵׁי תוֹרָה. אַרְבַּע אִמָּהוֹת. שְׁלֹשָׁה אָבוֹת. שְׁנֵי לוּחוֹת הַבְּרִית. אֶחָד אֱלֹהֵינוּ שֶׁבַּשָּׁמַיִם וּבָאָרֶץ.

חַד גַּדְיָא   חַד גַּדְיָא
דְּזַבִּין אַבָּא בִּתְרֵי זוּזֵי
חַד גַּדְיָא   חַד גַּדְיָא

וְאָתָא שׁוּנְרָא וְאָכְלָה לְגַדְיָא. דְּזַבִּין אַבָּא בִּתְרֵי זוּזֵי.
חַד גַּדְיָא   חַד גַּדְיָא

וְאָתָא כַלְבָּא וְנָשַׁךְ לְשׁוּנְרָא. דְּאָכְלָה לְגַדְיָא. דְּזַבִּין אַבָּא בִּתְרֵי זוּזֵי.
חַד גַּדְיָא   חַד גַּדְיָא

וְאָתָא חוּטְרָא וְהִכָּה לְכַלְבָּא. דְּנָשַׁךְ לְשׁוּנְרָא. דְּאָכְלָה לְגַדְיָא. דְּזַבִּין אַבָּא בִּתְרֵי זוּזֵי.
חַד גַּדְיָא   חַד גַּדְיָא

Who knows eleven?

I know eleven: Eleven stars;[158] Ten Commandments; nine months of gestation; eight days [until] circumcision; seven days of the week; six orders of the *Mishnah*; five books of the *Torah*; four Matriarchs; three Patriarchs; two tablets of the covenant; one is our God who is in Heaven and Earth.

Who knows twelve?

I know twelve: Twelve Tribes; eleven stars; Ten Commandments; nine months of gestation; eight days [until] circumcision; seven days of the week; six orders of the *Mishnah*; five books of the *Torah*; four Matriarchs; three Patriarchs; two tablets of the covenant; one is our God who is in Heaven and Earth.

Who knows thirteen?

I know thirteen: Thirteen attributes [of mercy]; twelve Tribes; eleven stars; Ten Commandments; nine months of gestation; eight days [until] circumcision; seven days of the week; six orders of the *Mishnah*; five books of the *Torah*; four Matriarchs; three Patriarchs; two tablets of the covenant; one is our God who is in Heaven and Earth.

One Kid. One kid.

Which father bought for two *zuz*.
One Kid. One kid.

A cat came and ate the kid, which father bought for two *zuz*.
One Kid. One kid.

A dog came and bit the cat, which ate the kid, which father bought for two *zuz*.
One Kid. One kid.

A stick came and beat the dog, which bit the cat, which ate the kid, which father bought for two *zuz*.
One Kid. One kid.

---

[158] Joseph dreamed that eleven stars would bow down to him together with the sun and the moon (Genesis 37:9).

וְאָתָא נוּרָא וְשָׂרַף לְחוּטְרָא. דְּהִכָּה לְכַלְבָּא. דְּנָשַׁךְ לְשׁוּנְרָא. דְּאָכְלָה לְגַדְיָא. דְּזַבִּין אַבָּא בִּתְרֵי זוּזֵי.

חַד גַּדְיָא חַד גַּדְיָא

וְאָתָא מַיָּא וְכָבָה לְנוּרָא. דְּשָׂרַף לְחוּטְרָא. דְּהִכָּה לְכַלְבָּא. דְּנָשַׁךְ לְשׁוּנְרָא. דְּאָכְלָה לְגַדְיָא. דְּזַבִּין אַבָּא בִּתְרֵי זוּזֵי.

חַד גַּדְיָא חַד גַּדְיָא

וְאָתָא תוֹרָא וְשָׁתָא לְמַיָּא. דְּכָבָה לְנוּרָא. דְּשָׂרַף לְחוּטְרָא. דְּהִכָּה לְכַלְבָּא. דְּנָשַׁךְ לְשׁוּנְרָא. דְּאָכְלָה לְגַדְיָא. דְּזַבִּין אַבָּא בִּתְרֵי זוּזֵי.

חַד גַּדְיָא חַד גַּדְיָא

וְאָתָא הַשׁוֹחֵט וְשָׁחַט לְתוֹרָא. דְּשָׁתָא לְמַיָּא. דְּכָבָה לְנוּרָא. דְּשָׂרַף לְחוּטְרָא. דְּהִכָּה לְכַלְבָּא. דְּנָשַׁךְ לְשׁוּנְרָא. דְּאָכְלָה לְגַדְיָא. דְּזַבִּין אַבָּא בִּתְרֵי זוּזֵי.

חַד גַּדְיָא חַד גַּדְיָא

וְאָתָא מַלְאַךְ הַמָּוֶת וְשָׁחַט לְשׁוֹחֵט. דְּשָׁחַט לְתוֹרָא. דְּשָׁתָא לְמַיָּא. דְּכָבָה לְנוּרָא. דְּשָׂרַף לְחוּטְרָא. דְּהִכָּה לְכַלְבָּא. דְּנָשַׁךְ לְשׁוּנְרָא. דְּאָכְלָה לְגַדְיָא. דְּזַבִּין אַבָּא בִּתְרֵי זוּזֵי.

חַד גַּדְיָא חַד גַּדְיָא

וְאָתָא הַקָּדוֹשׁ בָּרוּךְ הוּא וְשָׁחַט לְמַלְאַךְ הַמָּוֶת. דְּשָׁחַט לְשׁוֹחֵט. דְּשָׁחַט לְתוֹרָא. דְּשָׁתָא לְמַיָּא. דְּכָבָה לְנוּרָא. דְּשָׂרַף לְחוּטְרָא. דְּהִכָּה לְכַלְבָּא. דְּנָשַׁךְ לְשׁוּנְרָא. דְּאָכְלָה לְגַדְיָא. דְּזַבִּין אַבָּא בִּתְרֵי זוּזֵי.

חַד גַּדְיָא חַד גַּדְיָא

A fire came and burned the stick, which beat the dog, which bit the cat, which ate the kid, which father bought for two *zuz*.
One Kid. One kid.

Water came and extinguished the fire, which burned the stick, which beat the dog, which bit the cat, which ate the kid, which father bought for two *zuz*.
One Kid. One kid.

An ox came and drank the water, which extinguished the fire, which burned the stick, which beat the dog, which bit the cat, which ate the kid, which father bought for two *zuz*.
One Kid. One kid.

A slaughterer came and butchered the ox, which drank the water, which extinguished the fire, which burned the stick, which beat the dog, which bit the cat, which ate the kid, which father bought for two *zuz*.
One Kid. One kid.

The angel of death came and slew the slaughterer, who butchered the ox, which drank the water, which extinguished the fire, which burned the stick, which beat the dog, which bit the cat, which ate the kid which father bought for two *zuz*.
One Kid. One kid.

The Holy One, Blessed be He, came and killed the angel of death, which slew the slaughterer, who butchered the ox, which drank the water, which extinguished the fire, which burned the stick, which beat the dog, which bit the cat, which ate the kid, which father bought for two *zuz*.
One Kid. One kid.

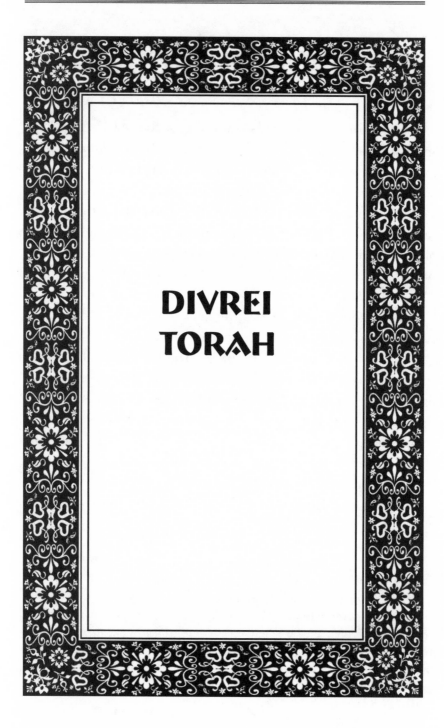

DIVREI
TORAH

THE UNITY OF THE JEWISH PEOPLE

The *Torah* emphasizes the unity of the Jewish people in Egypt. Pharaoh said, "Come let us deal craftily with *him*."[159] This reference to the nation in the singular suggests that the Jews were so united that the Egyptian king viewed them as one entity rather than as a group of individuals. Another verse states that, "They placed upon *it* tax collectors,"[160] again referring to the Jews as one collective unit. Again, after the Jews emerged from the Reed Sea and sang praises to *Hashem*, the *Torah* records that they said, "*I* will sing to *Hashem*"[161] rather than "*We* will sing."[162]

Pharaoh sought to destroy this unity. He ordered the Jewish slaves to build cities on unstable ground where the buildings would either collapse or sink.[163] The Egyptians also forced women to do men's work and vice versa.[164] By imposing such conditions, Pharaoh and his advisors hoped to create so much anguish and frustration that the Jews would begin squabbling among themselves.

Pharaoh had several motives for pursuing a program aimed at destroying the unity of the Jews.

First, he wished to prevent Jews from having more child-

---

[159] Exodus 1:10.

[160] Exodus 1:11.

[161] Exodus 15:1.

[162] *Ohr Hachaim* ad. loc. Rabbi Shimshon Raphael Hirsch notes that when describing the seventy Jews who descended into Egypt, the *Torah* calls them "seventy soul" (נֶפֶשׁ) in the singular, stressing the feeling of unity which prevailed among them (Exodus 1:5). By contrast, in Genesis 36:6, the *Torah* refers to the six members of Esau's house in the plural (נַפְשׁוֹת) (Commentary on Exodus 1:5).

[163] B.T. *Sotah* 11A.

[164] B.T. *Sotah* 11B.

ren, something he viewed as a threat to his own people.[165] As the *Haggadah* explains, the phrase, "[God] saw their affliction,"[166] refers to cessation of marital relations. By crushing the spirit of the people, the Egyptians hoped to create discord so that feelings of love and friendship — including marriage relationships — would be destroyed.

Second, Pharaoh sought to damage the unity of the Jewish people to prevent the Jews from escaping. He reasoned that whoever might plot an escape would be reported by others. Moreover, it would be impossible to coordinate any uprising without the loyalty and cooperation which unity fosters.

On a deeper level, the concepts of unity, harmony, and good will are antithetical to polytheism. The *Rambam* explains that ancient pagans, such as the Egyptians, believed in a Supreme Being. However, they also believed that *Hashem* is detached from the universe and leaves subsidiary "gods" in charge.[167] To the Egyptians, the apparent chaos of the universe results from conflicts between the sun-god and the moon-god, the peace-god and the war-god, and so forth. Disagreement and disharmony are the normal condition of the universe, not peace and unity.

By contrast, if only one God exists, then it follows that everything in the universe functions in a harmonious, unified manner even if it is not always apparent to human beings how this is so. Pharaoh's unsuccessful attempts to interfere with the solidarity of the Jewish people reflected a deep-seated opposition to monotheism.

The *Midrash* teaches that the plague of hail consisted of hailstones filled with fire. Ordinarily, water cannot coexist with fire. For the purpose of punishing the Egyptians, however, *Hashem* made peace between them and they functioned harmo-

---

[165] Exodus 1:9.
[166] Deuteronomy 26:7.
[167] *Yad Hachazakah, Hilchoth Avodah Zarah* 1:1-2.

niously.[168]

God punished the Egyptians measure for measure. They sought to destroy the unity of the Jewish people and to deny that God controls everything. He punished them by creating cooperation between substances which ordinarily do not work together.

The *Midrash* teaches that one of the reasons *Hashem* rescued the Jews from Egypt was that they did not speak evil of one another or inform against each other to their Egyptians masters.[169] The *Midrash* also makes the surprising assertion that even if Jews worship idols, *Hashem* will not punish them if there is peace among them.[170]

How can peace counteract the evil of idolatry — the absolute antithesis of Judaism?

When people cooperate with one another and peace reigns among them, they have the ability to understand the concept of unity. They will eventually come to realize that one God alone controls the universe. *Hashem* does not punish them because even if they presently worship idols, at some point they will recognize the truth and repent.

The *Zohar* states that Israel, the Holy One, Blessed be He, and the *Torah* are one.[171] When Jews act together as one harmonious unit, they have something in common with God Himself — they are one.

It was this recognition that God is one that the Egyptians sought to attack. They realized that even if the Jews sank to the deepest depths of depravity, God would still save them if they maintained their unity. The only way to destroy the Jewish people was to destroy their unity.

The role which Jewish unity played in the supernatural redemption from Egypt is reflected in the Hebrew term for

---

[168] *Shemoth Rabbah* 12:4.
[169] *Vayikra Rabbah* 32:5.
[170] *Breishith Rabbah* 38:6.
[171] *Zohar* III:73A.

supernatural — לְמַעְלָה מִן הַטֶּבַע — which literally means "above nature." The letters of the Hebrew alphabet which precede those of the word "nature" (הַטֶּבַע), i.e., are above it, are דחאס. These letters can be rearranged as ס' אֶחָד, meaning "sixty are one." The sixty myriads of Jews who were mired in Egyptian slavery acted in complete harmony, as if they were one person. Measure for measure, *Hashem* acted above and beyond nature and miraculously rescued them.

THE THEME OF FOUR

The *Seder* features Four Cups of wine, Four Questions, and Four Sons. What is the meaning of this repeated emphasis on the number four?

A Jewish holiday does not merely commemorate an ancient event. Rather, it serves as a conduit through which we draw spirituality into the world again and again every year. As the *Haggadah* states, "In each generation a person must view himself as though he left Egypt."

The holidays could not exist without a calendar which fixes them in time so that they can be celebrated year after year. On the fourth day of Creation, *Hashem* created the heavenly bodies which people use to measure time and to set the calendar. Thus, it was on the fourth day of Creation that God created the potential for the holidays to exist.

As the very first Jewish holiday, Passover was the first time when the power of the calendar was unleashed. God therefore gave Moses the *Mitzvah* to declare the first day of the month (ראש חֹדֶשׁ) just before the Jews departed from Egypt.[172] By granting the leaders of the Jewish people this authority, *Hashem* agrees to

---

[172] Exodus 12:2.

their decisions concerning when the holidays fall out.[173] The Jews thus gained control of time. That is why they could leave Egypt after only two hundred ten years even though God had told Abraham that the exile would last for four hundred years.

The Jews left Egypt in such a hurry that their dough did not have time to rise. This rapid departure was another sign that they were given a supernatural ability to transcend time.[174]

God told Moses, "I appeared to Abraham, to Isaac, and to Jacob as God Almighty, but My Name, *Hashem*, I did not make known to them."[175] This Name (י-ה-ו-ה) derives from three words which mean "was, is and will be" (הָיָה הֹוֶה יִהְיֶה). *Hashem* is above and beyond time, encompassing past, present, and future all at once.[176]

On Passover, God revealed this aspect of Himself and gave Israel a connection to it by granting the nation a degree of control over time. The rabbis alluded to this by invoking the theme of four throughout the *Seder* — a number which recalls the fourth day of Creation.

The number four also hints at the chariot which Ezekiel saw in his prophetic vision. That chariot had the faces of four creatures: a lion, an eagle, an ox, and a man. These four faces represent the concept of kingship. The lion is the king of wild beasts, the eagle is the king of the birds, the ox is the king of domesticated animals, and man is king over all Creation by virtue of God's instruction to "fill the Earth and subdue it."[177] Thus, in his vision, Ezekiel beheld the Divine Presence which represents

---

173 *Rosh Hashannah* 2:9.

174 *Maharal, Divrei Negidim*, on *"Yachol Merosh Chodesh"* (יָכֹול מֵרֹאשׁ חֹדֶשׁ).

175 Exodus 6:3.

176 *Likutei Amarim Tanya, Sha'ar Hayichud Veha'emunah*, Chapter 7 (82A).

177 Genesis 1:28, according to B.T. *Chagigah* 13B.

kingship.[178]

God's kingship finds expression through His interaction with the universe because it is through such interaction that people come to recognize Him and submit themselves to His authority. The process of liberation from Egyptian slavery focused upon causing Pharaoh and his people to recognize *Hashem's* authority and the reality that He interacts with the universe. The number four reflects this idea because it alludes to Ezekiel's vision of God's kingship.

THE TEN PLAGUES

Many commentators ask why *Hashem* hardened Pharaoh's heart, and how He could punish Pharaoh if He Himself apparently forced him to sin? There are several answers:

A. Once a person sins repeatedly, it is difficult for him to repent. The sin becomes second nature to him, and he no longer recoils from it.[179] This does not mean that repentance is impossible, but it is human nature to follow habit and routine. Pharaoh and his people had become so heavily engrossed in sinning that repentance became extremely difficult.[180]

When Moses asked permission for the Jews to leave for

---

[178] *Tikunei Zohar* 60A.

[179] B.T. *Yoma* 87A. *Hashem* helps a person along the path he chooses in life (B.T. *Makoth* 10B).

[180] The *Midrash* notes that *Hashem* announced the coming of each plague in advance. Even at the very end, He instructed Moses to tell Pharaoh that the death of the first-born would occur around midnight on the fifteenth day of *Nissan* (Exodus 11:4-5). The purpose of this advance notice was to permit the Egyptians time to repent (*Shemoth Rabbah* 13:6). Repentance was possible, but very difficult.

several days to offer sacrifices, Pharaoh asked who would be going. When Moses told him that he wanted the entire people to depart, Pharaoh suspected that the slaves were not merely seeking a temporary leave, and he accused Moses of plotting an escape.[181]

The Egyptians had no justification for enslaving the Jews because Jacob and his family originally came to Egypt at Pharaoh's invitation, and the Jews had done nothing to harm their hosts. Nonetheless, Pharaoh had so convinced himself that he had every right enslave the Jews that he accused the Jews of "wickedly" seeking to escape. According to his twisted mentality, Moses was really the wrongdoer — a criminal trying to steal *his* slaves. This frame of mind made it virtually impossible for Pharaoh to repent.

B. The *Midrash* explains that once a person sins and then rejects an opportunity to repent, God may take away his free will in order to punish him. During the first five plagues, Pharaoh was free to change his mind but chose to harden his heart. After that, God decided to punish him with the last five plagues, and Pharaoh no longer had the choice to repent. Only then does the *Torah* speak of God hardening Pharaoh's heart.[182]

The *Maharal* offers an interesting explanation for this phenomenon. Since human beings are transitory, their actions possess a transitory nature. Sins therefore lack an element of permanency and when a person repents, his or her misdeeds are erased. If, however, a person is warned to change but refuses to do so, his or her actions assume a more permanent character. *Hashem* then permits them to remain permanent by cutting off the ability to repent.

The reason for this is that when sins derive from the physical body, they are transitory like the body. Once a person rejects

---

[181] Exodus 10:10, according to *Onkelos; Shemoth Rabbah* 13:5.
[182] *Shemoth Rabbath* 13:3.

warnings not to sin, however, he shows that his mind is attached to the sin. Since one's mind is closer to spirituality than his body, and therefore possesses an element of permanency, his sins gain an element of permanency as well.[183]

C.   Rather than eliminate Pharaoh's free will, the act of hardening Pharaoh's heart actually permitted him to choose between good and evil. The plagues were so terrifying that any normal person would have released the Jews out of fear. God caused Pharaoh not to feel that fear so that he had to decide whether to release the Jews based solely upon moral considerations of right and wrong. In this way, rather than impinging upon Pharaoh's free will, God enhanced it.[184]

D.   The Jews who entered Egypt were all righteous people led by Jacob and his sons. Their descendants fell to the forty-ninth level of spiritual impurity due to the negative influence of the Egyptians. The Egyptians were responsible for repairing the spiritual damage they caused and could only do so by suffering punishments which would restore the faith of the Jews.[185]

מַכַּת בְּכוֹרוֹת
THE FIRST-BORN

The theme of the first-born is central to the *Haggadah*. During their very first meeting, Moses warned Pharaoh that

---

[183] *Gevuroth Hashem*, chap. 31. One might add that one may sin due to a lack of appreciation of the gravity of his actions. Once he has been properly admonished yet refuses to repent, it becomes clear that he sinned willfully. God then punishes the individual by removing his free will.

[184] *Gevuroth Hashem*, chap. 31.

[185] *Anaf Etz Avoth* 5:4 citing *Ohel Yaakov, Parashath Bo* 17A.

Hashem regarded the Jewish people as His first-born and that unless Pharaoh released them, the Egyptian first-born would perish.[186] Later on, before destroying the Egyptian first-born, God instructed Moses concerning the *Mitzvoth* which pertain to first-born crops, animals, and people.[187]   He ordained these commandments to commemorate the departure from Egypt.[188]

The importance of the first-born is also a theme throughout the rest of the *Torah*. For example, Jacob purchased the first-born rights from Esau[189] and referred to himself as the first-born when he sought the blessings from Isaac.[190] The *Torah* commands that a first-born son receive double the share his brothers receive from his father's estate.[191]   Initially, first-born males were designated to perform the Temple service, a right they forfeited to the descendants of Aaron after they participated in the sin of the golden calf.[192]

What is the meaning of this emphasis upon the first-born? What is the significance of *Hashem* designating Israel as His first-born, and why did the Ten Plagues culminate in the slaying of the Egyptian first-born?

The *Mishnah* teaches that *Hashem* created the universe by means of Ten Utterances,[193] as the Psalmist says, "By the word of the *Hashem* the Heavens were made, and by the breath of His mouth all their multitudes."[194]

---

[186] Exodus 4:22-23.

[187] Exodus 13:2. These *Halachoth* include redeeming each first-born Jewish male by paying five silver coins to a *Kohen,* donating the first-born of all *Kosher* livestock to a *Kohen,* redeeming first-born donkeys by giving a sheep to a *Kohen,* and bringing the first-fruits to the Temple.

[188] Exodus 13:14.

[189] Genesis 25:31-34.

[190] Genesis 27:19.

[191] *Shulchan Aruch, Choshen Mishpat* 277:1.

[192] *Shemoth Rabbah* 31:8.

[193] *Pirkei Avoth* 5:1.

[194] Psalms 33:6.

Each Hebrew letter, or combination of Hebrew letters, corresponds to an emanation of God's Divinity which passes through many stages, or worlds, until it is transformed into part of the physical universe. A stone, for example, derives its existence from a spiritual source represented by the letters of the Hebrew word for stone (אֶבֶן).[195]

The letters of the Hebrew alphabet total twenty-seven if one includes the five final letters (ךמןףץ). These twenty-seven letters can be divided into three sets of nine each. The first nine letters, א through ט, have numerical values from one through nine. The next nine letters, י through צ, have numerical values from ten through ninety. The last nine letters, ק through ץ, have numerical values of one hundred through nine hundred.[196]

The initial letters of each of these three sets are א, י, and ק. They represent God Himself initiating the creation of the universe.

The letter *Alef* (א) represents God because it has a value of one, corresponding to the One God. In addition, *Alef* (א) is related to the Hebrew word *"Aluf"* (אַלּוּף), meaning commander, and *Hashem* is the Commander of the universe.

The letter *Yud* (י) also represents God because it has a numerical value of ten, and *Hashem* filters His Divinity through ten spiritual realms during the process of creating and sustaining the physical world. In addition, *Yud* (י) is the first letter of *Hashem's* Name (י-ה-ו-ה).

The letter *Kuf* (ק) alludes to God because it has a numerical value of one hundred. Each of the ten spiritual realms contains aspects of all the others, and ten times ten equals one hundred.[197]

---

[195] *Likutei Amarim Tanya, Sha'ar Hayichud Veha'emunah*, Chapter 1.

[196] In this system, the final letters ךמןףץ follow ת and have values of 500, 600, 700, 800, and 900 respectively.

[197] *Be'er Mayim Chaim, Parashath Shemoth*, Chapter 4. He also notes that the numerical value of the letter א spelled out — אֶלֶף — is one hundred eleven, the same as the combined numerical values of א, י, and ק. The related word *"Elef"* (אֶלֶף) means one thousand, and one thousand is the product of 1 x 10 x

The second letters of each of the three sets are בּ, כ, and ר, the root of the Hebrew word for first-born (בְּכֹר). Just as the first letters of each set represent God Himself, the second letters of each set represent the first phase of Creation — a move away from God.

This can have either a positive or a negative connotation depending upon the attitude of humankind.

As the first stage of Creation, these letters can symbolize that the first-born is just a step away from God Himself, just as a first-born son can be an extension of his father if he chooses to emulate him.

King David states that God made people "a bit less than the angels."[198] Every human being has the ability to draw close to God if he or she so chooses. Israel is God's first-born because, as a nation, it has realized this goal and recognizes that God is the Source of all Creation.[199]

The letters בכ"ר can take on a different meaning, however. These letters represent the first step in the process which leads away from *Hashem* — Who transcends all physical and spiritual realms — toward the creation of a physical universe. In this sense, they can be the initial stage of a move away from recognizing God's unity. When people fail to recognize that all Creation derives from God, this becomes a source of evil.

Esau, for example, despised the privilege of being first-born.[200] Rather than understanding the status of a first-born as being but a step away from *Hashem* and striving to unite with

---

100. This hints that א, י, and ק are all encompassed by the letter א.

[198] Psalms 8:6.

[199] The *Midrash* hints at this when it states that the Creation was initiated with the letter "*Beth*" (ב) because that letter stands for "blessing" (בְּרָכָה). The root letters of the Hebrew word for "blessing" (בְּרָכָה) are the same as those of "first-born" (בְּכֹר) (*Breshith Rabbah* 1:10, cited by *Be'er Mayim Chaim, Parashath Shemoth*, Chapter 4).

[200] Genesis 25:34.

Him, Esau viewed his being first-born as the beginning of an opportunity to move away from God.

The *Zohar* states that God gave Egypt's guardian angel dominion over the angels of all the other nations of the world.[201] Egypt thus possessed first-born status.[202] When Pharaoh asked, "Who is *Hashem* that I should listen to His voice,"[203] he showed that he viewed the role of the first-born as moving away from the Creator, not toward Him. As a result, God chose to attack the Egyptian first-born.[204]

The *Midrash* hints at these dual aspects of the first-born when it refers to the Patriarchs as a chariot or vehicle (מֶרְכָּבָה) for the Divine Presence. Abraham, Isaac, and Jacob developed such an extreme closeness to *Hashem* that they were, so to speak, an extension of Him — a vehicle for performing His will in the world. The Hebrew root of the word for chariot (רֶכֶב) has the same letters as the root of the word for first-born (בְּכֹר).

By contrast, the *Torah* tells how Pharaoh's army, which he assembled to pursue the escaping Jews, included six hundred choice chariots.[205] In his eagerness to destroy Israel, he personally prepared his own chariot rather than waiting for servants to do so.[206] These actions allude to Pharaoh's attitude of rebellion against *Hashem* — his twisted understanding of the concept of the first-born as moving away from and denying the unity of God.

---

[201] *Zohar* II 16B.

[202] See *Sha'arei Orah, Hasha'ar Harishon, Hasefirah Ha'asirith.*

[203] Exodus 5:2.

[204] *Ohev Yisrael, Parashath Bo.*

[205] Exodus 14:7.

[206] Exodus 14:6, according to *Rashi*, citing *Mechilta.*

> ## טוֹבָה כְפוּלָה וּמְכֻפֶּלֶת
> # HOW MANY BENEFITS, DOUBLED AND REDOUBLED, HAS THE OMNIPRESENT BESTOWED UPON US!

Doubling is a theme repeated throughout the *Haggadah.* The *Seder* service calls for drinking Four Cups. The Second Cup may be viewed as a repetition of the first one. The participants then drink two more cups, thereby repeating the repetition — doubling and redoubling.

The miraculous growth of the Jewish population in Egypt also reflects this idea. The *Torah* states that when Jacob and his descendants entered Egypt they numbered only seventy.[207] The censuses taken in the Sinai Desert showed that there were over six hundred thousand adult men.[208] Since the *Midrash* relates that four-fifths of the Jewish population died during the plague of darkness, the adult Jewish males must have numbered over three million near the end of the enslavement. It is reasonable to infer that there were also three million adult women and millions of children.

The verses of *Hallel* reflect this same theme of doubling and redoubling because they frequently repeat the same concept. For example, "He raises the downtrodden from the dust; from the trash heap He raises the destitute. To position them with princes, with the princes of His people." There is also a custom to repeat certain verses in the *Hallel,* and when reciting *Hallel* with a group, those present repeat what the leader recites.[209]

Repeating something shows that it is considered impor-

---

[207] Exodus 1:5.
[208] Exodus 38:26; Numbers 1:46 and 26:51.
[209] *Shulchan Aruch, Orach Chaim* 422:3 based on B.T. *Sukkah* 38B.

tant.[210] It also symbolizes strengthening. For example, if a person has the same dream twice, it is likely to come true, as Joseph told Pharaoh, "Concerning the repetition of the dream to Pharaoh twice, [it is] because the matter is certain from God, and God hastens to do it."[211] The *Shulchan Aruch* rules that, under certain circumstances, if a person says twice that he will do something, it counts as an oath (שְׁבוּעָה).[212]

Doubling also represents the concept of redemption.[213] The very first time that a Jew left exile was when Abraham migrated from Ur to the Land of Israel. *Hashem* told him, "You shall surely go from your land" (לֶךְ לְךָ)[214] — a redundant phrase. When Jacob prayed to be rescued from Esau, he said, "Save me from the hand of my brother, from the hand of Esau."[215] When God first announced that He would deliver the Jews from Egypt, He said, "I have surely remembered" (פָּקֹד פָּקַדְתִּי).[216] Later, He used the four redundant expressions, "*I will take you out* from under the burdens of Egypt, and *I will save you* from their servitude, and *I will redeem you* with an outstretched arm and with mighty judgments. And *I will take you* to Me as a people."[217]

---

[210] *Anaf Yosef* states that is why we recite certain verses of *Hallel* twice.

[211] Genesis 41:32.

[212] *Shulchan Aruch, Yoreh De'ah* 237:5.

There is also a rule that certain stipulations are not valid unless repeated in both positive and negative terms (B.T. *Kiddushin* 61A). For example, it was not sufficient for Moses to proclaim that if the men of Gad and Reuben assisted the rest of the nation in conquering the Land of Israel west of the Jordan River, they would receive territory on its east bank. To make the stipulation binding, Moses had to reiterate that if the men of Gad and Reuben failed to assist in the conquest of the Land of Israel west of the Jordan River, they would not receive territory on its east bank (Numbers 32:29-30).

[213] See *Pirkei D'Rabbi Eliezer* 47.

[214] Genesis 12:1.

[215] Genesis 32:11.

[216] Exodus 3:16.

[217] Exodus 6:6-7.

Why does repetition, or doubling, symbolize redemption?

A pair has two possible implications: (a) one item which has split into two; or (b) two items which have joined together. God is an absolute unity, so the uniting of two items represents recognition of Him. Conversely, splitting one item into two symbolizes a failure to recognize God's unity.

Pairs represent an affirmation of Divine unity when two entities merge into one. The cave in which the Patriarchs and Matriarchs are buried is called the "Double Cave," or "Cave of Pairs" (מְעָרַת הַמַּכְפֵּלָה). Each pair of people buried there — Adam and Chavah, Abraham and Sarah, Isaac and Rebecca, Jacob and Leah — were so devoted to one another that their unity enhanced the spiritual unity of the world.

According to *Kabbalistic* tradition, the letters of the Hebrew alphabet represent combinations of spiritual forces. The Book of Creation refers to seven paired, or doubled, letters — seven letters which have two alternate pronunciations. Those letters are בג"ד כפר"ת.[218]

Each of these seven pairs represents two concepts such as wisdom and foolishness, wealth and poverty, life and death, or peace and war.[219] At first glance, these concepts appear to be irreconcilable opposites, but this is not necessarily true. If everyone were a brilliant genius, no one would recognize or appreciate genius. It is the existence of foolishness which makes genius identifiable. The same applies to other pairs of opposites. As the *Zohar* states, it is only possible to recognize light because darkness exists.[220]

This means that evil can serve good and enhance it by making it recognizable. Only when evil is not subdued by good

---

[218] *Sefer Yetzirah* 4:1-4:3. As an example, ב is pronounced "v" while בּ is pronounced "b." Knowledge of the differences in pronunciation for some of these pairs has been lost in most Jewish communities.

[219] *Sefer Yetzirah* 4:1-4:3.

[220] *Zohar* III 47B.

does it become irredeemable. Pairs of opposites represent separa-
tion from *Hashem* when they do not join together to complement
one another. When they function harmoniously, however, they
enhance human recognition of God's unity.

When *Hashem* subdued the Egyptians, evil became subservient to good and augmented it. The bitter darkness of the
Egyptian servitude made the brilliant light of redemption brigh-
ter. Likewise, the spiritual darkness of Egyptian idolatry made
the light of Divine revelation shine more brightly in the eyes of the
liberated Jews. This is the connection between pairs and redemption.

The sages of the *Talmud* questioned how earlier rabbis
could have instituted the drinking of Four Cups since anything
done in pairs attracts demons — the negative spiritual effects
which dividing into pairs can produce. They answer that Passover night is a "night of guarding" — a night when only a positive
spiritual outcome can occur.[221] This is because on Passover evil
becomes subservient to good and enhances it.

There is another concept behind this statement of the sages. Although the concept of pairs as one unit divided into two
ordinarily represents evil, it can also mean something else.

God transcends all physical and spiritual universes so that
they, and all they contain, do not affect Him. At the same time,
Hashem is present everywhere, giving life and existence to everything and guiding all which transpires.

This concept is beyond human understanding because it is
self-contradictory to say that God does both. There is, however, a
way in which people can partly grasp how something infinite can
have a relationship with something finite.

Suppose that a grasshopper is resting one hundred meters
from a wall. If it jumps half that distance, it will now rest only
fifty meters from the wall. If it then jumps half the remaining

---

[221] B.T. *Pesachim* 109B.

distance, it will land twenty-five meters from the wall. If the grasshopper could continue this pattern of jumping half the remaining distance, it would never reach the wall because there is no smallest number — every number can be divided in half. At the same time, however, one hundred meters is a finite distance, one which humans can easily comprehend. This is an example of something finite which contains something limitless, somewhat analogous to how *Hashem*, Who is infinite, nevertheless permeates the finite physical and spiritual realms.

The miracles of the Exodus hint at this because each one was divided into many others. The miracle of turning the Nile River into blood, for example, had many subdivisions. When a Jew and an Egyptian drank from the same pitcher, the Jew would receive water, but the Egyptian got blood. When the Egyptians dug wells for water, blood filled them. Even when an Egyptian spat, blood came forth.[222]

The *Haggadah* presents rabbinic opinions that whereas there were ten plagues in Egypt, there were fifty at the Reed Sea, or two hundred, or two hundred fifty. It then goes on to say, "How many benefits, doubled and redoubled, has the Omnipresent bestowed upon us!" Just as a finite distance contains an infinite number of subdivisions, each miracle *Hashem* performed during the Exodus had an infinite number of subdivisions.

Our recognition of the infinite acts of kindness with which *Hashem* has graced our nation — our reciting the tale of the departure from Egypt each year and constantly discovering new insights in it — is the ultimate way of uniting with God because it reflects the inclusion of the infinite in that which is finite.

Since this concept of division hints at God's unity, rather than the opposite, Passover night is a time when pairs can have only a good connotation.

---

[222] *Shemoth Rabbah* 9:10-11.

WHY GOD DESTROYED THE EGYPTIANS

The angels began to sing praises to *Hashem* when He split the Reed Sea, but He silenced them, saying, "How can you sing when My creatures are drowning?"[223]

One could raise the following question about this: If *Hashem* did not want to kill the Egyptians, why did He? He used a pillar of fire to keep the Egyptians away from the Jews during the night before the splitting of the Reed Sea. Why not simply keep the pillar in place and continue to prevent the Egyptians from attacking the Jews? Why permit them to enter the sea and perish?

There are three possible answers:

A. The *Torah* tells how Moses killed an Egyptian taskmaster who assaulted a Jew.[224] Moses had supernatural means at his disposal which he could have used to immobilize the Egyptian.[225] Why did he kill him?

The *Torah* states that before slaying the Egyptian, Moses "looked this way and that, and he saw that there was no man."[226] *Rashi* explains this to mean that Moses used his prophetic powers to see whether the Egyptian would eventually have worthy offspring. When he saw that he would not, he slew him.

Hashem deals with the wicked in the same manner. If He determines that they are utterly irredeemable, He may destroy them. God would have preferred not to kill the Egyptians, but when He saw that they would never improve, He decided that there was no point in sparing them.

---

[223] B.T. *Megillah* 10B; B.T. *Sanhedrin* 39B.

[224] Exodus 2:12.

[225] According to one view, Moses used one of *Hashem's* Names to kill the Egyptian (*Shemoth Rabbah* 1:29).

[226] Exodus 2:12.

What led to this harsh conclusion?

The *Gemara* gives a puzzling account of how the Egyptians decided upon drowning as the method for murdering Jewish babies.

The Egyptians knew that *Hashem* punishes measure for measure. If they put the Jews to the sword or burned them, they feared that they would meet a similar fate. Since God had sworn never to bring another flood upon the world, however, they reasoned that if they drowned the Jews, God would not punish them.[227]

What kind of game were the Egyptians playing? Did they really think that they could fool *Hashem*?

Ancient pagans such as the Egyptians knew that *Hashem* created the world.[228] However, they also believed that after God created the universe, He left various natural forces in charge of it. That is why they worshiped the sun, wind, rain, and other powerful forces.

When Pharaoh asked Joseph to interpret his dreams, Joseph repeatedly told him that dreams are messages from God. Pharaoh never claimed not to know about God, and he accepted Joseph's assertions.[229] Nevertheless, when Moses confronted Pharaoh and demanded the release of the Jews, Pharaoh answered, "Who is *Hashem* that I should listen to His voice to send forth Israel?"[230] He meant that although he believed in God, he also believed that God does not care about or supervise what goes on in the world. According to his way of thinking, there were certain rare instances, such as the Flood, when God intervened in human affairs. As long as one took care not to trigger such intervention, he could do as he pleased. Pharaoh and his people

---

[227] B.T. *Sotah* 11A.

[228] In his "Guide for the Perplexed" (מורה נבוכים), the *Rambam* quotes philosophical proofs of God's existence from the Greek philosopher Aristotle.

[229] Genesis 41:16, 25, 28, and 32.

[230] Exodus 5:2.

stubbornly clung to this belief even after repeated warnings and even after a chain of events which proved that *Hashem* is deeply concerned with what happens in the world.[231]

When interpreting dreams for Pharaoh, Joseph referred to God by the Name *"Elohim"* (אֱ-לֹהִים), a term which denotes God acting through nature. The message of the dreams reflected this because cycles of famine and prosperity have occurred throughout history and can be viewed as natural phenomena.

By contrast, when Moses and Aaron spoke to Pharaoh, they used the Tetragrammaton (י-ה-ו-ה), a Name which alludes to *Hashem* acting in ways not governed by the laws of nature.

Pharaoh understood how God might act in natural ways to cause famine or plenty, so he never questioned Joseph's references to God, but he could not accept the idea that God would transcend the laws of nature to rescue the Jews from Egypt.[232]

If a person sins, there is usually hope that he may eventually repent. God permits such a person to survive in the hope that he will repudiate his past. By clinging to the false belief that *Hashem* does not care about what happens in the universe despite abundant evidence to the contrary, the Egyptians showed that they would never change. Accordingly, *Hashem* decided to destroy them.

B. The *Torah* records that, "A new king arose over Egypt who did not know Joseph."[233] Rav and Shmuel offer differing interpretations of this verse. One held that there actually was a new king, while the other maintained that the old king continued to rule but is called new because he directed new decrees against the Jews.[234]

---

[231] When they chased after the Jews to the Reed Sea, the Egyptians clung to the false hope that their idol, *Ba'al Tzefon*, would help them (Exodus 14:2-3, according to *Rashi*).

[232] See *Targum Yonathan* on Exodus 5:2.

[233] Exodus 1:8.

[234] B.T. *Sotah* 11A.

Even a new king would have known about Joseph, whose position in the Egyptian government had been second only to Pharaoh. Therefore, the statement that he did not know Joseph must mean that the king behaved *as if* he knew nothing of him. He ignored all that Joseph had contributed to the country and invented excuses to enslave the Jews.[235]

Ordinarily, God might have forgiven the Egyptians for enslaving the Jews because slavery was a common feature of almost every ancient society. One of the purposes of Creation, however, is for people to recognize and serve *Hashem*. The desire to do so is driven by the natural human emotion of gratefulness. When a person recognizes how much God has done for him by creating all the wonderful things he enjoys, he seeks to praise and serve Him.

By showing such extreme ingratitude to Joseph and his family, however, the Egyptians demonstrated that even if they had eventually recognized that *Hashem* supervises and controls the universe, they would not serve Him. This meant that there was no reason for their continued existence.[236]

C. Rabbi Shimshon Raphael Hirsch offers a novel explanation about why the *Torah* states that, "A new king arose over Egypt who did not know Joseph."[237] He suggests that a foreign nation invaded Egypt, overthrew its rulers, and installed its own king who knew nothing about Joseph. The purpose of the new king's anti-Jewish policies was to consolidate his hold over Egypt

---

[235] *Etz Yosef.*

[236] *Hashem* spared Pharaoh's daughter, Bathya, from the fate of the other Egyptian first-born because she did not share this attitude. After rescuing Moses from the Nile River, the *Torah* records that, "She called his name Moses [מֹשֶׁה] and said, 'because I drew him from the water [מְשִׁיתִהוּ]'" (Exodus 2:10). Bathya thought it important to give Moses a name which would remind him of his origin so that he would be thankful for having been saved and, in turn, feel compassion toward others (Rabbi Shimshon Raphael Hirsch on Exodus 2:10).

[237] Exodus 1:8.

by directing the resentment the Egyptians felt towards their conquerors at a convenient target.[238]

This would explain the anomaly of the harsh treatment directed at the Jews. Ordinarily, a slaveholder would want to treat his slaves decently to preserve their value. In this instance, however, the enslavement was only one part of a program of genocide motivated by a desire to gain power.

Hashem might have forgiven the Egyptians for enslaving His people to benefit from their labor because that was a common feature of ancient society. However, He was not willing to forgive genocidal oppression motivated by political considerations.

THE UNIQUE *HALLEL* OF PASSOVER

Whenever the entire *Hallel* is recited on other occasions, it is read all the way through without any interruptions. On Passover night, however, we read the first two Psalms of *Hallel* before the meal and the rest after the meal. The reason for this is that the sages wanted the children at the *Seder* to participate in eating the *Matzah*. Since young children might fall asleep before the *Seder* is completed, one must interrupt the *Hallel* to consume the *Matzah* and have the meal.[239]

Shammai's Academy held that one should say only the first Psalm of *Hallel* before the meal, but Hillel's Academy ruled that one must recite the first two, and that is the practice followed today.[240]

The Jerusalem *Talmud* points out that the second Psalm of *Hallel* talks about the Exodus, starting with, "Upon the departure of Israel from Egypt." There is a principle that once one begins to

---

[238] Commentary to Exodus 1:8-9.

[239] *Tosafoth Yom Tov* and *Tifereth Yisrael* on *Pesachim* 10:6.

[240] *Pesachim* 10:6.

perform a *Mitzvah*, he or she should finish it. The Academy of Hillel therefore held that once a parent starts the story of the Exodus, he should complete it by reciting *Hallel* to the end of this Psalm.[241]

Why did Hillel's Academy hold that the concept of finishing a *Mitzvah* took priority over making sure that the children remain awake to eat the *Matzah*?

The idea of not delaying the fulfillment of a commandment is integral to the *Mitzvah* of eating *Matzah*. The *Torah* commands that, "You shall guard the *Matzoth* (הַמַּצּוֹת) [against becoming leavened]."[242] Rabbi Yoshaya notes that one may read this phrase as, "You shall guard the *Mitzvoth* (הַמִּצְוֹת)." When a *Mitzvah* comes to hand, one should not allow it to "leaven," but immediately seize the opportunity to perform it.[243]

One who takes a leisurely approach to *Mitzvah* performance demonstrates that *Mitzvoth* are not of primary importance to him. Conversely, by immediately seizing the opportunity to fulfill a *Mitzvah*, a Jew shows where his priorities lie.

This concept was especially important at the time of the Exodus because the Jews lacked sufficient merit to warrant their rescue. When God ordered them to slaughter the Passover sacrifice and consume it with *Matzah* and *Maror*, they eagerly raced to obey. This attitude of keen willingness made them deserving of redemption.

On a deeper level, time is a physical attribute which is as much a part of Creation as any other aspect of the physical universe. By delaying or interrupting the performance of *Mitzvoth*, a person contaminates them with physicality.

One aspect of the conflict between the Jews and the Egyptians centered upon whether God created and controls time.

---

[241] J.T. *Pesachim* 10:5.

[242] Exodus 12:17 according to *Rashi*.

[243] *Mechilta, Parashath Bo* 9.

Despite their belief in other deities, the idolatrous nations of the world believed in a Supreme Being who created the entire universe with one exception — time. According to Aristotle and other ancient philosophers, God and time have always co-existed.[244]

This false belief served as the basis for astrology because people use heavenly bodies such as the sun, moon, and stars to measure time. If time is a force independent of God, then He does not control the future and one can use astrology to predict or perhaps even to change future events.

This explains why Pharaoh repeatedly turned to astrology throughout the story of the Exodus. His astrologers predicted the birth of a boy who would rescue the Jews, but that this redeemer's downfall would come about through water. Hearing this, Pharaoh decreed that all male babies be cast into the Nile River.[245] At one point, Pharaoh warned Moses that the Jews could not escape Egypt because "evil (רָעָה) is opposite your faces."[246] *Rashi* explains Pharaoh's statement as meaning that, in Pharaoh's view, a celestial body called "evil" (רָעָה) opposed the Jews.[247]

When Moses demanded that the Egyptians release their Jewish slaves, Pharaoh angrily responded, "Who is *Hashem* that I should listen to His voice to send out Israel?"[248]

The Divine Name י-ה-ו-ה used in this verse refers to *Hashem's* trait of transcending time.[249] Moses had ordered the release of the Jews in the name of a God Who transcends time. Since, in Pharaoh's view, such a Being did not exist, there was no

---

[244] In his "Guide for the Perplexed" (מורה נבוכים), the *Rambam* presents numerous philosophical arguments to disprove Aristotle and uphold the view of the *Torah*.

[245] B.T. *Sotah* 12B.

[246] Exodus 10:10.

[247] *Rashi* on Exodus 10:10; *Yalkut Shimoni* 392. According to Egyptian mythology, Re or Ra (רָעָה) was the sun-god.

[248] Exodus 5:2.

[249] This Name alludes the words הָיָה הֹוֶה יִהְיֶה, meaning "was, is and will be."

reason to obey.

Moses informed Pharaoh and his advisors that the death of the first-born would occur at approximately midnight[250] even though it happened exactly at midnight.[251] The rabbis explain that whereas God knows the precise moment when midnight occurs, humans might miscalculate it. Had Pharaoh's astrologers erred in their calculations, they would have believed that the plague did not occur precisely at midnight, but slightly before or after that time. They would then accuse Moses of fictitiously claiming that God had caused the death of the first-born. To avoid such a possibility, Moses told them that the plague would happen near midnight.[252]

At first glance, this makes little sense. Why would Pharaoh and his people conclude that God did not cause the death of the first-born just because it appeared to them that it happened a few moments before or after the time Moses predicted? Why would such a small discrepancy mean so much to them?

The Egyptians continued to insist that *Hashem* had no control over time. Had the promised event not occurred at precisely the moment predicted by Moses, they would have stubbornly clung to this false belief.

This explains why the *Torah* interrupts the story of the Exodus to describe how *Hashem* commanded the Jewish nation to sanctify the new moon and proclaim the beginning of each lunar month. One of the rules connected with this *Mitzvah* is that if the *Sanhedrin* accepted testimony from witnesses and decreed that the new month begin on a certain day, its decision is valid even if astronomical calculations or other objective considerations indicate that the month should start on a different day.[253]

God gave this commandment just prior to the departure

---

[250] Exodus 11:4.

[251] Exodus 12:29.

[252] B.T. *Berachoth* 4A.

[253] B.T. *Rosh Hashannah* 25A.

from Egypt to emphasize that He controls time and that, through Him, Jews can control it too. The Hebrew expression for being above time (לְמַעְלָה מִן הַזְּמַן) hints at this. The letters of the Hebrew alphabet which precede — are above — the word for time (הַזְּמַן) are ד ו ל מ. These letters can be rearranged as מוֹלָד, a word which refers to the "birth" of the new moon.

Finally, this explains why Pharaoh only agreed to free the Jews after the plague which destroyed the first-born. The Egyptians had suffered staggering losses during the earlier plagues, but held firm against releasing the Jews. What made this final plague more convincing than any of the others?

Although the destruction of the first-born was the final plague, *Hashem* had warned Pharaoh about it from the very beginning. Moses told Pharaoh that God regarded Israel as His first-born and that if Pharaoh did not permit the nation to leave, He would kill the Egyptian first-born. Pharaoh arrogantly rejected this demand because he did not believe that God had any control over time and, therefore, that He had no control over any beginning or first thing. Only when God carried out His threat did Pharaoh finally acknowledge that he was mistaken.

Hurrying to do *Mitzvoth* and not interrupting their performance infuses the *Mitzvoth* with the characteristic of transcending time. Conversely, delaying or interrupting *Mitzvoth* contaminates their spiritual quality with physicality by subjecting them to the limitations of time. *Matzah* in particular symbolizes this because it alludes to the idea of hurrying to perform *Mitzvoth*. This point might be lost if one were to interrupt the *Mitzvah* of telling the story of the Exodus in order to eat *Matzah*.

וָא'מַר לָךְ בְּדָמַיְךְ חֲיִי
AND I SAID TO YOU,
"BY YOUR BLOOD SHALL YOU LIVE"

The blood of the Passover sacrifice and the blood of circumcision caused the Jews to merit redemption from Egypt.[254] It seems fairly obvious why the merit of the Passover sacrifice helped the Jews. Since the ancient Egyptians worshiped lambs, the act of slaughtering a lamb displayed rejection of their idolatry. Circumcision, however, does not appear to have any particular connection to the Exodus. How did the merit of this *Mitzvah* contribute to the liberation from Egypt?

When Rabban Yochanan ben Zakkai was about to die, his disciples asked him for a blessing. He replied, "May it be God's will that you fear the scrutiny of Heaven as much as that of people."

"Is that all?" asked the disciples.

Rabbi Yochanan ben Zakkai answered, "I firmly wish it! Take note that when a person is about to commit a wrong, he will say, 'I hope no one sees me.'"[255]

The *Mitzvah* of circumcision applies to a part of the body which is covered. This teaches that *Hashem* is aware of and concerned about every aspect of a person's life, even private matters about which no one else knows. The act of circumcision thus contradicted the Egyptian belief that God created the world, but does not supervise it, leaving matters up to subordinate deities.

On a deeper level, one may define every object in the universe as having seven dimensions. Six of them — front, back, top, bottom, right, and left — represent the object's physical

---

[254] *Pirkei D'Rabbi Eliezer,* chap. 28.
[255] B.T. *Berachoth* 28B.

aspects. The center of the object, its seventh dimension, symbolizes its spiritual nature, for the *Torah* teaches that every physical object emanates from a corresponding spiritual source.

The sequence in which *Hashem* created the universe reflects this. During the first six days, He created all of the physical elements of the universe. He then created *Shabbath*, a time of spiritual inspiration, on the seventh day.

The number eight, however, represents the supernatural, that which transcends both the physical and the spiritual — none other than God Himself. Since circumcision takes place on the eighth day of a baby's life, it reflects the special connection of the Jewish people to God.[256] By circumcising themselves before departing Egypt, the Jews reaffirmed their commitment to God, Who transcends both the physical and spiritual universe.

וַיַּעֲבִדוּ מִצְרַיִם אֶת בְּנֵי יִשְׂרָאֵל בְּפָרֶךְ
THE EGYPTIANS WORKED THE
CHILDREN OF ISRAEL WITH HARSHNESS

When Moses and Aaron first demanded that Pharaoh release the Jews, he did not simply refuse. He angrily ordered the Egyptian taskmasters to stop providing the slaves with the straw needed to reinforce their bricks, while requiring the Jews to maintain the same level of production. This made the already unbearable situation of the hapless slaves even worse.[257]

Moses then asked *Hashem*, "Why have You done evil to this people? Why have You sent me? Since I came to Pharaoh to speak in Your Name, he did evil to this people and You have not

---

256 See *Maharal, Tifereth Yisrael* 2.
257 Exodus 5:6-11.

saved Your people."[258] God responded, "Now you will see that which I will do to Pharaoh, for with a strong hand he will send them and with a strong hand he will drive them from this land."[259]

How does *Hashem's* response answer Moses' question? True, the fortunes of the Jews were about to change radically, but why did things initially get worse?

A deterioration in Israel's circumstances is a prerequisite for every redemption. As the sages teach, before the final redemption the world will reach a remarkably low point where insolence will greatly increase and those who fear sin will be despised.[260]

Why should this be so?

The *Klee Yekar* explains that certain natural forces in the universe constantly oppose one another. When one of those forces is about to overcome its rival, that rival fights back mightily. As an example, the world grows unusually dark just before dawn breaks forth. Likewise, it often happens that one who is mortally ill revives somewhat just before he or she dies.

The Egyptians represented certain spiritual forces of evil. When they sensed their imminent demise, they increased their oppression of the Jews, only to later collapse in the face of the plagues God brought upon them.[261]

This still leaves a question: While natural phenomena struggle with one another in this way, surely *Hashem*, whose power is absolute, is not subject to this principle. Why did He not simply reveal Himself immediately? Why permit the Egyptians to increase their oppression?

If a lit match were held next to the sun, the light of the match would be as nothing. In a similar way, God's holiness is so great that were He to fully reveal Himself in the world, nothing could exist. Rather, everything would be nullified in the Source of

---

[258] Exodus 5:22-23.

[259] Exodus 6:1.

[260] *Sotah* 9:15.

[261] *Klee Yekar* on Exodus 6:1.

all existence.[262]

To prevent this from occurring, *Hashem* reveals Himself to the world in a pulsating manner, revealing a bit and then withdrawing, just as Ezekiel envisioned angels "running and returning" (רָצוֹא וָשׁוֹב).[263] The numerical value of that expression equals "*Torah*" (תּוֹרָה) because one can study the *Torah* with many different levels of understanding, sometimes grasping more, sometimes less. Moreover, even after a point seems clear, a question may arise which clouds the matter again. This resembles the way in which God's presence in the universe ebbs and flows.[264]

At times when God is more fully revealed in the universe, the forces of evil recede. When God withdraws or reduces His presence, those forces surge back into dominance.[265] This ebb and flow phenomenon explains why Egyptian oppression increased immediately before the redemption. *Hashem* revealed Himself when He sent Moses and Aaron to appear before Pharaoh and demand the release of the Jewish slaves. He then withdrew a bit, permitting the forces of evil to temporarily dominate, only to reveal Himself in even greater glory to liberate His people.

---

[262] Cf. *Likutei Amaraim Tanya*, chap. 33. Something like this occurred at the Giving of the *Torah* when the revelation of God so overwhelmed the Jews that their souls left them (*Shemoth Rabbah* 29:4).

[263] Ezekiel 1:14.

[264] See *Mavo L'Chochmath Hakabbalah*, Part I, Introduction. The *Tanach* hints at this when it states that "You shall speak in it day and night" (Joshua 1:8) — both when the light of understanding is present and when it is absent.

[265] *Torah Ohr, Parashath Breishith* 2C-D.

> כָּל הַבֵּן הַיִּלּוֹד הַיְאֹרָה תַּשְׁלִיכֻהוּ
> ## EVERY SON WHO IS BORN
> ## YOU SHALL CAST INTO THE RIVER

Amram divorced his wife, Jochebed, after Pharaoh ordered the drowning of all baby boys, reasoning that it was preferable not to bear children who would be killed.

Amram's five year-old daughter, Miriam, prophesied that her mother would give birth to a redeemer. She then argued that Amram's decree was worse than Pharaoh's. Pharaoh only decreed against males, but Amram's decision also applied to females. In addition, because Pharaoh was wicked, his decree would not stand, whereas God might fulfill the decree of a righteous person. Finally, Pharaoh decreed only with respect to this world, but Amram's decree would also affect the world to come.[266]

Miriam's arguments convinced Amram to remarry Jochebed. Although Jochebed was one hundred thirty years old, she experienced a miraculous rejuvenation. Her wrinkles disappeared, and she regained her youth.[267] When Amram and Jochebed remarried, the ministering angels sang, "He positions the barren lady of the home as a joyful mother of children."[268]

This presents two difficulties. First, why was it any more of a miracle for Jochebed to give birth to Moses at the age of one hundred thirty than it was to give birth to his sister, Miriam, at the age of one hundred twenty-five, or to his brother, Aaron, at the age of one hundred twenty-seven?[269] Secondly, Jochebed was not

---

[266] There is a *Mitzvah* to produce children. By performing that *Mitzvah*, the Jews would gain a share in the world to come even if the Egyptians murdered their offspring.

[267] B.T. *Baba Bathra* 120A and B.T. *Sotah* 12A.

[268] Psalms 113:9.

[269] *Anaf Yosef* on B.T. *Baba Bathra* 120A raises this question.

barren — she already had two children, so how does the verse which the angels sang apply?

The *Talmud* warns that a person "should not open the mouth of the *Satan*," the Accuser. When an individual mentions the possibility that something bad may happen, he or she causes the Heavenly Tribunal to deliberate about whether it should occur.[270]

This principle applies especially to *Tzaddikim* because *Hashem* may fulfill their words even when they do not fully intend what they say. When Laban accused Jacob of stealing his idols, for example, Jacob declared that whoever took them would die. Thus, he unwittingly brought about the death of Rachel.[271]

Although Amram reversed his decision, remarried his wife, and sought to have a son, he may not have succeeded because *Hashem* might have fulfilled his decree even after he rescinded it.   The miracle of which the angels sang was not that Jochebed gave birth at an advanced age, for she had already done that. The miracle was that God set aside Amram's decree.

אֶחָד מִי יוֹדֵעַ
WHO KNOWS ONE?

This hymn associates major *Torah* concepts with numbers. The number two, for example, alludes to the two stone tablets inscribed with the Ten Commandments. Numbers three and four refer to the Patriarchs and Matriarchs. When the song reaches nine, however, it mentions the nine months of pregnancy. How is this topic related to Judaism?

The *Talmud* frequently uses the number nine as a metaphor

---

[270] B.T. *Berachoth* 19A.
[271] *Rashi* on Genesis 31:32 citing *Breishith Rabbah* 74:4.

for virtually all. For example, the *Talmud* states that ten measures of witchcraft descended into the world and that nine — virtually all — went to Egypt.[272]

There are three partners in creating a child: the father, the mother, and *Hashem*.[273] A person's character and talents are partly God-given and partly the result of his or her upbringing.

God may bestow such traits as a good memory, physical strength, an artistic eye, or great intellect. Parents may train a child to be polite, to read, or to swim. They may teach him *Torah* and set an example of what is right. However, all of this is only nine-tenths of the story because no person is complete unless and until he makes his own choice between right and wrong. Neither *Hashem* nor a person's parents make that decision.

This is the *Torah* concept hinted at by nine months of pregnancy. While God and family upbringing may account for virtually all, the final decision about who we are and how we act belongs to us.

This point holds special importance with respect to the Exodus because the Jewish people in Egypt were like a fetus in its mother's womb.[274]

The legacy of their righteous ancestors had taught the Jews much. God helped them to develop spiritually by sending Moses and Aaron to guide them and by displaying great miracles in Egypt. Even so, the final decision to accept their role as God's special people was theirs alone. They showed their acceptance of that mission when they obeyed *Hashem's* commandments to circumcise themselves and to sacrifice the Passover lamb.

---

[272] B.T. *Kiddushin* 49B.

[273] B.T. *Kiddushin* 30B.

[274] The sages teach that, "in the merit of the righteous women of that generation, Israel was redeemed from Egypt" (B.T. *Sotah* 11B). The special role of women in the Exodus underscores its similarity to the process of giving birth.

PARABLES

The stories in this section are fictional parables. Any similarity between people or events in these stories and any real person, living or dead, is purely coincidental.

THE RECITATION OF THE
FIFTEEN ELEMENTS OF THE *SEDER*

Reciting the elements of the *Seder* before starting to read the *Haggadah* helps orient the participants by giving them a preview of what they will be doing, but perhaps this custom also hints at something more profound.

In a small cottage in eastern France, sixteen year old Rachel Silver sat in a wicker chair as she chatted in quiet tones with an elderly lady. Suddenly, her little brother burst through the front door.

"Don't make any noise, David," cautioned Rachel, placing a finger to her lips. "Mrs. Cartier and I are discussing something important."

"I didn't even open my mouth," protested the boy.

"Come to the table," said Mrs. Cartier gently, "and I'll get you some apples and milk."

Little David smiled with delight as he took his seat at the table. Quickly downing the milk, he took the apples to the fireplace where Mrs. Cartier's green-eyed cat lazily flicked its tail to and fro. David enjoyed twirling his apples on the stones near the hearth before eating them.

Mrs. Cartier poured tea for herself and Rachel.

"I don't want to alarm your little brother," said Mrs. Cartier between sips, "but we must discuss tonight."

"Well, we obviously can't go trekking through the forest to the Swiss border in the middle of the night without a proper guide," answered Rachel. "Perhaps we can wait a day or two

until your nephew arrives from Marseilles…" Her voice trailed off as she observed Mrs. Cartier shake her head solemnly.

"The Nazis have started constructing a new barbed wire fence near the border and plan to commence extra patrols," explained the older woman. "If you wait a day or two it may be too late."

Rachel glanced at her little brother. The boy had eaten one of the apples, and now swung the core like a pendulum before the cat's watchful eyes. "But can I manage it with David? I mean, to go with a guide is one thing, but on my own?"

"You'll be fine. I'm afraid I'm too old or I would guide you myself, for I know these woods as well as I know every nook and cranny of this cottage. Pay attention, and I'll tell you exactly how to go."

At the end of their conversation, Rachel called David to the table. "We have a little surprise for you," said Rachel.

The boy hooted with glee.

Mrs. Cartier smiled kindly at the youngster. "You get to stay up late tonight."

"How late? Can I stay up till dawn and feed the chickens?"

"You're going to stay up very late anyway. Past midnight."

"Are you staying up late, too?" he asked his sister.

"Of course, silly." She hesitated. "Tonight is . . . well, tonight is a special night."

"Yes," put in Mrs. Cartier. "Tonight you get to take a long walk through the forest."

The boy's eyes grew wide. "A walk through the forest at night! That sounds scary."

Mrs. Cartier took the boy's sticky hand in her own. "There is nothing to be afraid of. Rachel will be with you, but you must listen carefully and do everything she says."

David looked up at his sister. Although the two women had made this expedition sound like some sort of game, he sensed that it was not. "Of course," he said in a serious tone. "Of course I'll listen."

Just after midnight, Mrs. Cartier led Rachel and David to the edge of the forest. The light of the full moon glimmered upon the old woman's face as she hugged Rachel. "Now don't forget any of the landmarks I told you about. As long as you follow those, you'll be fine." When she stepped back, she saw traces of tears glistening on Rachel's face. "Don't cry, girl. This war won't last forever. Be brave tonight, and with God's help, everything will be fine in the end."

Rachel embraced Mrs. Cartier again, too choked with emotion to respond. David tugged at his sister's skirt, anxious to start the adventure. Mrs. Cartier watched silently as the two

entered the forest.

Walking was a tedious affair. Without a flashlight, Rachel had to feel her way slowly along the darkened path. At one point, she tripped over a root, but she remembered in time to stifle a scream. She dusted herself off as she got up. "*Baruch Hashem*, I'm okay," she whispered to David.

After fifteen minutes of tiresome walking, Rachel and David reached a clearing. "There's the tree stump," exclaimed Rachel with delight. "Just as Mrs. Cartier told me." She pointed in the moonlight. "There's the 'X' carved into it."

Though he understood enough to realize that this trip was not a game, David could not resist climbing on top of the stump and declaring in a loud whisper, "I'm the king of the forest!"

'Perhaps this really is not so bad,' thought Rachel to herself. 'We haven't gone very far, and we've already found the first landmark.'

Remembering Mrs. Cartier's instructions about which path to take when leaving the clearing, Rachel continued walking with her brother. If David heard a scary sound, she would tell him, "It's probably some old owl. Just say *Shema* quietly to yourself, and it will go away."

Another twenty minutes brought the two siblings to a shallow creek — the second landmark. Quietly slipping off their shoes and socks, they waded across, the icy water stinging their feet.

"Too bad it isn't daylight," whispered David as they replaced their footgear on the other side. "We could see if our feet turned red from the cold water."

Under other circumstances, Rachel might have responded derisively to such a childish remark. Tonight, however, she had to play the role of a mature sibling. "Perhaps when we are safe in Switzerland," she whispered back, "we will find a stream to wade across during the day and do just that."

So the journey continued, Rachel growing more and more

confident with each landmark they passed until, at last, they reached safety on the other side of the Swiss border. Many years later, when Rachel Silver recounted her wartime adventures, she always added, "If it had not been for those directions Mrs. Cartier gave me with all those landmarks, I never would have made it. Even if I could figure out where I was going, I would never have had the courage to continue."

Exile and enslavement are scary propositions. Had the Jewish people faced them with no idea about how they would play out or when they might end, they may well have given up hope and never have survived. For this reason, *Hashem* told Abraham, "Know most certainly that your offspring shall be a stranger in a land which is not theirs, and they will enslave them and torment them [for] four hundred years. Also the nation which they will serve I will judge, and afterwards they shall go forth with great riches."[275] God's outline of the Egyptian enslavement to Abraham made it bearable for the Jewish people. Even as slaves, the Jews maintained the traditions of their ancestors and knew that their ordeal would not last forever.

The *Talmud* tells how Rabbi Akiva and his colleagues once visited the ruins of the Temple. Upon reaching Mount Scopus at the edge of Jerusalem, they tore their garments in mourning. When they reached the Temple Mount, they observed a fox emerge from the Holy of Holies. The other sages wept at this disgrace, but Rabbi Akiva laughed. He explained this seemingly inappropriate behavior by pointing out that just as the Prophets had predicted the destruction of the Temple, so had they predicted its restoration. Since the prediction of destruction came

---

[275] Genesis 15:13-14.

true, the prediction of restoration will also come true.[276]

Reciting the fifteen stages of the *Seder* service before it begins recalls the way in which God told Abraham in advance about the Egyptian exile and subsequent redemption. It also expresses our confidence that *Hashem* will redeem us from the present exile.

מַה נִּשְׁתַּנָּה הַלַּיְלָה הַזֶּה מִכָּל הַלֵּילוֹת?
WHY IS THIS NIGHT DIFFERENT FROM ALL OTHER NIGHTS?

The *Haggadah* starts with the Four Questions, but rather than responding to them, the paragraphs which follow talk about how the Jews were slaves and how their ancestors worshiped idols. The *Haggadah* never answers two of the questions — why we recline or why we dip our food twice — and it only explains the purpose of the *Matzah* and *Maror* much later on. A brief parable clarifies why the *Haggadah* does this.

Many years ago in Eastern Europe, one could find young Jewish orphans wandering about the streets. One such child was a young girl named Sprintza, who begged here and there for scraps of food. Her thin frame and sunken eyes showed that she frequently found nothing at all and went hungry. The typical housekeeper would have refused to use the tattered rags Sprintza called clothing to wipe the floor. The poor girl had no decent place to sleep, instead making do with any filthy corner she could find.

---

[276] B. T. *Makoth* 24B.

One day, a wealthy matron out for a stroll with her husband, a successful merchant, noticed Sprintza wandering the streets and took pity on her. The couple immediately agreed to take the young girl into their home. After several years, one could hardly tell that Sprintza had ever suffered hardship. Besides looking clean, healthy, and content, she had developed fine manners.

Eventually, the matron told Sprintza, "My husband and I have come to love you dearly. Many years have passed since you were a sickly beggar sleeping in the gutters. We have given you all the fine things of life. Now we want you to do something in return. We want you to join us for a banquet because ..."

"You don't have to bother explaining," interrupted the girl. "After all you've done for me, I'd be only too glad to travel to the ends of the Earth to do anything you ask."

There are many important and readily understandable reasons for every detail of the *Seder*. However, as with all *Mitzvoth*, because God's wisdom is infinite, human beings can never fully comprehend their significance. The *Haggadah* responds to the Four Questions by describing how *Hashem* saved us from Egyptian slavery and weaned us away from idolatry because we are so delighted that He did so that we do not care *why* He commanded us to perform the rituals of the *Seder*. Just as Sprintza agreed to do anything her benefactors might request without worrying about explanations, Jews willingly carry out the commandments of the *Seder* whether they fully understand the reasoning behind them or not.

הֲרֵי אָנוּ וּבָנֵינוּ וּבְנֵי בָנֵינוּ מְשֻׁעְבָּדִים הָיִינוּ
SURELY WE, OUR CHILDREN, AND OUR CHILDREN'S CHILDREN WOULD HAVE BEEN ENSLAVED

The *Haggadah* teaches that if the Holy One, Blessed be He, had not intervened, Israel would never have left Egypt. A standard question about this segment of the *Haggadah* is why the sages were so certain that the Jews would have remained enslaved. Many enslaved peoples have gained their freedom, albeit not through supernatural means.

Josh and Yoni were walking to the *Yeshivah* dormitory.

"So, what do you think about *Rebbe's* idea of having our class divide into teams to play basketball?" asked Josh.

Yoni, who was pudgy and unathletic, shrugged his shoulders. "I don't mind shooting some hoops, but I'm not really into sports." As the two boys entered their room, Yoni's shoulder bumped into a metal handle.

"Ouch!" cried Yoni. "What's this thing?"

David, another roommate, walked around from the other side of the Super Deluxe Weightlifter Ten Thousand. "Isn't it cool?"

"I don't know," said Yoni, rubbing his shoulder. He and Josh moved cautiously around the gadget, eyeing all the weights, cables, and levers. "You sure this isn't some antique torture device you picked up at a yard sale somewhere?"

"Oh, come on, Yoni," said David. "My dad has a friend who sells exercise equipment. He agreed to lend it to us so that we can get into shape for the basketball tournament."

Josh picked up the instruction booklet, pushed at the glasses on his nose, and started reading.

Yoni tugged at a cable. "You sure this thing is safe?"

"Of course it's safe. Just lie down on this bench."

Yoni sat down and felt the plastic-covered padding sink beneath him. "Feels comfortable enough." He lay back on the bench.

"Caution!" read Josh aloud from the instruction book. "Be sure to position your body on the center of the exercise bench to ensure proper equilibrium. Failure to do so could cause injury."

Yoni abruptly sat up. "I knew it! This thing is dangerous!"

"Stop fooling around," said David. "Lay back down and you'll see how easy it is."

Yoni complied as Josh continued to read: "Position head between pads at end of bench and place both hands firmly on exercise bar above you."

Yoni ran his tongue along his lips as he grasped the bar.

"Now push upwards slowly and evenly with both hands," continued Josh.

Yoni grunted as he pushed at the bar. His face reddened. Slowly, the bar lifted away from his chest.

Josh looked up from the instruction book. "Hey, you're doing it. It says you should push until your arms are fully extended and then slowly let the bar back down."

Sweat broke out on Yoni's forehead. At last, he managed to push the bar all the way up. Letting out a blast of air, he eased the bar back down. "There!" exclaimed Yoni as he slid off the bench. "You were right. It wasn't so difficult. How much weight was I pressing?"

"Ten kilos," answered David dryly. "The lowest setting the machine has. You're supposed to start with that and work your way up."

"The book says you should repeat the exercise twenty-five

times," said Josh.

"Twenty-five times!?!" exclaimed Yoni. "But I don't need to." He placed his hand on his bicep. "You should feel this baby. I may look weak and overweight, but after all that exercise, this arm's turned to pure muscle."

"Very funny," said David.

Josh flipped another page in the instruction book. "The book says to practice twenty-five times each day at the lowest setting until you get used to it. Then, you increase the number of times by ten each day until you can do two hundred. After that, you increase the weight by five kilos and repeat the process."

"Look," said Yoni. "I thought we were supposed to have a basketball tournament, not a weight lifting contest."

"But you need to develop strength in your arms if you're going to play well," explained David.

"But if my arms get sore from working with this equipment, I won't be able to play at all."

David clapped his hand to his forehead. "You're impossible, Yoni. Haven't you ever heard the expression, 'No pain, no gain?' It's like learning *Gemara*. Sometimes it starts off hard, but eventually you get it. Anyway, it's a *Mitzvah* to try to stay healthy."

Yoni snapped his fingers. "That gives me an idea. Doing *Chessed* is a big *Mitzvah*. Why don't we do some other team a favor and let them have this machine!"

"I already told you to stop clowning around. Now get on there!"

Yoni barely managed to do the twenty-five exercises. "Now I'm guaranteed to lose weight," he moaned as he accompanied Josh to the dining hall.

"Yeah, it was great exercise," agreed Josh, who had also worked out on the machine.

"That's not what I mean. My arms are so sore, I'm not sure I'll ever be able to lift any food to my mouth again."

Deep down, Yoni certainly knew that exercise was good for him. He may even have secretly envied other boys who were good at sports. The problem is that Yoni — like most people — was a bit lazy and did not want to exert any more effort than necessary.

Despite all the horrors and hardships of slavery in the American South, relatively few slaves rebelled against their masters. Those who did were often betrayed by other slaves.[277] The vast majority preferred the certainty of the life they knew to the uncertain future that freedom meant.[278]

The attitude of many Jews in Egypt was the same. The *Midrash* teaches that many members of the nation were so complacent about their situation that they did not want to depart. Those individuals perished during the plague of darkness.[279] Even those who survived were not enthusiastic about leaving.[280]

To some extent, all of us suffer from the same problem. Every loyal Jew recognizes the importance of becoming an accomplished *Torah* scholar and a *Tzaddik*. But how many are prepared to make the sacrifices necessary to accomplish those goals?

By explaining that had God Himself not intervened, Israel would have remained enslaved indefinitely, the *Haggadah* teaches us the importance of rejecting complacency. A Jew's mission is to constantly strive to better himself.

---

[277] This happened with Gabriel Prosser, a Virginian slave who tried to lead a revolt in 1800.

[278] Even the famous Nat Turner, who led an unsuccessful rebellion in 1831, had only about seventy-five followers.

[279] *Rashi* on Exodus 10:22, citing *Shemoth Rabbah* 14:3 and *Tanna D'bei Eliyahu Rabbah* 7.

[280] This explains why they complained so much during the journey through the wilderness on the way to the Land of Israel.

לְמַעַן תִּזְכֹּר אֶת יוֹם צֵאתְךָ מֵאֶרֶץ מִצְרַיִם
כֹּל יְמֵי חַיֶּיךָ

IN ORDER THAT YOU REMEMBER THE DAY OF YOUR DEPARTURE FROM THE LAND OF EGYPT

This verse refers to the *Mitzvah* of mentioning the departure from Egypt every morning and evening throughout the year. Discussing the departure from Egypt in detail on Passover night is completely independent of this year-round *Mitzvah*. Why, then, does the *Haggadah* mention it?

Eleven year old Bentzi Goldfarb lifted his baseball cap off his head and mopped the sweat from his forehead with the back of his hand. Little trickles poured down the sides of his face. The next minute, he hardly noticed the heat as two of his teammates came up to him with beaming faces.

"That play you made tagging that runner going to second base was terrific!" exclaimed Sammy. The two boys slapped each other's hands.

"How did you learn to do that?" asked Yossi. "I'm the tallest guy in our class, but I don't think I could have leaped like that!"

"I don't know," answered Bentzi modestly. "I guess I just practice a lot."

"By the way," said Sammy, "Yossi and I made a bet about you."

"What kind of bet?"

"Everyone in school knows you're the expert when it comes to knowing just about every statistic there is about profes-

sional baseball and football players," said Yossi. "I bet Sammy that you wouldn't know which player in the National Basketball Association scored the most baskets last season."

"Oh, that's nothing," said Bentzi. "What a silly bet! Everybody knows it was Blair Larkins."

"Dang!" shouted Yossi, slapping his thigh.

"Time for you to treat me to a snowball," said Sammy gleefully.

"Sorry to make you lose," said Bentzi, trying to stifle a self-satisfied smirk. "It's true I don't know as much about basketball as I do about baseball and football, but why don't you think of a harder question if you want to make a bet?"

Yossi slapped Bentzi on the back. "Don't worry about it! Let's go over to the Kosher Mart, and I'll treat you to a snowball too."

Bentzi enjoyed the snowball immensely as his friends continued to ply him with questions about sports heroes. When he got home, however, his mood suddenly changed.

"Bentzi," said his mother sternly, "I need to talk to you."

Bentzi did not like the solemn tone of his mother's voice. "Whatever Sarah says I did, it isn't true. I wasn't even home until just now."

"Sarah isn't your problem today." Mrs. Goldfarb took Bentzi into his bedroom and closed the door. "I got a telephone call from your *Rebbe* today."

"My *Rebbe*?" Bentzi sounded puzzled.

"Yes, you remember. The man who's supposed to teach you *Chumash, Mishnah,* and that sort of thing."

"Hah, hah! That's a good one, Mom!" Bentzi forced a smile.

"Well, what I'm about to say may not be so funny."

Bentzi tried to look serious, but it was difficult. He had a good idea of what he was about to hear.

"Rabbi Shuman says that you failed the last Hebrew

vocabulary test even though I spent so much time going over the flash cards with you."

"I don't get it, Mom. How's it possible?"

"I'm not sure myself, but the problem is that unless you improve drastically by the end of the year, you may have to repeat the fifth grade."

Bentzi let out a real groan this time. "What does everybody want out of me?"

"Well, I don't know what else I can do, so Abba and I have decided to hire a tutor for you."

"You mean a music teacher?'"

"A music teacher?"

"Yeah. Isn't a tutor someone who teaches people how to toot?"

"That's enough clowning around, Bentzi. This is very serious. Go get washed up for dinner. Rabbi Nataneli will be here at 7:30, and I expect you to pay close attention to everything he tells you. Your father and I are paying good money for this."

Three weeks later, Mrs. Goldfarb called Bentzi's tutor with incredible news. "It's unbelievable, Rabbi Nataneli! Bentzi got an 'A' on his Hebrew vocabulary quiz. He's never gotten an 'A' before in any subject. I don't know how you did it, but I'm really thankful."

"I'm delighted to hear about Bentzi's improvement," answered the tutor. "Actually, the secret is quite simple. You told me about Bentzi's amazing ability to memorize statistics about sports players. Someone who can do that obviously doesn't have a defective memory.

"The key is that Bentzi finds sports interesting, so he focuses all his attention on it and succeeds. To get him to do well with Hebrew, I had to figure out a way to get him interested in it. Some kids are fine using flash cards and lots of repetition, but that clearly wasn't the way to grab Bentzi's attention, so I decided to devise a little game. I drew a baseball diamond and we pretended

that some of the flash cards were players. Then we moved the cards around as though we were actually playing a game. That caught Bentzi's attention, and he ended up memorizing every single vocabulary word without a problem."

❖ ❖ ❖ ❖ ❖ ❖ ❖

The *Torah* lists four types of sons to whom a father must teach the story of the departure from Egypt. The *Mitzvah* of teaching one's children about the Exodus must be done in a way which best suits each child. The *Haggadah* discusses the separate and distinct commandment of remembering the Exodus daily as a way of alluding to this concept. For some children, a very brief and simple explanation, repeated daily, will prepare them to participate in the *Seder*. Others may require a different approach. Some may need to be offered treats and rewards to participate, while others will be drawn in by discussion of a puzzling question. How the job gets done is not important, only that it gets done.

כְּנֶגֶד אַרְבָּעָה בָנִים דִּבְּרָה תוֹרָה
THE FOUR SONS

The wise son asks, "What are the testimonies, laws, and statutes which *Hashem*, our God, commanded you?"[281] The wicked son asks, "What is this service for you?"[282] These questions sound almost identical. What makes one son wise and the other wicked?

❖ ❖ ❖ ❖ ❖ ❖ ❖

[281] Deuteronomy 6:20.
[282] Exodus 12:26.

Over a hundred-twenty years ago, a train chugged steadily through the Ural Mountains of western Russia. One of the passengers, the venerable Rabbi Rabinowitz, widely renowned for his brilliant *Talmudic* scholarship, had just finished his morning prayers. As he carefully put away his *Tallith* and *Tefillin*, the door to his compartment suddenly opened. In walked a gentleman who, for all appearances, could pass for a wealthy Gentile. The stranger wore impeccably tailored clothing of the latest style and carried a fancy walking cane. His manner and bearing radiated an attitude of smug self-assurance as he boldly greeted the rabbi.

"Good morning, rabbi!" exclaimed the rich gentleman.

"Good morning," answered Rabbi Rabinowitz, smiling pleasantly.

"My name is Ludwig Hoffman. Years ago, when I was a *Yeshiva* student, it was Lazer Hoffman."

"A fellow Jew. I'm most delighted." He turned to an elderly woman whose hair was covered with a long scarf of antiquated design. "Rivkah, we have a guest."

The lady, who had been observing the mountain scenery through the train window, nodded to the gentleman. When she smiled, heavy wrinkles appeared around her eyes. "I'm afraid that is one of the inconveniences of traveling. At home I would offer you something to eat and drink, but here I cannot do that," she said.

"I am traveling to a meeting of the rabbinical council in Kovna," explained the rabbi, "and my wife and I will also be visiting our daughter's family there."

"Yes, I have heard much about your great learning rabbi." Ludwig Hoffman clasped his fancy cane between his right arm and abdomen as he adjusted his burgundy cravat. "When I discovered you were riding this train, I felt I had to introduce myself. I must admit that I no longer observe the folk customs of our people and with your reputation for intellect, I did expect to find, with all due respect, a much more modern gentleman."

The rabbi had finished putting away his *Tallith* and *Tefillin* by this time. "Please sit down for a while with me. Why do you call the commandments of the *Torah* folk customs?"

"I left the *Yeshiva* when I was sixteen years old, having realized that its teachings did not suit me. I studied medicine at the University and have become a highly respected doctor. Over the years, I have developed a hobby of investigating the medical traditions of primitive cultures and, in my opinion, Jewish customs differ little from those found among other peoples.

"Let me give you an example of what I mean. It is very common in unenlightened societies to try to cure disease by use of an object which has some property similar to the disease. This is known as homeopathic medicine. For example, someone with a red skin rash might consume food that has a reddish color, assuming that the color can somehow cure the disease.

"The *Talmud* abounds with similar remedies. As a case in point, it says that if a person is bitten by a mad dog, he should eat from the lobe of its liver.[283] I do not mean to be offensive, but surely a man of your great intellect can see how primitive such an approach is — purely without scientific basis."

The shocked look on the face of the rabbi's wife made it clear that she did not approve of such talk.

"Perhaps we should retire to the smoking car, rabbi," suggested Dr. Hoffman. "No doubt your wife finds it difficult to appreciate this type of intellectual discussion. I'm afraid the education Jewish women receive ill prepares them to understand complex topics."

"You certainly seem to have given this matter a lot of thought, Ludwig," replied the rabbi smoothly. "It is all right for me to call you Ludwig?"

"Certainly, rabbi."

"I think you will find that my wife is completely at ease

---

[283] B.T. *Yoma* 84b.

discussing such issues. Women, as a rule, tend to have greater faith in God than men. As you may recall, the *Talmud* teaches that it was through the merit of the righteous women who lived at the time when the Jewish people were slaves in Egypt that God saved them."

Dr. Hoffman stifled a laugh. 'How quaintly naive,' he thought. "You know," he said aloud, "most old-fashioned Jews would respond to what I have said with anger, but I can tell that you have a genuine curiosity for the truth."

"My husband is right," said *Rebbetzin* Rabinowitz, quickly regaining her composure. "You are perfectly welcome to continue your conversation here. In fact, my husband has always found the medical field fascinating. You may be surprised to know that many people consult him for medical advice."

'How typical of ignorant people,' thought Dr. Hoffman smugly.

"It certainly is wonderful that we have found the opportunity to meet a University trained physician," continued Mrs. Rabinowitz. "While you are here, perhaps you could explain something to me about which I have always been curious."

The doctor grinned proudly. Here was a couple quite a bit older than himself to whom he could display his vast knowledge. Not only that, but his pupils included a prominent rabbi. Enlightening him would surely advance the cause of science in the struggle against unsophisticated superstition. "I would be most delighted to discuss medicine with you, Madam." Dr. Hoffman seated himself comfortably on the cushioned train bench, hoping that he would not find her question too simple-minded.

"Well," continued Mrs. Rabinowitz, "of course, as you yourself pointed out, I have no scientific training, but I have always wondered about inoculation. It seems to have developed into a very important and widespread medical practice. How exactly does it work?"

The doctor veritably swelled with pride. What a simple

question indeed! "Inoculation is a well-established medical principle founded upon modern scientific experimentation," he began. "You see, the way it works. . ." It was then that the good doctor's jaw dropped and a look of astonishment filled his face.

It was now Mrs. Rabinowitz's turn to grin. "I believe that what you were about to tell us was that a dead or weakened form of the disease is refined and injected into the patient, whose body then develops an immunity to it — a process similar to what the *Talmud* prescribes for treating the bite of a mad dog as you yourself just mentioned.

"Furthermore, since dogs are not *Kosher*, the rabbis of the *Talmud* are divided about whether it is permissible to use this remedy because it is not guaranteed to work. That was probably because people in ancient times did not have the ability to refine the microbes as we do today. Perhaps the sages of the *Talmud* knew a bit more than you suppose!"

"Although my wife has no fancy scientific degree," added the rabbi, "she is quite well read. Why don't you tell the gentleman about that young man who visited us from Berlin?"

"One time," said the *Rebbetzin*, "we had a guest who was a student at the University there. The *Midrash* teaches that the reason we wish people good health after they sneeze is because, at one point in history, a person who sneezed would die.[284] Our young guest thought the *Midrash* was far-fetched until I pointed out to him that certain Native American peoples were almost wiped out by the common cold which spread among them after they came into contact with Europeans. They had never developed any immunity, so they sneezed and died.

"Of course, not everything our sages say is meant to be taken literally, but one must always bear in mind that they possessed the highest level of wisdom."

---

[284] *Pirkei D'Rabbi Eliezer*, chap. 51.

The question of the wise son contains one very important element which is missing from the nearly identical question posed by the wicked son. The wise son mentions God. He may have questions. He may wonder about the meaning of *Torah* concepts. But he also knows that the *Torah* comes from *Hashem*. The wise son respects the authority of the *Torah* and is confident that any questions he has result from his own lack of knowledge and not from any defect in the *Torah*.

By contrast, the wicked son arrogantly asks, "What is this service to you?" He makes no mention of God because he does not believe in the Divine origin of the *Torah*, and he assumes that he is so clever that he can come up with questions which "disprove" it.

מָה הָעֵדֹת וְהַחֻקִּים וְהַמִּשְׁפָּטִים

WHAT ARE THE TESTIMONIES, LAWS, AND STATUTES WHICH *HASHEM*, OUR GOD, COMMANDED YOU?

One of the marks of piety of the wise son is his willingness to accept all of the *Mitzvoth* of the *Torah* as Divinely ordained.

The reasons for many commandments are readily understandable. Testimonies (עֵדֹת) refer to those *Mitzvoth* which commemorate a historic event, such as eating *Matzah* in memory of the food the Jews ate when they departed Egypt. Statutes (מִשְׁפָּטִים) refer to commandments which control how people deal with one another, such as those which regulate business activities.

Laws (חֻקִּים), however, are *Mitzvoth* the reasons for which are not known, such as the prohibition against breaking the bones

of the Passover sacrifice.[285] It requires special effort to obey commandments which fall into this category because human beings are rational creatures who possess a natural aversion to doing anything they do not understand.

The wise son recognizes that all of the commandments of the *Torah* have a Divine source and that he must perform those he does not comprehend with as much willingness as the ones he does.

One could raise a serious challenge to such piety. Why should Jews reject or criticize other religious systems? Surely, they contain nothing more contrary to reason or apparently illogical than our own? Why does the wise son accept the *Torah* with blind faith, yet reject other religions?

Mrs. Fried sat on the living room couch having a serious conversation with her young son, Yankie, a first-grader. Yankie's big brother, Avi, already over *Bar Mitzvah* age, sat a few feet away in an armchair, concentrating intently on his homework.

"I've been hearing in the news lately about some kidnappings, so I want to make sure you know how to protect yourself," explained Mrs. Fried.

Little Yankie smiled. "If anybody tries to kidnap me, I'll zap him with my super laser alien assault rifle."

Without looking up, Avi started erasing something in his notebook, and said in a tired voice, "That super laser alien assault rifle is just a toy, but even if it were real it would probably only work on aliens, so you'd better listen to what Mommy is telling you."

Yankie's smile vanished. "Okay."

"Now if anyone ever comes to the door," continued Mrs.

---

[285] *Abudraham.*

Fried, "you already know to ask who it is before opening it. Don't ever let a stranger come into our house."

Avi put down his pencil and looked up. "I heard someone say that if a stranger tries to get inside your house, you should yell, 'Bob get the shotgun!'"

"That's a good idea," said Mrs. Fried.

"But who's Bob?" asked Yankie.

"There isn't any Bob or any shotgun," explained Mrs. Fried, "but the stranger won't know that and will leave."

"Oh," said Yankie. "Would it be okay to shout, 'Avi, get the shotgun?'"

Avi chuckled. "I wouldn't know how to use a shotgun even if we had one, but I think it would work just as well."

"Now another thing you need to know," continued Mrs. Fried, "is that sometimes people try to kidnap children by getting them to ride with them in a car. If someone stops and asks you to ride with him, you should run straight home."

"What if they just want directions or something?" interjected Avi.

"Adults should ask other adults for directions. They shouldn't be asking small children. Whatever the person says, Yankie, just run straight home."

The next Sunday afternoon was pleasant and sunny, but Avi did not go outside to play. Instead, he decided to build a model airplane on the dining room table. Suddenly, he heard a loud commotion as someone opened the front door, then slammed it shut. The next moment, Yankie raced in almost breathless, shouting, "Avi, get the shotgun! Avi, get the shotgun!"

"What happened? Is someone chasing after you? Did you lock the front door?"

"It's Rabbi Seidler! He just tried to kidnap me!"

Avi frowned. "Rabbi Seidler? Isn't that your *Rebbe*?"

"Yes. He pulled his car up to the curb, rolled down the

window, and called my name."

Now Avi started to smile. "Why would Rabbi Seidler want to kidnap you?"

Yankie paused for a few moments, still trying to catch his breath. "I don't know. Maybe he locks kids in his basement and forces them to learn *Chumash*. You'd better call 911!"

Avi's smile turned into a broad grin. "Look, Yankie, all that stuff Mommy was telling you about not talking to a grown-up who stops his car and tries to speak to you only applies to strangers, not to people we know."

When strangers tell incredible stories about the miracles their religious leaders supposedly performed, we have every right to be skeptical. Who knows what motives these people have for spreading such tales? Who knows whether they are exaggerating some incident or inventing a complete fiction? Who exactly is it that witnessed these alleged events?

By contrast, Jews have a long and reliable tradition that their ancestors received the *Torah* from *Hashem* many centuries ago. God gave the *Torah* in the presence of the entire Jewish nation of several million people. Other religions base their claims on the "testimony" of a handful of individuals.

Moreover, the traditions of the *Torah* have been faithfully transmitted from father to son for generations.[286] A stranger may have devious reasons to lie or mislead, but a father can be trusted to impart the truth to his son. For this reason, Jews are justified in accepting every detail of the *Torah* and believing that even parts

---

[286] Even many non-Jews acknowledge the authenticity of the *Torah*. Archaeologists have discovered items such as *Torah* scrolls and *Tefillin* thousands of years old which are identical to those in use today. There are even ancient stone monuments carved by Gentiles which refer to events recorded in the *Tanach*.

which appear illogical are the word of God whose logic humans cannot fathom.

People often wonder how any person could deny that the Holocaust took place. After all, there is hardly any Jew alive who has not had contact with someone who experienced it first-hand. Moreover, tens of thousands of non-Jews were also in the death camps and witnessed what the Nazis did. There were also tens of thousands of soldiers who liberated the camps and saw the gas chambers used to murder millions of Jews. After World War II, when the Allies put Nazi war criminals on trial, most tried to claim that they were not responsible for these atrocities, but not one claimed that they never happened.

Even so, there are anti-Semites who contend that the Jewish people fabricated the Holocaust. True, the Nazis hated the Jews, they argue, but they never set up a program to systematically murder them.

What makes matters even stranger is the fact that other mass murders have occurred during recent times, yet none deny that they took place. During the 1930's, the Stalin regime killed millions of Russian peasants who refused to cooperate with his government's farm collectivization program or who were suspected of disloyalty. In the 1970's, the Communist regime in Cambodia killed approximately two million intellectuals whom it feared might rebel. Sadly, many other instances of mass murder and genocide have taken place throughout the world. No one has ever questioned the fact that such events occurred except when it comes to the destruction of European Jewry during World War II.

Why should this be so?

Perhaps *Hashem* is teaching us the very point made above. Many question the authenticity of the *Torah*. How could a civilized nation such as Egypt permit the cruel enslavement of another people, slaughtering babies to provide blood for Pharaoh's baths, burying people alive in the walls of pyramids, throwing helpless infants into the Nile River to drown? How is it that so

few Egyptian records of these events have survived? How can Jews be sure that God defeated the Egyptians by supernatural means? Perhaps the plagues were nothing more than peculiar natural phenomena.

The answer is that Jews possess an authentic tradition. Just as some Gentiles deny the Holocaust — although no rational person could seriously doubt that it occurred — some deny the events of the Exodus even though they certainly happened.

This explains why the *Haggadah* calls the son who excludes himself from the community wicked. Such a son seems misguided. He has a poor attitude. But wicked? What has he said or done which is so terrible that his father tells him that had he been in Egypt, he would not have deserved to leave?

The entire foundation of the Jewish religion rests upon a belief in the authenticity of the tradition of the community. One who thinks that the chain of tradition is not relevant to him, and who does not view himself as a link in it, challenges the truth of the *Torah* itself. And a Jew who does not believe in the *Torah* is lost.

מְלַמֵּד שֶׁהָיוּ יִשְׂרָאֵל מְצֻיָּנִים שָׁם
THIS TEACHES THAT THE JEWS
WERE DISTINGUISHED IN EGYPT

The *Haggadah* praises the Jewish people for retaining their unique identity despite their lengthy servitude in Egypt. The *Midrash* explains that the Jews were redeemed because of four things: (a) they continued to speak Hebrew; (b) they continued to use Hebrew names; (c) they did not speak ill of one another, being especially careful not to betray their comrades to their Egyptian masters; and (d) they did not engage in immoral practices as the

Egyptians did.[287]

Why was the fact that Jews remained distinct from the Egyptians so praiseworthy when most of the differences had nothing to do with Judaism? The above description sounds a lot like the "bagels and lox Jews" of today — people who observe little or nothing of the Jewish religion but are culturally Jewish. Such individuals have Jewish-sounding names and may know a smattering of Yiddish or Hebrew. They tend to stand up for their fellow Jews, just as the slaves in Egypt did not speak ill of one another. Some oppose intermarriage, just as their ancient counterparts rejected Egyptian promiscuity. One would think that there is little to praise about such a highly superficial attachment to the Jewish people. Why would maintaining this type of Jewish identity merit a miraculous rescue from Egypt?

A neatly dressed waiter carrying a silver tray laden with a teapot and cakes approached Mrs. Eisen and Mrs. Berman as they sat waiting for their taxi in the hotel lobby.

"The hotel manager asked me to serve you these with his compliments," said the waiter with a heavy Polish accent.

Mrs. Eisen smiled politely as she poured out some of the tea. "I'll just have something to drink. I don't care for any cakes, but please thank the manager anyway for his thoughtfulness."

"Ah," said the waiter with a smile. "You American ladies are always on a diet, aren't you?"

Mrs. Eisen returned the smile politely, but said nothing. She wondered how the waiter would have reacted had she explained that she could not eat the cakes because they were not *Kosher*. Would he even know what *Kosher* meant?

"And you, madam?" The waiter turned to Mrs. Berman,

---

[287] *Vayikra Rabbah* 32:5.

who was staring out of the window at the cramped streets of the small Polish town. The stocky middle-aged woman had taken no notice of him. She seemed to gasp slightly as she turned toward the waiter. "I beg your pardon. I wasn't listening."

"Some cakes and tea, compliments of the manager."

"Oh, no thank you," she answered in Polish, immediately returning to gaze out the window.

The waiter, appearing a bit surprised to be addressed in his native tongue, opened his mouth to say something, but Mrs. Eisen interrupted.

"I'm afraid my companion is a bit excited. It's been many years since she lived in Poland, and this is her first time returning."

"I see." The waiter withdrew with his tray.

"I'm glad you didn't tell him anything more about me or our trip," said Mrs. Berman quietly when the waiter was out of earshot.

"I know how much this trip means to you, Sophie, but you really should try to remain calm. The waiter was just trying to be friendly."

"No one here is friendly without a reason, Rivkah." She lowered her voice. "He's probably an agent of the secret police."

Mrs. Eisen settled her teacup and saucer on a low table near the couch where the two women were seated. During the 1960's, it was certainly possible that secret police might trace the movements of two American tourists in Communist Poland. "I just hope you won't be too disappointed if it turns out to be a different Henryk Kowalski than you were expecting. I mean, that must be a fairly common name in Poland."

"You're right, and this isn't the same village where I left Sarah, but I can't help having a certain feeling that I've found her."

Mrs. Eisen placed her hand gently on her friend's arm. "Don't forget that they never responded to your letters."

Mrs. Berman turned her gaze back to the window. Just then, a taxi pulled up to the hotel. "It must be for us," she said.

Inside the taxi, Mrs. Berman gave the driver his instructions. It was a short ride to the shabby apartment building which was the destination of the two tourists. Outside, a ragged crowd of children paused in their games to stare as the two foreign ladies, wearing very fancy clothing by local standards, emerged from the taxi.

As they climbed to the second floor of the building, Mrs. Eisen said, "Don't be too disappointed if no one is home right now, Sophie. They don't have a telephone, so we couldn't call ahead."

Mrs. Berman made no response except to say, "This must be it." A young man, who looked to be no more than twenty, answered the door. He was unshaven, wore a stained undershirt, and held a smoldering cigarette in one hand.

"I am looking for Mr. Henryk Kowalski," said Mrs. Berman cautiously.

"I am he," answered the young man, raising his eyebrows in astonishment.

The expression on Mrs. Berman's face mirrored his surprise. "There must be some mistake. The Henryk Kowalski I know would be well into his fifties."

"Oh," the young man scratched at his shoulder with the hand that bore the cigarette. "You must mean my father. I am Henryk Kowalski, Jr."

"Is your father available, then?"

The man shook his head. "I'm afraid you would have to visit the cemetery to meet him."

"The cemetery?"

"Dead these past nine years."

"I'm sorry. I didn't know."

"Quite understandable. Were you an acquaintance of my father?"

"Yes. My husband and I were sent off to a concentration camp during the war, and we left my little daughter with your family. After all these years, I finally managed to trace you here."

"I'm afraid there must be some mistake. I was born during the war and I don't recall my parents telling me anything about keeping a little girl. I am sure you know how common a name like Kowalski is in Poland."

"What about your mother? Is she also..."

"No, no. Mother is alive, but I'm afraid she isn't quite well. She suffered a nervous breakdown and lives at the state mental hospital. You are welcome to visit her, but whether she could give you any information or even recognize you..." The man shook his head sadly.

"Do you perhaps have relatives living in this part of Poland who might know something?" Mrs. Berman could not keep her voice from wavering with disappointment.

"My sister, Maria, is about six years older than me. She lives in an apartment at 16 Mariski Street. I don't know what she could tell you. Most of our other relatives still live in Kutno."

Mrs. Berman's face lit up. "Kutno is the little village where I left my daughter. I must speak with your sister."

Another short taxi ride took the two ladies to 16 Mariski Street. This time, however, the women were not so lucky. No one was home, and they were forced to return to the hotel.

Mrs. Eisen prepared a meal as best she could. Since *Kosher* food was difficult to find in Poland, the women had brought along some cans of tuna and purchased fruits and vegetables locally.

"It's terrible that so few people in Poland have telephones," said Mrs. Eisen as she cut up the fruit. "We could save so much time and trouble if you could simply call Maria Kowalski and find out if she knows anything about your daughter. At least we could have written a note and left it at Maria's apartment."

"It looks suspicious to the government when foreigners leave notes," said Mrs. Berman. She shook her head. "They only

gave us a visa for two weeks. There is hardly time to do anything."

"Perhaps we should go straight to Kutno. After all, that is
where you left Sarah before..."

"No, no. I must speak to Maria. Something tells me that I
must."

"It's doubtful she's going to know anything more than her
brother. She would have been a small child when you left Sarah
with her family — if this is the right family."

"Sarah was only four when I left her. It sounds as if Maria
is the same age as Sarah would be. Her brother says the family
came from Kutno."

Mrs. Eisen stopped cutting the fruit, her face filled with
surprise. "Are you saying that you think that Maria Kowalski is
your Sarah?"

Mrs. Berman spoke slowly and with determination. "I'm
sure of it."

"Let's eat and try going out there again this evening."

Though it was past nine o'clock, the sun had not yet set,
for the day ends late during the summer in the part of Poland
Mrs. Eisen and Mrs. Berman were visiting. As the two women
rode in their taxi, Mrs. Eisen could not help noticing how many
people were out strolling, most appearing to be in good spirits as
they enjoyed the cool breeze that preceded the onset of evening.
"Poland is a poor country, but the weather and the countryside
are quite nice," she remarked to her companion. "It's difficult to
imagine what happened here."

Mrs. Berman did not reply. She could only think of the
number tattooed on her forearm and how she hated everything
about Poland. She could not put such thoughts into words,
though. There were the secret police to worry about, and she
must find Sarah.

Mrs. Eisen read her friends thoughts. "Please don't take it
so hard. So much happened here..."

"I understand. You are trying to tell me that anything could have happened to Sarah. Despite my efforts to hide her, the Germans could have found her. I know that, but something just tells me that I must go on. Does that sound strange to you?"

"Not at all. The sages say that when a person dies, his relatives forget about him after a year. Since you cannot forget your daughter and are willing to spend so much time and money pursuing her, perhaps it is a sign that she is still alive."

For the first time during the entire journey, Mrs. Berman smiled. When the two women knocked at the door of 16 Mariski Street, Mrs. Berman's heartbeat picked up as she heard the sound of footfalls inside the apartment. The door opened.

"Maria Kowlaski?" inquired Mrs. Berman hesitantly.

"Yes."

"Your hair!" Mrs. Berman could not help saying this as the dying rays of the sun caught in Maria's hair. She was sure it was the same color as that of her long lost daughter.

Maria frowned at her caller. "My hair? What do you mean?"

"We visited your brother, Henryk, earlier today," said Mrs. Berman. Regaining her composure, she explained the purpose of her visit.

"I'm afraid I cannot help you. I know nothing of a Sarah Berman. It's a shame you weren't able to make your trip to Poland some years ago when our father was still alive and my mother had her health."

"You don't remember anything?" Mrs. Berman's voice was filled with emotion.

The young woman continued indifferently. "I don't recall either of my parents mentioning anything about hiding a little girl or taking one in. Of course, so much went on during the war. Perhaps she was moved to another family at some point."

Tears welled up in Mrs. Berman's eyes as she looked into Maria's. She was sure she saw her daughter in those eyes.

"Aren't you my dear little one?" she asked in Yiddish.

Maria looked quizzically at the older lady. "I don't understand what you're saying?"

"I know you are my daughter," continued Mrs. Berman in Polish. "How can you not remember the Yiddish we spoke at home?"

Maria seemed a bit shaken, but she said, "I'm sure I never saw you before in my life. I'm sorry about your situation, and I wish I could be more helpful, but. . ."

Mrs. Berman's face lit up. She opened her handbag and pulled out a stuffed bear which had one eye missing. "Don't you remember your toy bear? I... I used to tuck you into bed with it every night."

Maria looked blankly at the stuffed animal.

No longer able to contain herself, Mrs. Berman started to sing *"Shema Yisrael"* with the same tune she had used so many years before when she put Sarah to sleep. Tears flowed freely down her cheeks.

Maria's jaw suddenly dropped as a wave of recognition swept over her face. "Dubie! I used to call that bear Dubie! Mama, it's really you!"

Mother and daughter embraced.

"Sarah!" exclaimed Mrs. Berman in a hoarse voice. "You remember!"

A tattered stuffed bear and faint recollections of her mother's lullaby, trivial though they were, restored Sarah Berman's memory of who she was.

Before *Hashem* saved the Jewish nation from Egyptian slavery, the Jews had strayed far from His ways. The *Satan* questioned why the Jews should be saved, seeing as some had worshiped idols. Had the Jews lost every last trace of their

identity, it would indeed have been impossible for God to redeem them. It was because the Jews managed to retain some remnants of their identity — however minor or superficial — that God was willing to save them. He knew that if He did so, they would ultimately remember who they were.

וַנִּצְעַק אֶל ה'
WE CRIED TO *HASHEM,*
GOD OF OUR ANCESTORS, AND
HASHEM HEARD OUR VOICE

This verse indicates that it is proper to cry out to God in times of difficulty. As the *Rambam* writes, it is a *Mitzvah* to cry out to *Hashem* whenever trouble befalls a community.[288]

On the other hand, when the Jews reached the Reed Sea and cried out to God to save them, Moses replied, *"Hashem* will fight for you, so be silent!"[289] God Himself also disapproved, saying, "Why do you cry out to Me? Speak to the Children of Israel, and let them go forward!"[290]

How can one explain this apparent contradiction? Was it right for the Jews to cry out to *Hashem* or not?

Leon, a poor European peasant, sat in a filthy dungeon upon a pile of straw, his eyes filled with tears.

"Come, come, man," said another prisoner, who shared the wretched cell. "Surely a poor man such as yourself cannot find these accommodations so terrible. If anyone should weep, it is I, Count Maximillian. Throughout my life I have never rested my head upon anything but the finest silks. Just looking at this dung heap makes me nauseous."

"But I just don't understand it, Your Grace?" sobbed Leon. "Why did the king imprison me?"

---

[288] *Yad Hachazakah, Hilchoth Ta'anith* 1:1.
[289] Exodus 14:10 and 14:14.
[290] Exodus 14:15, according to Rabbi Avraham Ibn Ezra, who says that *Hashem* was referring to the Jewish nation, not to Moses.

"Hah!" The count slapped his thighs and laughed. "Do you think your little act can fool me, a man of noble blood? Caught stealing by the looks of it, weren't you?"

Leon's face reddened as he stared angrily through his tears at his fellow prisoner. "A poor farmer I may be, as were my fathers before me, but one can be poor and yet be honest."

The count shrugged his shoulders. "Perhaps. Are you then telling me you have no idea whatsoever why you are in prison?"

"The king visited our village as he is accustomed to do once each year on his way to his summer palace. As poor as we peasants are, we always manage to clean the place up nicely for the royal visit. Everyone dresses in his best clothing to honor the king. We all gather — men, women and children — in the village square where the king dismounts from his royal coach and greets us. Then he enters the mayor's mansion for a special luncheon before proceeding on his way."

"Very nice." Count Maximillian already felt himself growing weary of Leon's story.

"Yes, it is a lovely custom the king has," Leon continued, not noticing the count's unenthusiastic response. "My farm lies adjacent to one of the royal forests where none may hunt without the king's permission."

The count turned, his eyebrows raised in astonishment. "A peasant seeks to hunt in the royal forest? Why of all the temerity!"

"Oh, no, Your Grace," came the brisk reply. "Certainly not. It's just that there is a huge black bear which lives in the forest. All of the villagers are afraid of it, but it rarely bothers anyone except me because my farm lies so close to the forest. At night, it romps through my field destroying my crops. One morning, when my poor wife went to milk the cow, she caught sight of it and fainted dead away. When the king visited our village, I fell upon my knees and begged that he send the local

sheriff with his men to kill the bear and rid us of this dangerous menace. That is when the king angrily ordered his men to arrest me and cast me into this dungeon." Leon finished his tale with a burst of sobbing. "Who knows when I may see my family again!"

Count Maximillian stroked his brown goatee and shrugged his shoulders. "Indeed you're right. I don't understand it. As for myself, my family is well known to His Majesty. That can be a great help at times, but harmful at others. You see, being close to the crown also means being trusted. The king put me in charge of certain funds from the royal treasury." He shook his head wearily. "Gambling was my vice. When I found myself in great debt, I made the mistake of borrowing from the funds His Majesty had entrusted me."

A look of horror swept over Leon's face. "Then it will be the gallows for you surely!"

The count laughed. "Nonsense! You peasants have such foolish ideas! My family has already raised enough money to replace what I took, and with my connections to the throne, I should be out in a matter of weeks."

The count gave the straw scattered on the dungeon floor a kick with his fur-trimmed boot. "Not that I don't regret my misdeeds. One night in this hole is enough to make any man repent. The very thought of even sitting down here revolts me!"

The count thrust his hands behind his back as he paced to and fro in the cell. "Still, I don't understand what happened in your case. The king is a rather temperate man. It's not like him to simply fly off in anger at anyone, high or low."

The count smiled to himself thoughtfully as he continued this soliloquy. "I remember being in His Majesty's presence one time when an extremely old woman petitioned him. She must have been half crazy — told the king that the sound of the dogs barking in her village frightened her cat. She even claimed that it caused the cat not to have kittens and requested that His Majesty issue an edict forbidding dogs to bark. Realizing that she was not

right in her mind, His Majesty spoke gently with her and then had his courtiers escort her from his presence. He even had them send her away with a basket of food. No, it is most unlike him to react with anger."

"I found it strange as well, Your Grace," said Leon. "As you know, the king holds an open audience in the capital once each month when any subject may approach him. When I attended last month and asked His Majesty for the same thing, he agreed without any sign of displeasure."

Count Maximillian clapped his hand to his forehead and rolled his eyes heavenward as he burst out in a gale of laughter. "You foolish idiot! It's all too clear why the king imprisoned you! How ignorant can you peasants be?!? The king is a man of supreme integrity. When you appeared at his open audience last month and he granted your request, you should have trusted him to fulfill his promise. By asking again when he came to your village, you showed that you question the king's word. Surely such insolence deserves to be punished!"

The *Torah* says that, "the Children of Israel groaned from the servitude and cried out, and their clamor from the servitude rose to God. God heard their cry, and God remembered His covenant with Abraham, Isaac, and Jacob."[291]   Initially, it was perfectly proper for the Jews to cry out to *Hashem* to save them from Egyptian slavery. God then sent Moses with the message that "I am *Hashem*. I will take you out from under the burdens of Egypt, and I will save you from their servitude, and I will redeem you with an outstretched arm and with mighty judgments."[292] Once the King of Kings assured the Jews that He would take care

---

[291] Exodus 2:23-24.
[292] Exodus 6:6.

of matters, it was impertinent on their part to cry out yet again at the Reed Sea. That is why Moses said in a severe way, "*Hashem* will fight for you, so be silent!"[293]

וַיִּזְכֹּר אֱלֹהִים אֶת בְּרִיתוֹ

GOD HEARD THEIR CRY, AND GOD REMEMBERED HIS COVENANT WITH ABRAHAM, ISAAC, AND JACOB

Young Prince Frederick looked quite pompous as he galloped on his beige stallion across the king's riding grounds. His horse jumped over hurdle after hurdle effortlessly. Handing the reins to a stableman after dismounting, the young prince patted the horse with a white-gloved hand.

"Not bad for a beginner," commented Prince Frederick's older brother, Prince Wilhelm.

"A beginner?" replied Prince Frederick, indignantly drawing off his gloves. "I've been riding since I was eleven."

"All of three years then," said Prince Wilhelm sarcastically. "How would you rate our brother's horsemanship, Ernst?"

Prince Ernst stifled a yawn to demonstrate how unimpressed he was. "I was far better when I was his age!"

Prince Frederick angrily stuffed his riding gloves into the deep pockets of his gold-embroidered jacket. "That's not what my instructor tells me."

Prince Ernst waved at his brother with the back of his hand. "He's just telling you that you're good to encourage you."

The young prince wagged his forefinger at his two older brothers. "I can ride just as well as the two of you at any time and

---

[293] Exodus 14:14.

under any circumstances."

A smirk of mild amusement played on Wilhelm's face. "What if we give you a chance to prove it?"

Frederick mashed his fists into his hips defiantly. "Gladly!"

Wilhelm broke into a mischievous grin as he beckoned to Frederick to follow him.

"Where are we going?" asked Frederick as he sauntered after his brothers.

"To prove that you're the greatest rider in the kingdom," said Ernst matter-of-factly.

Within a few minutes, the princes reached a broad fenced-off area near the royal stables. Tallest of the three brothers, Ernst lazily crossed his arms as he leaned on top of the fence. Wilhelm smugly folded his arms across his chest as he watched little Frederick climb up the fence so he could see over it. Inside the pen stood a pure white stallion gnawing at a knot of wild grass and shaking its mane furiously.

"Lightning," said Prince Wilhelm, for that was the name of the horse.

Prince Frederick glowered at his brother. "Is that it, then? You think I can't ride him?"

Wilhelm scratched his nose for a moment. "I doubt it," he answered coolly. "You know father's men captured that stallion in the western mountains. Even now he's barely tame. Some of the stablemen won't even go near him, let alone try to ride him."

Frederick jumped down from the fence. "What do stablemen know about riding?" he sneered.

"Then let's make a wager," continued Wilhelm. "You ride Lightning thrice around this pen and I'll give you the sword Sir Felix presented to me for my birthday."

Young Frederick's eyes widened. Even Ernst started to pay attention.

"Sir Felix used that sword in the Battle of Dusselheim,"

said Ernst. "How can you give away something so valuable?"

Wilhelm laughed. "I'm not giving anything away. Do you really think our little toad of a brother can ride that horse?"

Ernst shrugged his shoulders, but Frederick bristled at his brother's insulting remark. "Done!" he cried, shooting out his hand to shake with his brother.

"Not so fast." Prince Wilhelm continued to maintain a cool facade. "A fair wager requires that both parties put up something."

Frederick lowered his hand. "And what do you want from me?"

"If you lose," Wilhelm spoke in a slow, meaningful way. "If you lose, you shall sleep in the stables for a fortnight."

"I shan't lose." Hotter and more indignant than ever, Frederick thrust out his right hand, this time to be firmly clasped by that of his brother. No sooner had they finished shaking than Prince Frederick was over the fence cautiously treading in his tall leather riding boots towards the half-wild stallion.

"Now there's a good horse," cooed the boy. He dipped his hand into the pocket of his fancy riding jacket and pulled out a lump of sugar he had stored there for his own mount. As Frederick inched the sugar towards Lightning's mouth, the stallion caught sight of him and shook its mane violently. Despite the wild look in its eyes, the horse did not seem to mind.

"You'll let me ride you, won't you?" cajoled the young prince as the stallion licked at the sugar. He patted the horse's neck tentatively. "I'll be gentle with you."

In the end, Frederick managed to mount Lightning, but no sooner did he touch his heels to its belly than the horse reared violently and threw him off. Laughing uproariously, Princes Wilhelm and Ernst clambered over the fence and ran carelessly to their brother only to find to their horror that the boy was dead of a broken neck.

◇ ◇ ◇ ◇ ◇ ◇ ◇

"Kneel before me!" commanded the king. Princes Wilhelm and Ernst glanced at one another nervously. Never before had their father addressed them in such a fierce tone. They knelt. "I don't think I need to explain why I have summoned you," continued the king.

"But father," said Ernst, holding back tears. "We never meant..."

"How dare you interrupt your sovereign!" roared the king. His Majesty beckoned to the royal scribe to approach the throne. To his sons, he said, "You may rise."

"Father, you must let us explain," implored Wilhelm. "We never meant to harm Frederick..."

"Silence!" commanded the king. "I have already considered what you have done, and your decree has been sealed. Proceed scribe."

The royal scribe bowed to the king. "Your Majesty," he began. Then he bowed to the princes. "Your Royal Highnesses."

"Leave out the niceties," ordered the king impatiently. "Just read the decree."

"Yes, Sire." The scribe cleared his throat. "In as much as their Royal Highnesses, Prince Wilhelm and Prince Ernst, have betrayed our trust and committed acts against our sovereignty and against the peace and welfare of the kingdom; now, therefore, with the consent of the Royal Privy Council, we hereby decree that the rights and titles of said princes are annulled and their possessions forfeited to the Crown; and further, that the said princes are hereby banished to the far lands of the north beyond our borders to remain there forever and never to set foot again in our domains under pain and penalty of death!"

A sob burst forth from the distraught queen who sat upon a throne next to the king, her face buried in her handkerchief. "My dear husband," she cried, "I beg you not as a woman of royal

blood, but as your loyal wife and as a mother! Is it not enough that I am bereft of poor Frederick? Shall I lose my other sons as well?"

Touched, the king motioned to several ladies-in-waiting near the queen's throne. "Trust me, Martha," he said quietly, "I am as sad about this whole affair as you are, but the law is clear. These ladies will escort you to your quarters."

After the queen departed, the king said to his sons, "Very well! You have heard the decree. I knew there would be tears from your mother, but I expect you to comport yourselves as men. The captain of the royal guards awaits you outside the palace grounds to conduct you to your exile."

The next morning, the king sat glumly at breakfast without the company of the queen. After he heard nothing from her during the next two days, however, he said to his personal chamberlain, "Really, this has gone far enough. I understand my wife's grief, but she must overcome it at some point. Go fetch her."

When the chamberlain returned, he said, "The queen's chambers are deserted, but I found this note. Shall I read it for Your Majesty?"

"Never mind," snapped the king. Seizing the note, he read: "My Dearest Husband and Most Sovereign Liege: I know you love me as much as I love you, and you must not think me wrong or disloyal for behaving this way. I know that you are right and that our sons deserve punishment for what they did to their brother. Still, as a mother, I could not bear what happened. I have betaken myself to the far lands of the north — there to reside in exile with my sons. Yours faithfully forever, Martha."

At once, the king folded up the letter and commenced giving orders. "Chamberlain, prepare my battle gear immediately! Have the stablemen prepare my steed! Command Sir Felix to round up his men and present himself before me without delay!"

Meanwhile, Wilhelm and Ernst found themselves penniless wanderers in the lawless country to the north of the kingdom.

They cast furtive glances back at the huge stone wall that marked the border as they trudged away to seek their fortune. Dejected and without weapons, the former princes were easily overcome by a band of coarse thieves who forced them into servitude. When Queen Martha arrived, they captured her as well.

'It is so not bad,' thought the queen as she scoured pots and dishes for hours in the squalid bandit hideout. 'At least we are together.'

Wilhelm and Ernst, chained together, crawled about on their hands and knees scrubbing the stone floor. The leader of the bandits entered the room with muddy boots that made fresh tracks on the floor. "You missed some spots," he said, pointing to the mess he just made. "What kind of cleaning is that?"

"But you just made those tracks yourself," protested Wilhelm indignantly.

"I'll teach you to talk back to your betters." The wicked man delivered such a fierce blow to Wilhelm's face with the back of his hand that the prince fell over, knocking down Ernst as well. Struggling against the chains, he tried to right himself.

"How dare you bully my son!" declared the queen, wiping her reddened hands on her apron.

"Silence, woman!" snarled the ruffian.

"How can I be silent when I see such injustice?"

"I'll teach you to answer me that way!" The villain raised his hand to strike the queen only to find himself suddenly confronted with a sword-tip poised at his neck.

"Touch that lady and your life is forfeit," declared the stern voice of Sir Felix.

The villain immediately raised his hands and drew back. "I meant no harm, really." He swallowed hard.

"I'm sure you didn't," came the cold, sarcastic reply. "Now get out of here at once before I run you through."

The king entered with several soldiers. "Are you all right, Martha?"

"Yes, thank God. You arrived just in time."

The king snapped his fingers. "Men, free my sons immediately!"

Soldiers hacked away the chains that bound Wilhelm and Ernst.

"My sons," said the king once they stood freely before him, "I am still not convinced of your innocence, nor that you do not deserve further punishment. Nonetheless, I cannot bear to see your mother in this condition. Since I am liberating her, I hereby grant you your freedom as well. You may return with me and resume your positions in the kingdom."

The *Haggadah* states that, "God remembered His covenant with Abraham, Isaac, and Jacob."[294] The term covenant in this verse refers to the Divine Presence (שְׁכִינָה)[295] — the revelation of *Hashem* in this world.

When God's people suffer, onlookers may get the false impression that the *Torah* is not true because they do not realize that Jews only suffer because they have sinned. This false impression causes the Divine Presence — the recognition of God in this world — to decrease. As the sages put it, the Divine Presence joins the Jewish nation in exile.[296]

By rescuing the Jews from Egyptian slavery and fulfilling the terms of His covenant with Abraham, Isaac and Jacob, *Hashem* made clear that He rules the universe. He thereby increased the manifestation of His Divine Presence in the world.

As the above parable stresses, the rivalry between Joseph and his brothers caused the Egyptian exile. On their own merit, the Jews did not necessarily deserve to be rescued. However,

---

[294] Exodus 2:23-24.

[295] *Zohar* I:120B.

[296] B.T. *Megillah* 29A.

when God took note that the Divine Presence would suffer if He did not fulfill His covenant with our ancestors, He decided to liberate Israel.[297]

וַיַּרְא אֱלֹהִים אֶת בְּנֵי יִשְׂרָאֵל וַיֵּדַע אֱלֹהִים
GOD SAW THE CHILDREN OF ISRAEL,
AND GOD KNEW

"I hope you boys will enjoy the park as much as I did when I was your age," said Rabbi Jacobs as he pulled his dark blue van loaded with tenth-graders to a stop.

"How did *Rebbe* even know about this place?" asked Yossi Dwek. "I don't see a single other car parked here."

"My father used to take us here when I was a kid. It was sort of our little secret. It's an unspoiled and very private part of the park."

"So how about a game of Frisbee tag over in that clearing?" asked Mendy Goldman, slapping a bright orange Frisbee against the palm of his hand.

"There'll be plenty of time for Frisbee tag," answered Rabbi Jacobs, exiting the van and stuffing the keys into his pants pocket. "First, I want to show you guys a trail down to the lake."

The boys raced down the trail, nimbly darting around large rocks and occasionally skipping from tree root to tree root. They held their balance as they maneuvered over a rotting log that lay over a shallow ravine. Rabbi Jacobs, who had planned a much more leisurely stroll, found himself completely out of breath trying to keep up. He could not even call out loudly enough to get the boys to slow down. To add insult to injury, when they

---

[297] This parable is based on *Zohar* III:297B.

finally arrived at the lake, the rabbi's charges failed to appreciate its scenic majesty.

"Hey, it's just a bunch of water, *Rebbe,*" said Yossi with a tinge of disappointment. "Besides, the lake at my summer camp was a lot bigger."

"Okay, so now that we've seen the lake, how about that game of Frisbee tag back at the clearing?" said Mendy.

Poor Rabbi Jacobs hardly had time to register a hoarse "Let's take it easy for a minute," before the young men had started racing back up the trail.

'At least they're letting off plenty of steam,' thought the rabbi as he wearily trudged up the trail. Wiping his forehead with a handkerchief as he reached the top of the hill, Rabbi Jacobs saw the boys already deeply engrossed in their game.

"I got you out!" declared one.

"No way!" shouted another. "It came this close." He held his forefinger and thumb almost touching one another. "But the Frisbee didn't get me."

"It had to have gotten you because it deflected when it came near you."

"Well, if it did, it barely grazed my shirt."

"A graze counts as an out."

"No it doesn't!"

"Here comes Rabbi Jacobs. Let's ask him."

Rabbi Jacobs sat down at the picnic table panting. As the boys gathered around to ask his opinion about what counted as an out, the *Rebbe's* eyes suddenly rolled back in his head and he lurched forward onto the table.

"Very funny, *Rebbe,*" said Mendy Goldman.

The other boys laughed at the sight of their teacher pretending to faint.

"Hey," winked a freckle-faced boy. "Let's pour some water on him."

"Stop clowning with us, *Rebbe,*" said Yossi Dwek. "Let's

take a break from Frisbee tag and have some lunch."

But Rabbi Jacobs' arms remained limp. The handkerchief had fallen from his hand, and Mendy noticed spittle dripping from his mouth. "*Rebbe*?" he asked in alarm. After getting no response, he nudged the teacher. "Aren't you carrying this a little too far?"

"Hey," said one of the boys in a frightened voice. "Hey! There's something really wrong with him. What do we do?"

"Let's not panic," said Yossi authoritatively. "That's always rule number one. He's probably just fainted."

"But how can we be sure it isn't something serious?" asked another boy.

"We can call for help on *Rebbe's* cell phone," said Mendy. "He always keeps it on his belt." Mendy detached the mobile phone. "How do you turn it on?"

"Let me see that," said Yossi, grabbing the phone. "Look. You press down on this button until it comes on. See?"

The phone beeped and Yossi dialed 911.

"It looks like he's breathing," said the boy with the freckles. "Maybe we should try putting a little water on his face."

"Shhh!" said Yossi. "Why don't I hear anything?"

One of the boys poured a few drops of water onto Rabbi Jacob's forehead. The rabbi reacted by moving slightly, but he did not awaken.

Yossi removed the mobile phone from his ear. "It's dead! What a time for a cell phone to stop working!"

"What should we do?" asked another boy in a panicky tone.

"Simple," said Yossi. "We'll carry *Rebbe* into the van and drive him out of the park. Once we're out, we can stop someone and use their cell phone to get help."

"But none of us knows how to drive," objected the boy with the freckles.

"Mendy," said Yossi, "you started driver's ed already.

You'll have to drive."

"Me?" Mendy looked flustered. "How can I do that? I just got my learner's permit, and I've only taken two classes. The only actual driving I did was around the parking lot with the instructor."

"That's more than any of us has done," replied Yossi.

"But I can't..."

"Well, what are we supposed to do?" insisted a tall boy with frizzy *Peyoth*. "Let *Rebbe* die?"

"Why can't some of us just walk out of the park and get help while some of us stay with *Rebbe*?" asked Mendy.

"This is an emergency," said Yossi. "The park entrance is at least three miles from here. Unless we get help right away, something serious could happen."

The boys lifted their limp teacher into the van. "Easy does it," said Yossi as he closed the door. "I got his keys out of his pants pocket. This must be the one for the van."

The whole group climbed in as Yossi passed the keys to Mendy. "This is crazy," said Mendy. "I don't know anything about what I'm doing."

"How difficult can it be?" answered Yossi as he strapped himself into the front seat next to Mendy. "We've all seen our parents drive thousands of times."

Mendy shook his head. "Somehow, I don't think that's all it takes."

Mendy turned the key in the ignition. The van made a grinding sound before the motor started. "Great," muttered Mendy. "I can't even start it smoothly."

"Yeah," said Yossi, "but the point is that you got it started."

Mendy placed the van into gear and it staggered forward.

"Use the brake pedal!" shouted Yossi.

"Yeah, yeah, that's right," said Mendy. He stamped his foot on the brake pedal and the van lurched to a halt. "The

instructor said to always keep your foot on the brake pedal when you start." Mendy eased his foot this time and the van went forward. The ride was not an elegant affair, but considering that Mendy had never done anything like it before, it was not too bad either.

"I just hope nobody tries to drive past us in the other direction," said Mendy. "I doubt I can control the van well enough to keep to the right on this narrow road."

"If somebody comes, we'll stop and get them to help us," said Yossi. "Slow down. We're coming to a curve." Mendy did slow down, but not enough to avoid going off the road. Fortunately, the area next to the curve was gravelly. Mendy did not run into anything and managed to get the van back onto the road without a problem.

Five minutes later, the boys found themselves at the park entrance. "What do we do now?" asked Mendy. "I barely made it this far. There's no way I can drive on a regular road with traffic."

"*Baruch Hashem*, you won't have to," said Yossi. "Look over there! Cops!" About fifty meters away stood a police cruiser. Yossi ran over to the open window of the police car and said, "Officer, you've got to help us! Our teacher fainted back in the park, and we've got to get him to a hospital!"

The police officer hurried to the van, examined Rabbi Jacobs, and then radioed to the other officer in the cruiser. "Turn on the siren, Murphy. Looks like we've got a 911 here."

"Roger. I copy," came the reply as the siren went on. "Where to?"

"Montgomery General."

"Roger."

"Slide over son," the police officer instructed Mendy as he took the wheel.

"Montgomery General is where my father works as a therapist," Mendy told Yossi. "*Rebbe* will be fine. It's got a good emergency room."

After the hospital technicians wheeled Rabbi Jacobs away, the boys sat down in the waiting area.

Fifteen minutes passed. One youngster with black hair pulled off his glasses and rubbed his eyes. "Seems like they're taking a long time in there," he muttered.

The tall boy with the frizzy *Peyoth* got up, thrust his hands into his pockets and paced back and forth.

"Do you really have to do that?" asked Yossi. "You're just making us all more nervous."

The tall boy did not answer. Instead, he sat himself down, folded his hands across his chest and stared at the floor.

Mendy Goldman's father showed up. "I would have come down sooner," he explained, "but I was right in the middle of helping a patient. Has anybody come out and told you anything yet?"

As if someone had read Mr. Goldman's mind, a door opened and a doctor emerged.

"It looks like your rabbi had a minor stroke," said the doctor. "He probably overdid it hiking with you boys, but the medicine I gave him should break up the blood clot without any problem. It's a lucky thing you brought him in when you did. Another half hour or forty-five minutes and he would probably have been permanently paralyzed, if he had survived at all."

Mr. Goldman put his arm around Mendy's shoulders. "That was some pretty level-headed thinking on your part, son."

"Actually, it was Yossi's idea. If he hadn't insisted, I doubt I would have had the guts to do what I did."

"Excuse me," said the police officer who had driven the van to the hospital. "Are you this boy's father?"

"Why yes," answered Mr. Goldman.

"I'm afraid I'm going to have to take your son down to the station."

"What for?"

"Well, he's broken a number of laws, and I'm afraid I have

to book him."

"Book him? You should be congratulating him!"

"I see things somewhat differently, Mr. Goldman. Your son drove a motor vehicle without a license. Furthermore, since the owner was unconscious at the time, he couldn't have had permission to use the vehicle even if he did have a license. Unauthorized use of a motor vehicle is a serious offence."

"That's absurd! My son saved a man's life and you're going to charge him criminally?"

"I'm sorry, Mr. Goldman, but that's the law."

Mr. Goldman's face turned livid, but Mendy tried to calm things down. "Dad, I don't mind going with the officer," he said. "I'm sure we can get this all straightened out..."

"You keep quiet!" commanded Mr. Goldman. "I'll have your badge for this, officer! My son is a hero!"

"Perhaps you think so, but the way I see it, he was endangering himself and whoever else was out on the road."

"But that's the whole point! No one else was in that part of the park. If someone had been, he wouldn't have needed to do what he did."

By this time, the officer had grown impatient. "Look, I'm just doing my job, and the rules about this are clear. Now stop interfering or I'll take you down to the station too!"

Two months later at the County Court, a serious looking Juvenile Magistrate tapped the end of her pencil against a pad of paper after hearing the police officer's testimony.

"Your Honor," began Mendy Goldman's lawyer, "may I say something in this boy's defense?"

The Magistrate shook her head. "I don't think that will be necessary." Looking over the rims of her narrow reading glasses at the police officer, she continued, "Officer, I understand you were just doing your duty by arresting this young man, and I'm not criticizing you for that. Nonetheless, it is plain to me that

there were extenuating circumstances here and that the boy had little choice but to act as he did. In fact, I only wish that all of my cases were this easy to decide. I'm going to enter a finding of 'not delinquent.'"

Mendy smiled as he shook hands with his lawyer. The police officer solemnly gathered some papers off the desk in front of him as he prepared to leave.

The rabbis teach that the Jews had sunk to a very low spiritual level during their enslavement. Although they had not reached the lowest level of impurity, they hovered just above it. When the time arrived for their departure, the Accuser raised an objection. Jews had worshiped idols and committed other sins. They really had no right to a miraculous rescue. Let them drown together with their Egyptian oppressors.

One cannot blame the Accuser for leveling this accusation — after all, it's his job. Nevertheless, the *Haggadah* states that "God saw the Children of Israel, and God knew."[298] The Supreme Judge saw the truth and recognized that extenuating circumstances existed. The brutal slavery had ground the nation down to the point where they did things they otherwise would not have done. The overwhelming influence of Egyptian culture had corrupted them. Although the Accuser's charges were technically true, they did not warrant the punishment he demanded.

Rabbi Yitzchak of K'far Katan trudged along beside his heavily laden donkey. Tired though he was, his heart grew light as he saw the outskirts of the Babylonian village of Punkasya rise

---

[298] Exodus 2:25.

before him. He planned to stay in the village overnight. Another day's travel would bring him to the last stop on his arduous journey from the Land of Israel.

An elderly man with a gnarled white beard hobbled toward him along the road, leaning heavily on a stout walking stick. After Rabbi Yitzchak greeted him, the elder spoke, "I see from your headdress that you are a *Torah* scholar. Thank God that our village has merited such a visitor. Perhaps you can rid us of the wicked demon who plagues us."

The rabbi sighed heavily. "I may perhaps be able to assist you. Tell me something of this creature."

"There is so much to tell that it's difficult to know where to begin. This demon calls himself Argomorph, and he fears nothing, sometimes striking even during the daytime. Almost every villager has had trouble with him."

"It is no small task you request. Can you give any more specifics? Perhaps I will learn something that will give me an idea of the demon's weak spot."

"I can only tell you how my poor father was desperately ill. Then the demon visited him and..." The old man broke off, tears streaming down his wrinkled face.

Rabbi Yitzchak placed a gentle hand upon the man's shoulder. "Now, then, I didn't mean to upset you. You've told me enough. I'm going straight into the village. I'll see what I can find out from the other folks there. Have faith that with *Hashem's* help I may be able to help you."

When the rabbi entered Punkasya and questioned the villagers about Argomorph, almost everyone had his own tale of woe.

"I saw it with my own eyes," said Hyrcanus, the wealthy landowner. "My poor neighbor, Moshe, became ill at the beginning of the harvest season — trapped in bed just at the time when he needed most to be out in his fields. It was then that Argomorph visited a whirlwind on his farm." Hyrcanus shook his

head bitterly.

"I, too, have a tale to tell," ventured a burly farmer. "I was with my young son just outside our home. The two of us were talking when Argomorph suddenly appeared and whisked the boy away. I've never seen my son since." The man's sad eyes bespoke the wrenching grief of a father who has lost a child.

So matters continued throughout the remainder of the day. Villagers of all shapes and sizes, rich and poor, high and low, poured out their wretched tales of sorrow to Rabbi Yitzchak.

That very evening, the rabbi immersed himself in the *Mikveh*, recited a special prayer, and strode calmly to the outskirts of the village to await the demon. Argomorph did not disappoint the sage. A fearsome blur of colorful fire, the demon towered above the lone man. Rabbi Yitzchak did not flinch, however, for he felt confident that, with his faith in *Hashem*, he would prevail.

"Rabbi," spoke the demon, in a harsh, rasping voice. "I sense that you have in your possession a special stone — the one we demons call the stone of truth. Show it to me."

The rabbi hesitated. "Swear first that you will stop harming these villagers."

The demon laughed. "I cannot swear until I see the stone."

"Then swear, at least, that you will not harm me."

The demon laughed again, louder this time. "You know very well that there is no need for me to make such an oath. I cannot harm you even if I wished to, for your *Torah* learning protects you."

"If my *Torah* learning protects me, then may it also protect the innocent inhabitants of this village. Swear, Argomorph, and I will show you the stone."

"You would have me swear not to injure the innocent villagers?"

The rabbi nodded.

"Very well. I wish to see the stone, so I swear."

Rabbi Yitzchak removed a phosphorescent stone from

beneath his cloak. The glow of the fiery demon caused the stone to emit a brilliant array of flashing color.

"How beautiful, rabbi," gloated Argomorph. "Now, let us gaze deeply into the stone."

Rabbi Yitzchak sensed that the demon was playing with him, yet he could not avert his eyes from the stone. In it, he beheld a vision of the old man who had first greeted him as he approached Punkasya. The man appeared at least twenty-five years younger and he was screaming at Argomorph.

"Wicked demon," shouted the man angrily. "My father lay upon his deathbed, but you revived him. Now my hopes of inheriting his money are gone."

In the vision, Argomorph's eyes reveled in this rebuke. "With the cure I gave him, he may live to be a hundred."

"It's unnatural. All know that the old must die to make way for the young. May a thousand curses befall you. I may never live long enough to inherit from the old man. Even if I do, he may use up all his money in the meantime. May a thousand times a thousand curses be upon you!"

The images in the stone changed. This time, it was Hyrcanus, the wealthy landowner, who faced the demon.

"You've wrecked my plans," complained the landowner in frustration. "Had Moshe been unable to harvest his grain, he would not have been able to pay back the hundred *Dinarim* he owes me, and I would have been able to seize his fields as I've always wished. Then you created a whirlwind which harvested all his grain and stacked it up neatly for him. May you descend to the deepest pits of hell where you belong!"

With a shriek of laughter, the demon again disappeared.

Once more, the images in the stone of truth shifted. Finally, Rabbi Yitzchak saw the burly farmer standing with his young son outside their cottage.

"You were late finishing your chores," screamed the father, his speech slurred from heavy drink.

The boy paled with fright, turned, and tried to limp away.

"I'll teach you to try to get away from me," shouted the farmer, his face crimson. He easily overcame the child, seized him, and gripped him firmly. "I said you were late finishing your chores."

The boy shook with fear as he fought to answer. "You know I have trouble walking after you crushed my leg…"

The farmer smacked the boy's face fiercely with the back of his hand. "I only discipline you for your own good, and I don't give you half of what you deserve."

Tears streamed down the child's cheeks, already badly bruised from prior beatings. In a choking voice, he said, "I did the best I could."

"You'll learn to do better when I'm finished with you." He raised his hand to strike again, when Argomorph suddenly appeared. The shocked farmer released his grip. Without a word, the demon seized the boy and disappeared.

The phosphorescent stone showed Argomorph depositing the child far away at the farm of an elderly, childless couple. These kind people took the child in, nursed him back to health, and cared for him as if he were their own son.

The next day, Rabbi Yitzchak of K'far Katan packed his donkey to continue on his journey. Sadly, he informed the villagers that he had been unable to rid them of Argomorph.

"I'm not surprised," said the innkeeper as he wished the rabbi farewell. "All the other great rabbis before you have failed to defeat the demon."

"I'm not surprised either," muttered the rabbi as he went on his way. "Argomorph only promised not to harm innocent villagers — and these people are hardly innocent."

This story illustrates how easy it is for people to twist

around facts to suit themselves. Moreover, human beings may not know enough facts to accurately judge a situation. Only God Himself, Who knows everything, can truly decide what is right and what is wrong.

The Egyptians had a very warped view of justice. They took the position that they were simply exercising a legitimate right of self-defense by enslaving foreigners whose loyalty they deemed questionable. Besides, since God Himself had decreed that the Jews suffer exile and servitude, the Egyptians thought that they were doing nothing more than fulfilling the Divine will.

The *Haggadah* states that, "God saw the Children of Israel, and God knew."[299] *Hashem* knew what was really happening. The Jews had done nothing to warrant suspicions of disloyalty. If anything, their presence benefited the Egyptians. As for fulfilling the Divine will, the Egyptians went far beyond compelling the Jews to work for them. They forced them to perform work which ordinary slaves would never have been required to do. They also tried to drown Jewish babies and committed other atrocities.

Just as the inhabitants of Punkasya could fool a visiting rabbi who did not know all the facts, the Egyptians could deceive themselves. They could not, however, deceive *Hashem*, Who saw what was happening to the Children of Israel and knew the truth.

---

[299] Exodus 2:25.

בְּיָד חֲזָקָה וּבִזְרֹעַ נְטוּיָה
WITH A STRONG HAND AND AN
OUTSTRETCHED ARM

The metaphors of a strong hand and an outstretched arm appear redundant. What is the difference between the two?

Sarah and Tovah were students together in high school. Unfortunately, they were not very attentive pupils, more interested in discussing clothing and video games than in academics. Although they were well-behaved, they frequently handed in assignments late or incomplete. Even then, their work showed that they had paid little attention to what they were taught.

At last, the principal called each girl into her office. She explained that without substantial improvement very soon, she would have no choice but to ask the girls to leave the school.

Sadly, Sarah and Tovah showed almost no concern about the principal's warning. The very next week, Tovah failed to hand in an important paper in history class. She could not tell the teacher that she had not worked on the paper because she was too busy hanging on the telephone talking to friends, so she made up a flimsy excuse. Neither the teacher nor the principal was willing to accept any of Tovah's excuses, however, and she was expelled.

Not long afterwards, Sarah's teachers noticed a remarkable change. Not only did she complete every assignment correctly and on time, but there were even a few occasions when she handed them in ahead of schedule. Her math teacher was so impressed that she said, "I thought I had given out some pretty difficult homework. How did you learn all the material so well?"

Sarah answered with two words: "From Tovah."

The teacher lifted her eyebrows in surprise. "From Tovah? She isn't even in school anymore! How could you learn anything from her?"

"What I meant was that when I saw what happened to her, I realized that I need to be more serious and pay attention to my work."

❖ ❖ ❖ ❖ ❖ ❖ ❖

The punishment of the Egyptians served several purposes. It forced them to release the Jews, and it was fair retribution. *Hashem's* "strong hand" represents those aspects of the plagues.

However, those punishments also served as a warning to the Jews of what might befall them in the future if they disobeyed God. Just as a father might raise his hand threatening to punish a child with an "outstretched arm," the plagues put Israel on notice about the possible consequences of rebelling against *Hashem*.[300]

לֹא עַל יְדֵי מַלְאָךְ
NOT THROUGH A MESSENGER

Hashem usually conducts events through intermediaries. Even when performing miracles, He typically employs agents such as prophets or angels. Why, during the final stage of the departure from Egypt, did God choose to act directly?

There once lived a king whose young son spent much time

---

[300] This story illustrates a point made by the *Yad Mitzrayim*.

playing with other boys near the royal castle.

One time, during a particularly exciting game, the prince tripped and fell in the mud. Hearing the commotion, the king looked out of his window and ordered his servants to take care of the boy. One servant led the child inside where another removed his dirty clothing. The royal laundrymaid took away the soiled garments while the royal valet fetched fresh ones. Another servant drew a bath for the prince. Thus, through their combined efforts, the palace servants restored the prince's dignity.

On another occasion, the king heard shouting outside. When he gazed out of the palace window, he observed the prince playing a wild game with several other boys who looked bigger and older. The game had grown quite rough. Worried that the other youngsters might injure his son, the king sent some servants to bring the prince inside.

On a third occasion, the king heard some commotion and looked out the palace window. This time, however, it was not the prince and his friends getting into mischief. Instead, a horde of fearsome bandits had swooped down and kidnapped him. By the time the king could react, they had carried the terrified boy off to their mountain hideout from where they planned to send ransom demands to the palace.

No sooner had the king witnessed this harrowing event than he donned his heavy armor and assembled his army. Seizing his weapons, he mounted his fastest charger and prepared to lead his soldiers to rescue the prince.

Observing the kings actions, an elderly attendant said, "Begging Your Majesty's pardon, but I could not help noticing that whenever the prince had a mishap in the past, Your Majesty always sent servants to take care of him. Why don't you let your servants and soldiers take care of this matter? Why do you insist on leading the army personally?"

"Don't be foolish!" snapped the king. "When the boy fell in the mud or his playmates got too rough with him, he was in no

real danger, and I could rely upon others to execute my commands. Now that the prince's life is truly in danger, I cannot rely
upon others. I will lead the rescue personally!"

In many situations throughout history, God used angels or
natural phenomena to save the Jewish people. When the Jews
were in Egypt, however, they descended to the forty-ninth level of
impurity. Had they stayed even a moment longer, they would
have been irredeemably lost — so mired in Egyptian culture that
they would never recover.[301] In this dire predicament, *Hashem*
saw fit to "personally" lead the rescue.

The *Torah* says, "You are children to *Hashem*, your God."[302]
Just as a loving father would not want to rely on servants to
rescue his child from mortal peril, *Hashem* did not want to rely on
angels. Rather, God acted "not through an agent, not through an
angel, but the Holy One, Blessed be He, in His glory, personally."

THE PLAGUE OF WILD ANIMALS

The *Torah* uses an unusual term to denote the plague of
wild animals which attacked the Egyptians. Rather than calling
them wild animals (חַיּוֹת), it calls them a mixture (עָרוֹב). The rabbis
explain that the *Torah* uses this designation because a variety of
predators roamed together through Egypt, terrifying Israel's

---

[301] *Maor Veshemesh, Parashath Tzav*, sub verba "*Umipethach*" (ומפתח). This is
why the *Haggadah* says, "If the Holy One, Blessed be He, had not taken our
ancestors out of Egypt, then we, our children, and our children's children
would be enslaved to Pharaoh in Egypt."
[302] Deuteronomy 14:1.

enemies.[303]

What was the significance of this?

One theme of the *Haggadah* is that forces which under other circumstances would oppose one another cooperated to defeat the Egyptians. Fire and water cannot coexist, but the plague of hail consisted of fire inside ice.[304] Ordinarily, different species of wild predators do not act in harmony. To serve *Hashem*, however, they cooperated in attacking the Egyptians.

There is another point to be made as well.

"Thanks for agreeing to go jogging with me," said Shaindy Finkel, an overweight girl.

"I like jogging," answered her friend, Rivkie Cohen.

A block further on, Shaindy called, "Wait up!"

Rivkie stopped. "But we've hardly done anything yet."

"Maybe you haven't," said Shaindy, panting, "but this is a lot for me." She bent over and rested her hands on her knees. "Let me catch my breath for a minute."

Rivkie paused. "Well, nobody says we have to jog the whole time. We can walk a little bit."

Shaindy forced herself to take a few steps along the sidewalk. "I just have to keep reminding myself how important it is for me to lose weight. If I don't do something about it now, when I get older, I'll have a real problem."

Just then, two large dogs, a golden retriever and black Labrador, trotted up on the lawn of a house they were passing.

"Yikes!" shouted Shaindy, moving off the sidewalk and into the street.

"What's the matter with you?" asked Rivkie.

---

[303] *Rashi* on Exodus 8:17, citing *Shemoth Rabbah* 11:2.
[304] Exodus 9:24, according to *Rashi*.

"I don't want to get bitten," explained Shaindy.

"Relax. They like us. See! They're wagging their tails. Besides, they can't leave the yard because the owner has an electronic fence."

"I don't see any fence."

"Read the sign on the lawn."

Sure enough, there was a sign that said, "Dogs contained by invisible electronic fence."

"Okay," said Shaindy, "but suppose the dogs can't read."

"Oh, stop being silly," replied Rivkie. "The dogs wear special collars that give them an electric shock if they get too close to the boundary."

"That doesn't sound very nice."

"It also doesn't seem to be working." The dogs had skipped out onto the sidewalk and headed straight for the girls.

"I told you they couldn't read."

Rivkie dropped down on one knee. "Here boys!" she called. The golden retriever approached and licked Rivkie on the face.

"Gross!" said Shaindy. "You let him lick you?"

"Sure. Our cocker spaniel at home always licks me. You know my older brother, Tzvi? He used to have trouble getting up in time for *Minyan* no matter how my father tried to wake him up. Finally, he trained our dog to jump up on the bed at precisely 6:30 and lick his face."

"Yuck!"

Rivkie shrugged her shoulders. "Well, at least he gets up on time."

While Rivkie affectionately patted the golden retriever, the black Labrador ambled over to Shaindy and started sniffing at her. The golden retriever joined him. "Looks like they like you better than me," said Rivkie.

"Sure. They figure I'll make a bigger meal."

"They're just being friendly. Go ahead and pat them."

Rivkie took Shaindy's hand and started rubbing it along the golden retriever's head and neck. The dog sat down, enjoying this treatment.

"Hey, I think you're right," said Shaindy.

"We'd better take these dogs back into their yard and let their owner know what happened. They shouldn't have come onto the sidewalk like that. Come on, boys." Rivkie clapped her hands. The two dogs obediently followed her up the walk to the door of their home. Shaindy followed at what she deemed a safe distance. A sign on the door read, "Gorovitz." When Rivkie rang the bell, the black Labrador yapped for a moment.

"You must be Mrs. Gorovitz," said Rivkie politely when a middle-aged woman answered. "You've got some really friendly dogs, but I thought you should know that they came out onto the sidewalk. Your dog containment system must not be working right."

The golden retriever jumped up, placed its paws on Rivkie's shoulders, and started licking her face again. "Good boy," said Rivkie, patting the dog with both hands.

"Seems like my dogs have really taken a liking to you," said Mrs. Gorovitz.

"Can they do any tricks?" asked Shaindy timidly.

"These are very smart dogs," explained Mrs. Gorovitz. "My husband and I have taught them all the usual tricks like 'sit,' 'play dead,' 'shake hands,' and 'fetch,' but they also know a few commands most other dogs don't. Watch!" Mrs. Gorovitz snapped her fingers and shouted, "Cry boys! Cry!" The two dogs lay on the ground and covered their eyes with their paws.

"Hey, that's pretty cool," said Shaindy. "Can I try one?"

"All right. Say, 'kiss.'"

"Kiss!" commanded Shaindy. Suddenly, both dogs were upon her, licking at her face. "Oh, yuck! Down boys! Down!" Shaindy wiped at her face while Mrs. Gorovitz and Rivkie laughed. "No wonder they like licking everybody in the face," mut-

tered Shaindy.

"What did you think they were going to do?" asked Mrs. Gorovitz.

"Maybe lick each other?" suggested Shaindy.

"Now watch this," continued Mrs. Gorovitz. "Run boys! Run!" The two dogs started scampering wildly up and down the yard, yapping merrily. "Here Happy! Here Lucky!" The dogs returned obediently to Mrs. Gorovitz and sat thumping their tails against the ground.

"Happy and Lucky?" asked Rivkie. "Those are their names?"

"Yes. The black one is Happy and the gold one is Lucky."

"I'll bet you really enjoy having such nice dogs."

"My husband and I do enjoy them, but I think they miss my children. My older ones are married, and my youngest is away at seminary. The dogs don't get to play with a young person anymore."

"I wouldn't mind playing with them," offered Rivkie.

"That's nice of you. Any time you girls are in the area, feel free to come into the yard and play with Happy and Lucky as much as you like."

A few days later, Shaindy Finkel and Rivkie Cohen already felt like a couple of pros as they jogged along the sidewalk.

On this particular occasion, Rachel Attar, a more experienced runner, joined her friends. When the girls reached an intersection with a red traffic signal, Rivkie stopped jogging and put her hands on her hips. Shaindy also stopped, letting out a deep breath of relief.

"You two shouldn't stop," said Rachel, jogging in place. "Just keep going like I am. That's what builds up the stamina."

Shaindy waved her hand dismissively. "I don't think I'm ready for that yet."

"You've improved a lot, though," said Rivkie. "Remember how you used to have so much trouble keeping up with me?"

"Yeah, I can feel my leg muscles strengthening."

A few blocks later, the girls found themselves confronted by two tough looking teenage boys who suddenly planted themselves menacingly on the sidewalk. Rachel, who was slightly ahead of her friends, stopped in her tracks when she saw them.

"Uh, oh," said Shaindy quietly. "I heard that some non-Jewish boys were picking on kids near the boys' day school."

"My brother, Tzvi, told me that one boy needed stitches after they got through with him," said Rivkie uneasily.

"Look who it is," sneered the taller of the two hoodlums. "Nice Jewish girls."

"Don't try to start anything," warned Rachel defiantly.

"My buddy and I just want to use the sidewalk, but you're in the way."

"We have as much right to use the sidewalk as you do."

"Oh, yeah?" The boy punched his fist into the palm of his hand menacingly.

"Something's not right with these guys," Shaindy whispered.

"That's putting it mildly," Rivkie whispered back.

"What I mean is, they're trying too hard to look tough." Both boys had on tattered jeans so badly stained and faded that it looked as if they never taken them off since they bought them. The sleeves of their sweatshirts had been ripped off, and the writing on one included some words Jews should not use.

"There are stores where kids can buy clothes like that," continued Rivkie in a low, nervous voice.

"Right," replied Shaindy, "but sometimes, when a person tries too hard to give a certain impression, it means that inside he's really the opposite."

"The only impression I'm getting is that these guys are a couple of jerks."

"What I mean is that inside they lack self-confidence. They're really cowards who scare easily. Go ahead and give a

whistle!"

"A whistle?" Then it dawned on Rivkie what Shaindy meant. The workers had still not come out to fix Mrs. Gorovitz's electronic dog fence.

Rivkie whistled.

"Look at the little Jew-girl's adorable ponytail," said the taller boy sarcastically.

"Aw, how cute," said the other bully.

"How about a little game of pull the ponytail." The bigger boy took a wild swipe at Rachel's head, but Rachel easily dodged out of the way.

"Get away from me!" shouted Rachel, backing away.

"Darn! Hold still!" complained the boy. "I need more practice." But just as the bully raised his hand for another attempt, Happy and Lucky came charging out of their yard. Happy did not look very happy, however. Neither did Lucky. The two dogs lowered their tails as they snarled menacingly at the hoodlums.

"What gives here?" demanded the taller boy, a frightened tone entering his voice.

"My dogs don't like it when they think I'm being threatened," explained Rivkie firmly.

The boys lifted their hands, trying to keep them out of biting range. "Well, call your dogs off us," said the shorter boy.

"Yeah, I was just playing," said the taller boy nervously. "Can't you girls take a joke?"

"Apparently not," answered Rivkie coolly.

Happy let out a low growl. "Look," said the shorter boy, his voice growing high-pitched. "I said call your dogs off."

"It's not so simple," explained Rivkie. "I can't always control them when they think me or my friends are being threatened."

"What should we do?" asked the taller boy.

"Try backing away real slowly."

The two supposedly tough guys took a few hesitant steps backwards, but Happy and Lucky continued to advance on them. "It isn't working," said the smaller boy desperately.

"Then I think the only other thing you can do," said Rivkie, "is...RUN!" Happy and Lucky responded instantly to Rivkie's command, scampering madly up and down the sidewalk.

"That girl's dogs have gone crazy!" exclaimed the taller boy.

"Let's get out of here!" shouted the smaller one.

The bullies sprinted away, but they were no match for the speed of Happy and Lucky who chased after them, snapping and yipping at their heels. After the dogs had gotten halfway down the block, Rivkie let out a shrill whistle and dropped to her knees. Happy and Lucky raced back, nearly knocking Rivkie over as she hugged and patted them enthusiastically. "Good boys!"

Shaindy got down on one knee and started patting Lucky, who licked her hard on the face.

"I thought you didn't like being licked on the face," said Rivkie gleefully.

"I guess I'm getting used to it."

In this story, Shaindy Finkel discovered that the very thing she originally feared saved her. King Solomon wrote that "When *Hashem* is pleased with a man's ways, even his enemies make peace with him."[305]

Ordinarily, wild animals do not discriminate among ethnic groups, and Jews have just as much reason to fear them as anyone else. During the Ten Plagues, however, they attacked only the Egyptians, leaving the Jews in peace.[306]

---

[305] Proverbs 16:7.
[306] Exodus 8:18.

The *Talmud* teaches that two angels — one good and one evil — accompany a person when he returns home from the synagogue on Friday evening. If everything is prepared nicely to greet *Shabbath*, the good angel says, "May it be God's will that it should be so next *Shabbath*," and the evil angel answers "*Amen!*"[307]

When a person serves *Hashem* properly, even those things he would least expect help from are at his service.

אִלּוּ קֵרְבָנוּ לִפְנֵי הַר סִינַי

IF HE HAD BROUGHT US BEFORE MOUNT SINAI, IT WOULD HAVE BEEN ENOUGH!

Why does the *Haggadah* state that if *Hashem* "had brought us before Mount Sinai but not given us the *Torah*, it would have been enough?" What benefit would the Jews have gained from traveling to Mount Sinai had they not received the *Torah*?

One time, a king needed to select an officer to handle palace security, a highly prized position. Besides supervising the palace guards, the king would expect the officer to constantly review and improve the palace's defenses. The officer would have to be adept at the use of swords, pistols, and other weapons, as well as hand to hand combat.

Choosing the right individual — a person who was shrewd, highly skilled, and immensely loyal — was not a simple task. As an initial step, the king decided to hold a series of con-

---

[307] B.T. *Shabbath* 119B.

tests. Any person in the land could compete in the sharpshooting match, wrestling, and other activities designed to identify the most likely candidates. After that, the king planned to check the background and integrity of the winners to select the new officer.

When news of the contest reached a tiny outlying farm village, everyone agreed that Will Stout should travel to the palace, for he was the most capable man there. As for strength, everyone knew that Will could chop down a whole acre of forest in half a day without feeling winded. As for leadership, no one in the village would think of making a serious decision for the community without first consulting Will, whose sound advice everyone respected.

All of the townsfolk felt proud and excited about their representative. The entire village pitched in to help with Will Stout's travel expenses, and not a single person failed to show up for his departure. Little children danced around him merrily as he set off for the capital with his heavily laden donkey.

Will Stout performed well in many of the contests at the palace, but, quite naturally, it was difficult to win against such a large number of highly qualified people. When the king announced the winners, everyone cheered. The king then thanked his other loyal citizens for participating and sent each one home with a gold coin as a token of his appreciation.

It was then that Will Stout spoke up. "Your Majesty," he said, "I think I speak on behalf of all of us who are going back home when I say that although we did not win this contest, it has been a huge honor and privilege just to be greeted by Your Majesty and to see the wonderful sights of our nation's glorious capital and Your Majesty's palace." At that, another cheer rose from the crowd.

Even if *Hashem* had not given us the *Torah*, just being greeted by His Divine Presence and observing the splendor of Mount Sinai would have been a tremendous honor and privilege all by itself.

פֶּסַח
THE PASSOVER SACRIFICE

It was King Dorian who first managed to free himself from the ropes which bound his hands and feet. Three hours of steady chafing against the sharp edge of a stone had paid off.

"Never has the air tasted sweeter," exclaimed the young king after removing the gag from his mouth. Sunshine filtering through the pine trees sparkled upon the beads of sweat which dampened the king's blonde hair.

King Dorian glanced around at his men. "I see fear in your eyes, Lord Blackwood." He stared hard at a man of vast girth, his face darkened by a stubbly black beard. "I suppose you can't mutter your silly incantations with your mouth stuffed. Anyway, I doubt your spells have ever proved useful." Lord Blackwood stared back at the king with imploring eyes.

The king turned his gaze to an elderly gentleman. "Pendergast presents a completely different aspect. It seems to me that you are smiling, my trusted friend, confident that you will shortly have your freedom."

Finally, King Dorian looked at his third companion, a tall man of athletic build, his face graced with a huge red moustache that curled at the ends. "As for you, Lord Crofton, I sense some frustration in your eyes. Upset that it was not you who freed himself first?" The edges of the red moustache which protruded from behind the cloth gag twitched. Dorian laughed. "Too bad

your brilliant network of spies didn't detect my brother's plotting before we were all abducted. I hope your skills as a general will prove better at winning back my throne."

The king sighed. Within thirty minutes, he had freed his companions. All four men paced back and forth, rubbing the places where the ropes had bitten into their flesh.

"Begging Your Majesty's pardon, but you should not speak disrespectfully of my spells," said Lord Blackwood at length. "They contain powerful magic that ..."

"Could not even release us from our fetters," finished King Dorian sarcastically.

"Your Majesty does not understand. If I had my potions with me..."

"Pendergast," interrupted the king, "we are without quill and parchment, but make a mental note to remind me the next time my brother Francis decides to kidnap us that I must insist that he have the courtesy to send along a supply of potions for Lord Blackwood."

"Your Majesty," spoke up Lord Crofton, "I hardly think Blackwood can be blamed. He doesn't have the practical turn of mind that a military man such as myself does. It's not his fault if he is a bit incompetent."

"Incompetent!" exclaimed Lord Blackwood in outrage. "Me? Incompetent? You miserable excuse for a general! You're just trying to divert the blame for all this from yourself!"

"Now, now, Blackwood." Lord Crofton laughed with the cold tone of one who is sure of his superiority. "Don't take on so."

"Pardon me, Your Majesty," interrupted Pendergast, clearing his throat. "We cannot waste any time with this type of conversation. We must figure out how to return to Arnbruck."

"Pendergast is right," announced King Dorian, his voice barely audible above the ranting of his other two adjutants.

"Very well," declared Lord Blackwood, turning from Lord Crofton, a purple vein throbbing in his right temple. "The first

thing to do is to pray to the gods of earth, fire, air, and water."

King Dorian planted his fists firmly upon his hips. "Didn't I just tell you to forget about your silly magic?"

"Your Majesty, I hardly think…"

"You can stop right there," interrupted Lord Crofton, sneering. "I quite agree. You hardly think." He paused stiffly before continuing. "Just look around. We are on an island where there is plenty of air, plenty of earth, and we are surrounded by water. Now if only I had some fire to burn you beard!"

"Your Majesty!" gasped Lord Blackwood, placing his hands on his stubbly beard.

"Oh, come now, Blackwood! You know Crofton would never do such a thing." The king stepped between his two councilors and placed his arms upon their shoulders. "Must you really act like foolish children? We are trapped in a deadly situation. We must work together." He nodded his head toward his elderly servant. "Pendergast, I would hear your counsel."

"Well, Your Majesty, it was quite dark when the rebels brought us to this island. I have no military training, nor am I conversant with the spirits, but my general sense of direction tells me that we should head this way." He pointed. "I think that is where we came from. Once we reach the edge of the island on that side, we can decide how to escape."

"Now you see, gentlemen," said the king amiably, "wasn't that simple?" With that, the men set off. Fortunately, very little undergrowth covered the ground, so an hour's march was all it took to reach the edge of the island.

"Ah!" exclaimed Lord Crofton. "It is clear where we are now."

"Yes," agreed King Dorian. "I know the place myself." He pointed towards a rocky coastline across a wide channel of water. "That narrow rock that juts up straight out of the sea is Icicle Point." Glancing about him, the king detected that only two of his men were with him. "What in blazes happened to Blackwood?"

"Here, Sire," came a cry from the woods. After a few moments, Lord Blackwood emerged, waving his right hand aloft to signal the others, his left hand mopping his forehead with a handkerchief. "Here, Sire. I just couldn't keep up with you."

"What were you doing back there?" demanded Lord Crofton. "Babbling more idiotic incantations?" But his voice sounded less harsh than it had earlier. Lord Blackwood merely glared at him.

"I beg Your Majesty's pardon for the delay," said Lord Blackwood as he planted his spacious person upon a piece of driftwood and panted heavily.

"Granted," said King Dorian smiling. "I do hope you'll come up with a spell some day that will help you reduce your girth."

After some discussion, the four men decided to build a raft to cross the channel. Although their craft sank during the voyage, it brought them close enough to the mainland so that they could swim ashore.

"Sire, I simply must rest," begged Lord Blackwood, letting off a tremendous sneeze. "That swim nearly did me in."

"We might not have sunk had you listened to Pendergast and not shifted your weight so." Nonetheless, King Dorian sat himself upon an outcropping of rock.

"I for one say we must continue pressing on," insisted Lord Crofton, casting a harsh look at Lord Blackwood.

"And why, pray tell, do you say so?" demanded the magician, still panting.

"Because that is the military way. When my men and I set out upon a mission, we make use of all available daylight to press on."

"Do I look like one of your soldiers, then? Am I a youngster of eighteen or nineteen years?"

Lord Crofton eyed Lord Blackwood's huge bulk. "You eat enough to feed an army! I'll wager that!"

"Balderdash! We simply must stop!"

The general's face reddened. "And I say we press on!"

"When we return home, I shall use my potions to turn you into a slimy worm!"

While Lords Crofton and Blackwood were thus engaged in yet another "gentlemanly" and "reasoned" discussion, King Dorian turned to Pendergast. "Well," he said, examining his damp clothing, "what say you, Pendergast?"

The elderly valet smiled. "Your Majesty knows that I am not trained in military matters as is Lord Crofton, nor very sharp at scientific inquiry as is Lord Blackwood, but the sun is low in the sky. Since we will very likely not get much further today and will not wish to make camp in the wild, I suggest we seek refuge in the Jewish village to the east."

"Jewish village to the east? You know how to get there?"

"May it please Your Majesty, your father and I had occasion to visit that village several times, and we were always greeted warmly by its inhabitants."

By this time, Lords Crofton and Blackwood had stopped arguing. Each sat with his arms folded, fuming and refusing to acknowledge the other. At the mention of the Jewish village, however, Lord Blackwood remarked, "You cannot go to Jews. They do not worship earth, fire, air, and water."

Unable to contain himself, Lord Crofton blurted, "I for one think we have all had quite enough of water for one day. We have no reliable way to make a fire and, thanks to you, we will be sleeping tonight on the hard earth out in the cold air."

At this, Lord Blackwood lashed out again, uttering an intricate curse vile enough to rattle the bones of Lord Crofton's departed ancestors, who seemed to be the target of the greater portion of it. Thus, the two men resumed their quarrel even more loudly and vehemently than before.

Meanwhile, King Dorian nodded at Pendergast, who began to walk with the king in the direction of the Jewish village. By this time, the irate general had Lord Blackwood by the collar and raised his fist threateningly. "I'll put a bruise on that fine mouth of yours that will keep your curses shut up for the longest while!"

"Look," said Lord Blackwood meekly, his eyes following King Dorian and the valet. "They're leaving us."

Lord Crofton released his grip, causing the magician to fall heavily upon some rocks and release a muted shriek. Within a minute, the two of them had caught up with the king.

"As much as I disdain Blackwood's opinion in most matters, Your Highness," said Lord Crofton, "I must caution you about the Jews. Their race is known to be devious and conniving."

"Then you would have us make camp in the middle of nowhere?" replied King Dorian mildly.

"It may be safer than putting ourselves at the mercy of people who might sell us to our enemies. If we are captured, your brother will surely have us killed."

"You have a point, Crofton," continued the king. "How well do you know the Jews of this village, Pendergast?"

The old valet looked with penetrating blue eyes first at the strutting general and then at the king. "Quite well, Your Majesty. Prince Francis has a rather broad reputation as a Jew-hater. Combine that with his reputation as an ill-tempered sot and wastrel, and I think you will find the Jews siding with Your Majesty."

"We shall take our chances with the Jews then," said King Dorian with a tone of finality.

The men made good time, reaching the Jewish village an hour before sunset.

"Look at all these people milling about the town square," commented the king as he strode into the village with his companions. "Their faces do not have a very merry cast."

"Lazy Jews!" muttered Lord Blackwood under his breath. "They probably do nothing but mill about all day long."

"I'd say you could teach them a lesson or two in that direction," hissed Lord Crofton.

King Dorian's trusted servants were about to enter upon another nasty quarrel when the shout of an elderly man interrupted them. "It's him! It's His Majesty!" The eyes of the square's inhabitants turned with astonished looks as the old man pointed towards the king. "Thank God, we're saved!"

"The king! It's the king!" Excited cheers raced through the crowded square.

A young man of about twenty seized the king's hand and, bowing low, kissed it. "Nathan Levy at your service, Sire." He turned and motioned to a much younger boy who jostled his way through the crowd. Trembling a bit at the sight of His Royal Majesty, the lad nevertheless managed to bow. "My brother, Isaac," said Nathan.

Two girls also came forward and curtsied politely before the king. Suddenly, the younger of the two burst into tears.

"Why, whatever is the matter, young miss?" asked King Dorian gently.

"Is it true what everyone is saying?" answered the girl, who could not have been much older than nine.

The king glanced with concern at his companions, then asked, "And what is everyone saying?"

"That Your Majesty has come to rescue us from Prince Francis."

King Dorian looked knowingly at Lords Crofton and Blackwood as if to say, "I suppose you won't be questioning the loyalty of the inhabitants of this village any longer."

"Take no offence at the words of my sister," spoke up Nathan, "but surely Your Majesty knows that Prince Francis has arrested dozens of Jewish leaders, including my father, Jacob." A slight tremor entered the young man's voice, and he lowered his eyes.

"Jacob Levy," said Pendergast thoughtfully. "No doubt he refers to Jacob the Jeweler, Sire."

"Your lordship knows my father then?"

"Most certainly. Finest jeweler in all Arnbruck in my opinion."

"Francis arrested him?" interjected the king.

"Together with many others. He issued an edict commanding all Jews to leave the kingdom within a fortnight. Any who remain will be burned at the stake...," the youth's voice trailed off, "...together with my father."

"Your Majesty will need food and shelter," spoke up the older of Nathan's sisters. "You must come to our home. It is nothing compared to a great palace, but ours is the largest in the village."

At dinner, it was young Isaac who proved most talkative, telling the king's entourage all about the plans for his *Bar Mitzvah* that would be coming up in six months. In his naive youth, he had forgotten the grave peril the Jews faced.

"I heard that Your Majesty is quite fond of dogs," said Isaac. "Is it true that your kennels house over a thousand of the finest in the world?"

The boy's high spirits made King Dorian laugh. "I'm afraid that rumor is a bit exaggerated, though I have my share of fine hunting dogs, and I am fond of them."

"We have a Great Dane, but mother won't let him inside the house. I have to keep him in our stable with the horses. Your Highness should see how I can make his coat glow when I wash and brush him."

"Really, Isaac, you should not distract the king and his ministers with so much talk," said Mrs. Levy as she placed cakes on the table for desert.

"Quite a satisfying meal, Madam," said Lord Blackwood, patting his huge mid-section with both hands. "I really doubt I have room for desert."

Lord Crofton opened his mouth to comment, but King Dorian nudged him sharply with his elbow. The general then wiped at his great moustache with a napkin and said, "I quite agree, Madam. An excellent supper."

"Would Your Majesty like to try some barley beer?" interrupted Isaac. "My father showed me how to make it, and I've got quite a supply out in the shed."

"Didn't I just tell you to leave these gentlemen alone, Isaac?" said his mother.

"It's quite all right, Madam," said the king pleasantly. "I'd be most delighted to sample your son's brew." Once the boy had left, he turned to the others. "It is clear that we must act quickly to stop Francis."

"I am at your service, Sire," said Nathan, who overheard the remark. "I am sure the other young men in the village would join me."

Lord Crofton looked doubtfully at the young man. "How are you at handling a sword?"

"A sword, sir? I've never done it, but I'm sure I could learn."

The general shook his head. "It's not as simple as it seems."

"What skills *do* you have?" asked the king.

"My father has trained me as a jeweler, Your Majesty. There isn't too much call for that trade in our village which is why he spends so much time in the capital. Still, I am good with my hands. I can do all manner of delicate work, fixing clockworks, mending locks. Things like that."

"Your intentions are noble," said Lord Crofton, "but I don't see how a man like you would help in a military campaign."

"What is your counsel, Pendergast?" asked the king.

The old valet smiled. "Once again, I'm afraid I know little of the strategies of combat, but it seems to me that we could have much use for a man who knows how to pick locks."

Lord Crofton's eyebrows rose. "Pick locks? He spoke of mending them."

"Do you suppose you could do that?" inquired King Dorian. "Picking open locks could prove most useful."

By this time, Isaac had returned with a decanter of dark beer and several small glasses. "He can pick open a lock, all right. He's even shown me how to do it."

"I say we find a way to send a message to Lord Frothing-ham," said Lord Crofton, pouring out barley beer for himself and the company. "I am certain that he remains loyal to Your Majesty and can organize the army so that as soon as we return to the capital, we can arrest Prince Francis and his cutthroats."

"A good plan," agreed the king, "but who will get the message there?"

"I'd gladly volunteer," said Nathan.

King Dorian sniffed at the beer in his glass. He looked at Isaac. "Smells quite strong."

"My special recipe," declared the boy proudly.

"If it's at all decent," said Lord Blackwood, "I shall have to add it to my own list of potions." With that, he downed the beer. "Mmmm...quite good, actually." He poured himself some more. "To the king!"

"To the King!" answered everyone present.

"For once I agree with Blackwood," said Lord Crofton. "The beer is quite excellent. I do not think it wise, however, to send young Nathan with a message to Lord Frothingham."

King Dorian gave the general a look of mild surprise.

"Oh, I do not question his loyalty, Your Majesty," continued Lord Crofton. "After all, his own father's life is at stake. But a young man entering the capital at this time would arouse too much suspicion."

It was then that Pendergast's gaze fell upon young Isaac. The king noticed this and also looked at the boy.

"Me?" asked Isaac, surprise and eagerness all jumbled up together in his voice.

Mrs. Levy came forward. "Why, of course, you could do it, Isaac. You know you're almost *Bar Mitzvah*." She turned to the king. "I have a stocking cap and breeches that would make him look like any peasant boy out of a thousand. No one would realize what he was up to."

"But entrusting the fate of the entire kingdom in the hands of a mere boy?" Lord Blackwood shook his head. "It oughtn't be done!"

King Dorian continued to gaze at Isaac. "He is young, but he has a courageous spirit, and that should count for something."

"Scrawny, I say," continued Lord Blackwood.

"Anyone would look scrawny compared to you," declared Lord Crofton.

Lord Blackwood opened his mouth to respond, but the king tapped him sternly on his foot beneath the table. "What then is your opinion, Crofton?" asked the king.

The general cleared his throat. "I did say myself that we

must send our instructions to Lord Frothingham discreetly." He hesitated. "Still, a boy, Sire?"

Isaac stood transfixed by all this attention. He suddenly sensed the true importance of his mission, and it sent shivers down his spine.

"And you, Pendergast?" continued King Dorian. "Your view?"

Pendergast nodded. "If I am any judge of character, he can do it, Your Majesty. I can see it in him."

"What about you, Isaac?" asked the king. "Can you promise never to betray your king, no matter what?"

The boy gulped and nodded.

"They may torture you if they catch you," said Pendergast. "Are you prepared for that?"

Isaac nodded again, adding almost in a whisper, "My life for my king!"

About mid-morning the next day, a ragged youngster, who looked no different from any of the hundreds of farmboys wandering about Arnbruck, strode along the king's highway. When the sun reached the middle of the sky, Isaac found a shady spot near a brook to eat a lunch consisting of black bread and a lump of cheese he had stored inside his stocking cap. No sooner had he finished this simple fare than three masked men rode up.

"What's your business here?" demanded the tallest of them.

'Bandits,' thought Isaac to himself. 'But what can they want of me?' Then aloud he answered, "My father is the freeman Rudolph. I'm on my way to check his flocks."

"You lie, boy," sneered the stranger.

"Why should I lie?" Isaac sensed something was wrong. "If it's gold you're after, you won't find any with me."

The two accomplices of the tall bandit dismounted and started to approach the boy. "Do you suppose Prince Francis has

no spies?"

Isaac's jaw dropped. He tried to leap across the brook, but in his panic, his feet slipped on a mossy rock. The men pounced upon him.

"Your real name, then, boy!" demanded the tall bandit.

"Peter!" Isaac gasped under the crush of the men. "The son of Rudolph. I don't know what you want. You can ask any in the village who I am."

The tall bandit approached with a casual air. "Turn him around" he said. The ruffians flipped Isaac around to face their leader. "You know, boy, you're rather puny. It wouldn't take much to break such small bones, and your pretences won't help you. Tell us the message King Dorian gave you!"

Isaac felt the blood rush to his face. 'So these devils know,' he thought to himself, but before he could say anything, the leader belted him in the stomach.

"Perhaps that will knock a few words out of you," he declared contemptuously. Isaac thought he could see the man's eyes smiling behind the mask. He had to think fast, but the blow had knocked the wind out of him, and his mind whirled. He felt nauseous.

"I don't know what you're talking about." Isaac managed to choke out the words.

The tall villain unsheathed a dagger from his belt. He ran his gloved finger along the shiny blade. "You don't seem to hear very well, young man. For that you may lose an ear!"

Isaac's jaw dropped in terror. He trembled wildly, but the hoodlums held him fast.

"Now, now," continued the bandit. "You needn't get upset. Just tell us the king's message and all will be well."

Isaac immediately clamped his mouth shut. A vision of his father leaped into his mind. 'Let them torture me,' he thought. 'I'll never betray the king!'

The leader of the villains nodded at one of the men who

held Isaac. The man wrenched the boy's arm up behind his back, causing him to yelp in agony.

"That's better," said the leader. "At least we are getting something out of your mouth now. Tell us who you are traveling to meet."

Isaac clenched his mouth shut again and tried to look defiant. A nod from the leader brought another wrenching pull at Isaac's arm. The boy wondered frantically how much more pressure his shoulder could bear before his arm popped out of its socket.

"Still nothing?" The leader shook his head. "I'm afraid you'll look rather poorly with your ears missing. I'll give you a moment to think it over." He paused. Isaac could tell that the fiend was savoring every moment of this. "Well? Will you talk?"

The pain in Isaac's arm and shoulder were unbearable now. Still, he managed to say, "I tell you I know nothing!"

"It's a pity," said the leader. "I'm afraid that leaves me with no choice." With that, he removed his mask.

"Nathan!" shouted Isaac. The other men released him and took off their masks as well. "King Dorian! Lord Crofton!"

Nathan started laughing. Isaac rubbed his sore shoulder. "Very funny! You just wait until we get back home!"

The king drew Isaac close and tousled his hair. "You don't understand, Isaac. We had to do it. Anyone can say that he is loyal to the king, but promises are often easily spoken and easily broken."

"Well put, Sire," agreed Lord Crofton.

Isaac, still probing his shoulder, continued to scowl at Nathan, but the king hugged the boy to him. "I'm sorry I had to put you through this, Isaac, but your mission is so important that I had to be absolutely certain you could handle it. I had to make sure that your courageous words of loyalty would be matched by deeds."

❖ ❖ ❖ ❖ ❖ ❖ ❖

The Jews in Egypt were like a boy before his *Bar Mitzvah*. Although he has received plenty of training and is full of the enthusiasm of youth, he is not yet obligated to observe the *Torah* and remains untested.

When Moses went to save the Jewish people from Egyptian slavery, he did so for the purpose of bringing them to Mount Sinai to receive the *Torah* and become *Hashem's* loyal servants. The Jews accepted this mission, as the *Torah* says, "The people believed and listened, for *Hashem* remembered the Children of Israel and saw their affliction, and they bowed and prostrated themselves."[308]

Affirmations of loyalty are not enough, however. *Hashem* wished to be certain that the Jews would *act* loyally as well. For this reason, He required them to take lambs — animals which the Egyptians worshiped — and slaughter them as sacrifices. Although this meant risking their lives and safety, the Jews willingly complied. It was this action which proved their loyalty to God.

בְּכָל דּוֹר וָדוֹר חַיָּב אָדָם
IN EVERY GENERATION
A PERSON IS OBLIGED TO VIEW HIMSELF
AS THOUGH HE EXITED EGYPT

Many nations celebrate holidays which commemorate historic events, but the *Haggadah* carries matters a step further. Passover is not simply a day devoted to remembering events of long ago. Rather, a person must view himself as though he personally departed Egypt. What does this really mean? What

---

[308] Exodus 4:31.

additional element does the *Torah* expect Jews to add to their observance of Passover beyond a historical commemoration?

Joe Grossman's eyes fluttered. He felt another hand pressing his own. It felt warm and comforting, yet somehow awkward and out of place.

"Joe, can you hear me?"

Taking a moment to focus his eyes, Joe realized that the hand belonged to his wife and that she was addressing him. "Yeah," he answered dully. "What's going on? Where are we?"

"In the hospital, Joe. *Baruch Hashem*, you've finally regained consciousness. You've been through quite a bit."

Joe wrinkled his forehead. Still trying to focus his eyes, he tried to raise himself. "Can you make this bed go up or something?"

"Of course." Mrs. Grossman touched a switch on the side of the bed that made the upper half rise. "That better?"

"Yes. I remember a crash and an explosion. How long have I been here?"

"About twenty-five years."

"Twenty-five years?" Excitement rose in Joe's voice.

His wife squeezed his hand. "The doctor says you shouldn't exert yourself. Try not to move around too much just yet."

"Twenty-five years," repeated the patient. "How can I have been here that long? Where are the children? Have they all grown up?"

Mrs. Grossman hesitated, a puzzled look on her face. "What do you mean? They were all grown up before the accident. With modern cryogenics, doctors can freeze and preserve a person for hundreds of years, if necessary."

"Cryogenics? Hundreds of years?" An agitated expres-

sion swept over Joe's face. "That's science fiction!"

Mrs. Grossman turned her face from her husband to hide her pained expression. "The doctor was afraid... I mean you had quite a bit of surgery. You probably need to rest."

"What about our bank account?   I remember we were almost overdrawn, and I gave you a check and a deposit slip.   Did you make the deposit?"

Mrs. Grossman turned back to her husband, tears welling up in her eyes. "A deposit slip? Oh, Joe..."

"What did I say? What's wrong?"

Their conversation was interrupted by the appearance of Dr. Weingutt. Joe Grossman's blurred vision had improved to the point where he could detect that the young doctor might be in his thirties. "Well, Mr. Grossman, your tests look pretty good. You can probably go home in another week."

"Sounds great, doc." Joe smiled stiffly, not only because he felt awkward, but also because the muscles in his face felt strange — as though they had not been used in a long time. "Can I ask you a question?"

"Of course."   Dr. Weingutt's voice sounded confident. "It's my job to answer your questions."

"My wife says I've been here for twenty-five years. Is that right?"

At this, the doctor's demeanor abruptly changed. Before he could answer, Mrs. Grossman interrupted. "Could I speak to you outside for a moment, doctor?"

Out in the hospital corridor, Mrs. Grossman said, "I'm terribly worried about him. How are his kidneys and his liver?"

"Well, as you know, they were completely destroyed by the explosion when his spaceship got too close to that black hole. The cloned organs I replaced them with appear to be doing fine. With computerized robotics, these types of transplants are so routine that anyone just out of medical school can manage it."

Mrs. Grossman nodded. "He seems all right physically,

but I'm worried about his mind. When I mentioned to him that he had been kept alive cryogenically, he shouted something about science fiction. Then he asked whether our children are grown when they were all over a hundred years old before he started that trip. Then he said something about a deposit slip."

"What's a deposit slip?"

Mrs. Grossman forced a sad smile. "I keep forgetting how young you are, Dr. Weingutt. Today, all bank deposits are made electronically, but more than a hundred years ago people used to fill out printed forms called deposit slips and go to the bank to deposit money. It's as if my husband thinks he's living back then."

Dr. Weingutt tapped the end of his polyscope against his forehead thoughtfully. "Let's hope it's only a temporary problem with his mind, as you say. I'm only a doctor, but every child knows that black holes have such tremendous gravitational pull that even light cannot escape from them. Time also becomes warped in their vicinity. I'm not an expert about the type of Rambasco generator used to power your husband's ship, but some scientists have hypothesized that if the super-photons used in those generators would come too close to a black hole, they might cause some kind of fracture in time itself."

Mrs. Grossman's eyes widened in horror. "You mean that it may not just be Joe's mind. He might actually somehow *exist* in another time period!"

Dr. Weingutt nodded. "But before we get carried away, let me speak to him for a moment." He paused. "You wait here."

The doctor returned ten minutes later looking pale and tense. "Physically, he's fine, and his responses to my questions reflect a normal frame of mind, but…"

"But what, doctor?"

"He continued to talk about things which don't exist. How old is your husband anyway?"

"One hundred fifty-two."

"Quite young by today's standards, yet he asked me to find out if you had taken care of changing the oil in his car."

Mrs. Grossman let out a gasp. "Gasoline powered cars haven't been used since before Joe was born!"

Joe Grossman tossed fitfully in the hospital bed. Suddenly, he found himself blinking his eyes and staring at his wife. "Is that you, Sarah?"

A smile lit up Mrs. Grossman's face as she leaned closer to her husband. *"Baruch Hashem,* this is the first time you've spoken since the accident."

Joe reached around to try to fluff up the pillows behind his back.

"Don't move too much, yet," said his wife. "You had quite a concussion. I'll raise the bed for you." She touched a switch that raised the top of the bed. "That better?"

"Yes, I had the strangest dream, Sarah..." A look of astonishment suddenly passed over Joe's face as he caught sight of himself in a mirror that hung over a nearby wash basin. "My face! Why do I look so old?"

Mrs. Grossman smiled gently. "You can't expect to look too young when you're over eighty."

"Over eighty? You know I'm over a hundred fifty, but with my DNA replacement grafts, I shouldn't look like this." His gaze turned back to his wife. "And you! You haven't looked so old in years."

Their conversation was interrupted by the appearance of a doctor who appeared to Joe as if he might be in his thirties.

Patting her husband gently on the hand and fighting back feelings of hurt and anxiety, Mrs. Grossman said, "This is Dr. Guttwein, Joe."

The doctor smiled. "Your test results look good, but I'm

afraid you'll have to stay in the hospital a bit longer."

"What's that black thing hanging around your neck, doctor?"

"Why, a stethoscope, of course."

"But if you're a doctor, why don't you have a polyscope?"

Dr. Guttwein gave a puzzled look and turned to Mrs. Grossman. "May I speak with you in the corridor for a moment?"

Outside, the doctor said, "It's fortunate the firefighters were able to drag your husband from that car wreck seconds before the gas tank exploded. Had he suffered any greater damage to his kidneys and liver, I couldn't have saved him."

"Your performance was wonderful, doctor. Physically, he seems all right, but that concussion...I think it may have done something to his mind. He seemed startled by his own appearance and muttered some nonsense about DNA replacement grafts. And did you see how strangely he acted about your stethoscope?"

"You wait here for a minute, while I check on him a little further."

Ten minutes later, Dr. Guttwein returned, visibly shaken. "His vital signs look fine, and he appears to respond normally when I speak to him, but..."

"But what?"

"He asked me to find out about the generator in his spaceship. He wants to know whether the super-photons have been properly recharged. He appears rational, but he's obviously hallucinating. When I asked him if he remembered what type of car he was driving when he had the accident and hit the railing, he gave strange blank look as though he thought I was crazy."

Yossel Grossman found himself staring vacantly at the silhouette of a woman created by the weak yellow light of a glass encased oil lamp. When she noticed his eyes flitting, she gave a

tiny gasp.

"Yossel, are you finally coming around?"

"Is that you, Sarah?"

"Yes, Yossel. *Baruch Hashem*, you're all right."

Mr. Grossman blinked his eyes. "Why is it so dark in here? Is the electricity out?"

"Elec...?" Mrs. Grossman paused. "What do you mean?" She carefully lifted the oil lamp and placed it on a small wooden table next to the bed. "That should make things better for you."

Yossel studied his strange surroundings. At last, he said, "Where am I?"

"Why, at home, of course." Mrs. Grossman's voice was now tinged with anxiety. "Don't you recognize it?" Before Yossel could respond, a bespectacled man wearing a frock coat, knee breeches, and a three-cornered hat came into the room. "Dr. Wuttgein!" exclaimed Mrs. Grossman. "I'm so happy you came. Look, Yossel is awake."

Yossel stared at the man. "You're a doctor? Did you just come from some sort of masquerade party?"

Dr. Wuttgein approached the patient, squinted a bit, and adjusted his spectacles. "As I explained to you, Mrs. Grossman, patients often become disoriented after entering a state of unconsciousness. Your husband had quite a bump on the head. No doubt he also feels weak after having been bled."

"Bled? What do you mean? Did I have a transfusion?"

Dr. Wuttgein glanced uneasily at Mrs. Grossman. "I think we had better speak for a few minutes in the parlor."

Outside the bedroom, it was Mrs. Grossman who spoke first. "I'm so thankful for all you've done, doctor. I do hope you'll take no offence at what my husband..."

"Think nothing of it," the doctor interrupted with a magnanimous gesture of his hand. "Quite to be expected."

"What did he mean by trans... trans... something?"

"I'm afraid he was speaking gibberish. Obviously, there is

no such thing."

"Before you came in, he uttered some other strange word. It sounded scientific, but I never heard it before. Elec... something."

Dr. Wuttgein spoke with calm confidence. "You must be patient with your husband. That was quite a nasty accident. No doubt the humors of the liver and kidneys have been severely disrupted. That can cause temporary delusions."

Mrs. Grossman did not draw much comfort from this diagnosis. "Are you sure that this is temporary, doctor?"

"Wait here a moment, and I'll check on him further."

Ten minutes later, Dr. Wuttgein returned, pale-faced and clearly disturbed. "I'm afraid his case is rather severe. When I asked him if he recalled anything about how he lost control of his horse before his wagon rolled down that ravine, he looked at me as though I were insane. Then he started raving about driving a machine that goes without horses — a Ford, whatever that might be — and saying that 'gasoline,' or some other gibberish word, caught fire and exploded." The doctor shook his head sadly. "A most severe case, I'm afraid, most severe."

Since ancient times, people have wondered about the mysterious nature of time and whether one can travel into the past or future.[309] Despite modern technology, time travel is no more feasible today than it was centuries ago, yet it continues to fascinate people. The above story takes matters one step further because the idea that the same person could somehow exist simultaneously during different time periods is even more bizarre than time travel.

---

[309] The *Talmud* records a story about Choni Hami'agel who slept for seventy years. When he awoke, he discovered that everything had changed radically and that no one recognized him (B.T. *Ta'anith* 23A).

For *Hashem*, however, time is not a mystery because He created it. From His perspective, the Exodus has never stopped happening and never will.

When Jews try to view Passover not as ancient history, but as something happening now, they create a special relationship with *Hashem*. Just as He is above and beyond time, they also, to a degree, place themselves above and beyond the constraints of time.

שֻׁלְחָן עוֹרֵךְ
THE FESTIVE MEAL

The *Talmud* states that each person should rejoice on a festival with what he or she enjoys. Men should drink wine, women should wear new clothing, and children should be given treats such as nuts.[310] Why does the *Talmud* specify these forms of rejoicing instead of giving a general instruction that people should celebrate and leaving it up to each individual to decide how to do so?

Back in the early 1930's, the famous gangster, "Light-Fingers Louie," sat on the bunk of his jail cell chewing on the end of an unlit cigarette.

"You're addicted to them things, ain't you Louie?" said his cellmate, Spike.

"Yeah," said Louie absent-mindedly. "Bad enough they coop you up in this hole. They won't even let a guy smoke."

Spike dealt out the cards for the umpteenth time. Louie

---

[310] B.T. *Pesachim* 109A.

glanced at his hand, then folded the cards and threw them down on the bunk. "You're losing your touch, Spike. That's the same lousy hand you dealt me last time."

"Hey, I can't help it if…"

"Knock it off, Spike! I knew you were a cardsharp before even you knew it, but a good cardsharp wouldn't deal the same lousy hand twice. Even the dumbest stiff wouldn't fall for that."

"Aw, knock it off yourself. I'll deal 'em out again."

"Naw, forget it." Louie whisked the cards off his bunk and onto the floor. "I ain't playing no more today. I got ten more years in this slammer to play with you."

Spike picked up the cards, tucked them into their worn box, and tossed them under his pillow. Louie lay back on his bunk, took the cigarette out of his mouth and fashioned fake puffs of smoke with his lips.

"I been thinking…" said Louie.

"So, you got a new hobby," said Spike sarcastically.

"Real comical, Spike." Louie continued to stare toward the ceiling, eyeing the imaginary clouds of smoke from his unlit cigarette. "No, I mean it. When the judge threw the book at me for that bank robbery, you know what he said? He said, 'Louie, it's too bad a man with your talent don't get a decent job. Society could use a man like you.'" Louie raised his head to observe Spike's reaction, but the latter simply snickered. "No, for real, Spike. He really said it. Maybe he put it in a little better language, but it was just like that. 'Louie, robbing banks ain't for you.' And I been thinking. Maybe he's right."

"That's a good one. I can see the headlines now. 'Light-Fingers Louie Goes Legit.' Maybe you'll open a comedy club. If that don't draw a laugh, nothin' will."

Louie turned his eyes towards his cellmate without moving. "You ain't never thought about going legit, Spike? Have a nice job, a nice family — everybody respect you?"

"You're full of baloney, Louie. Let's turn on the radio for a

while." Without waiting for a reply, Spike turned the dial.

"...and don't forget to enter our vacation sweepstakes contest when you order our service," said the radio announcer. "It's 11:15 a.m. Time for the local news. In a tragic story, five year old Linda Smithers was trapped today inside the vault of First National Bank downtown. According to police, the little girl wandered off when she accompanied her mother to the bank earlier this morning. The door somehow closed on the child, trapping her inside the vault. Bank personnel attempted to open the door by using the combination, but the lock became jammed. Police have been trying to communicate with the little girl, but are afraid that the oxygen inside will run out in just a few hours..."

Louie sat up in his bunk. "That's it!" He went to the barred door of his cell and started banging. "Hey, guard, come quick!"

One of the prison guards came to the cell, but he was not hurrying. "You need to make an emergency visit to the bathroom or something."

"No, listen, dummy. The radio just said there's a little kid trapped in a bank vault who's going to suffocate. Tell the warden to have somebody take me over there quick."

The guard placed his hands on his hips. "Have you been smuggling drugs into this joint, Light-Fingers? There ain't no warden who's going to let you go nowhere."

"But the child could die!"

By this time, Spike had come to the cell door. "Hey, Mack, how long would you say you've been working on this cell block?"

"Thirteen years."

"And how long has Louie been in?"

"I don't remember. Maybe five."

"So you know Louie as good as I do. There ain't no bank vault door that can keep out Light-Fingers Louie."

The guard hesitated. "You know what? You're right!" The guard removed his walkie-talkie from his belt and pressed a

button. "Margie? This is Mack over on cell block 3B. I know this is going to sound goofy, but a prisoner over here tells me he just heard about a little girl trapped in a bank vault downtown... Oh, you heard about it, too? Yeah, well, this prisoner is an expert at breaking into bank vaults. Can you ask the warden... What's that? In a meeting? Well, it's an emergency. Can't you just knock on the door for a second and see if he can do anything?" Mack nodded at Louie. "She says she's going to ask him."

After several tense moments, word got back that the warden agreed to have several guards transport Louie to the bank.

As soon as Louie entered the bank surrounded by guards, a red-eyed woman holding a handkerchief wet with tears ran up to him. "Thank goodness you got here! The bank manger told me they were bringing over a specialist."

The guards could not help smiling at one another. "He's a specialist, all right," said one.

"Knock it off," said Louie. "Can't you see the lady's upset?" He turned to the woman. "Don't worry. I'll get your little girl out safe and sound."

At the vault, the bank guards looked almost as distraught as the child's mother. "I don't see what this guy can do?" said one of them, shaking his head. "We've tried everything, but the door is jammed. Just ask Ms. King, the locksmith."

"They're right," said Wilma King. "I have more than twenty years of experience in this business. I've been trying for over an hour, but I just can't get it open. I don't know what anybody else can do."

Louie cracked his knuckles. "Your problem," he explained confidently, "is that you do not have light fingers."

Louie put his ear next to the vault door to listen to the tumblers as he maneuvered the dials of the combination lock. As he listened, he could make out the muffled sobbing of the little girl. "I can hear her in there," he told the crowd in a hoarse

whisper. Ever so gently, Louie turned the lock cylinders, listening for the clicking sounds that meant they were in the right position. The minutes ticked by, but there was hardly a sound as the tiny crowd held its breath to see what would happen. Beads of sweat formed on Louie's forehead. He closed his eyes, focusing every bit of concentration he could muster on his ears and fingers. Ten minutes later, a frightened young girl was hugging her mother, shaken but safe.

Back at the prison that night, Mack, the guard, came over to Louie's cell. "Pretty good work, Louie. You saved that girl's life."

Louie came over to the cell door. "It wasn't my biggest caper, but I'd say I did pretty good."

"So good, in fact, that you'll be leaving here next week."

"Leaving? You mean I'm being transferred to some place decent? I don't have to live in this hole no more?"

Mack grinned. "When the governor found out what you did, he decided to commute your sentence!"

When Adam and Chavah sinned, their misdeed affected all humanity. By observing the *Torah*, Jews correct that sin. The ideal way to correct a sin is to take the very thing which was misused and to use it for good.[311]

According to some opinions, the fruit of the Tree of Knowledge was the grape.[312] By using wine to celebrate during festivals, Jewish men help correct part of the sin.

Prior to sinning, Adam and Chavah were in such a state of purity that they did not need to wear clothing. Only afterwards, having descended from their lofty spiritual level, did they require

---

[311] See B.T. *Yoma* 86B.
[312] B.T. *Berachoth* 40A.

garments.[313] By wearing nice clothing in honor of the festivals, women do their part to help correct the same sin.

Children are not truly capable of sin because they do not fully appreciate the difference between right and wrong. They are only affected by sin through their parents, so they do their part in counteracting the sin of Adam and Chavah indirectly by rejoicing through eating nuts. The numerical value of the Hebrew word for "nut" (אֱגוֹז) equals that of "sin" (חֵט) when the latter is spelled defectively, without an *Alef* (א). Nuts hint indirectly at sin, just as children are tainted by sin only indirectly.

הַלֵּל
HALLEL

King David said: "What can I return to *Hashem* for all the good You have granted me? A cup of salvation I shall lift and call upon the Name of *Hashem*. My vows to *Hashem* I will fulfill before all His people."[314]

One who fails to fulfill a vow violates a serious *Torah* prohibition. If all that King David promised to do was to perform an obligation he was bound to fulfill anyway, how was he showing thankfulness to God?

Humphrey Hamilton Cromwell, III, a wealthy young spendthrift, sat in the rear of his limousine as his chauffeur sped along a coastal roadway through the black night. Just a few years before, at age twenty-five, he had inherited his family's fortune,

---

[313] Genesis 3:7.
[314] Psalms 116:12-14.

the management of which he left with certain accountants in the New England town from which he hailed. This permitted him to engage in what he considered the more important activity of jetting around the country from one party to the next.

"Are you quite sure you wish to stay at your beachfront bungalow tonight, Master Humphrey?" asked the driver. A man in his fifties, who had served the Cromwell family since his youth, he still referred to his young employer as "Master Humphrey," although the latter was no longer a boy. "I'm sure I could find suitable accommodations for you further inland."

"How many times must I remind you, James," replied Humphrey indignantly, "that you are my chauffeur, not my nanny?"

"It's merely a sound precaution, sir. They've been talking on the radio all afternoon about how the hurricane will make landfall tonight."

"I know about it. Just drive on. I need a good night's sleep, and I won't feel comfortable in a hotel. I'm afraid I must admit that I had a bit too much to drink tonight even by my standards."

"But, sir," persisted the chauffeur. "The forecasters are predicting widespread flooding."

"Oh, I've been through storms here before. A hurricane is nothing more than a big storm."

James knew better than to push the subject further. Humphrey was so pig-headed that once he made up his mind, the more anyone challenged him, the more steadfastly he stuck to his position.

When they reached the bungalow, James parked and opened the rear door for his youthful employer. The chauffeur had to hold onto his hat tightly with one hand to keep the wind from whipping it away. The sun had gone down almost three hours ago, but an observant onlooker could have made out that the sea had crept well up the sandy beach.

"Are you quite sure, sir?" yelled James above the sound of wind and sea.

The young Mr. Cromwell responded by glaring at him through the darkness. "Come for me in the morning at about nine, James," he snapped. With that, he stalked resolutely into the bungalow.

At about three in the morning, something cold and wet awakened Humphrey from a deep sleep. He tried to turn on the small lamp which stood on a night table next to his bed in the second story of the isolated bungalow, but it failed to respond to his touch.

The young man bolted upright in bed as he realized that he was surrounded by water and that the power was out. Getting out of bed, he found that the chilly water reached almost up to his knees. He slogged over to the window, but all he could see was darkness.

Fierce winds beat about like wild demons as torrents of rain rattled against the roof of the small building. Humphrey thought of opening the window and calling for help, but the nearest residence was a good two miles away. He had always thought this was such a nice spot on the beach — away from the crowd. Only now did he realize how such isolation could be a drawback. Panic seized him as he began to grasp the danger of his situation. He was a poor swimmer.

The water in the bedroom continued to rise. The entire building swayed. If the flood swept it away, Humphrey would almost surely drown, yet if he stayed where he was…

He was almost certain the water had already risen two or three inches in the few minutes since he had gotten up. It was just above his knees now. He felt a tremendous wrenching beneath him. The bungalow must be coming loose from its foundations.

What does a man do when he is about to die? The thought suddenly flashed through Humphrey's mind. Being so young, he had never made out a will, never considered what might happen

after he passed on. But what rubbish! Who did he care about enough to leave anything to? And if he was gone, what did it matter to him who got his money?

He had always assumed that someone confronted with imminent death would break down in uncontrollable emotion, crying and ranting, yet he felt amazingly calm. He gazed outside into the brutal darkness. The water continued to rise. 'That darkness is about to overwhelm me.' The thought was solemn, almost mystical. 'I will become one with the darkness.'

Just then, Humphrey heard a faint buzzing sound. What could it be? The electricity was out. Nothing could be running inside the bungalow. Was there something inside the building that functioned with batteries and had somehow gone on, or was this the sound that the Angel of Death made when it was about to snatch another victim?

The strange buzzing grew louder. The bungalow lurched. Do buildings buzz when they are being ripped from their foundations? Suddenly, as it grew louder, Humphrey realized what the buzzing was — an outboard motor. He immediately threw open the window and started shouting. Gusts of wind-driven rain greeted him. The roar of the storm outside was so great that he doubted anyone on a boat could hear him, yet amazingly, within moments, the boat came into view, its headlights distinct through the darkness.

"Help! Over here!" Humphrey's voice was hoarse with desperation. It hardly seemed possible that the person operating the boat could hear him, yet the boat, tossed wildly by the violent flood, pulled right up to the window. The skipper managed to throw a coil of rope through the window. Humphrey caught it in his wet hands and heaved with all his might to draw the boat as close as he could.

Everything was a blur as Humphrey scrambled through the window into the madly bobbing vessel where, panting and shivering, he took a seat. The master of the boat wasted no time

turning inland, racing at top speed away from the raging flood.

An hour and a half later, Humphrey Hamilton Cromwell, III sat wrapped in a blanket in the lobby of the Hotel Ritz, sipping hot coffee together with his chauffeur, James, and Captain William Stokely, for those were who his rescuers turned out to be.

"I suppose that was an adventure even for a seasoned mariner such as yourself," said Humphrey.

"I'm afraid my boat was badly battered," answered Captain Stokely. He looked like the type of weather-beaten man who could sit for hours on a pier smoking a pipe and spinning sea-tales for children. "I couldn't look to dock her properly, just had to ground her when we came in. May not even find her in the morning if this storm keeps up."

The storm already seemed distant and surrealistic as Humphrey sat in the luxurious surroundings of the hotel.

James put down his coffee mug. "I told Captain Stokely that you are a decent man who would treat him fairly if he rescued you, Master Humphrey."

"Oh," shrugged Humphrey. He was certain he detected a tone of remonstration in the chauffeur's voice. 'Aching to remind me that he told me so,' thought Humphrey. Then aloud, he said, "You name your price, my good man," but his voice lacked enthusiasm. Almost as an afterthought, he added, "You did save my life, after all."

"I'll need to see what happens with my boat," replied the captain, still looking very much like he should be smoking a pipe as he stroked his chin with a coarse, weathered hand.

A month later, Humphrey Hamilton Cromwell, III sat at the dining table in his New England mansion, hale and hearty, consuming luncheon with James. James usually ate with the other help in the kitchen — an arrangement James himself seemed to prefer. However, in as much as Humphrey had been feeling a bit lonely for company — his next exciting social event not coming up until the end of the week — he had talked the chauffeur into

joining him. The young globe-trotter had just finished entertaining his luncheon guest with an account of the woes he was experiencing trying to update his wardrobe for the new season when the doorbell rang.

"James, would you mind?" asked Humphrey.

"I'm a chauffeur, not a butler."

"But Livingston is off today and the cook is in the middle of..."

James raised a hand to silence his employer. "Fine, fine, I'll get it." He felt relieved to interrupt the one-sided and terribly boring conversation. Moments later, James returned and said, "It's Captain Stokely, sir."

"Stokely? The fellow with the boat? What does he want?"

"I believe he's here to see you about money."

"Money? What money?"

James looked hard at Humphrey. "Don't you recall my telling you in the hotel lobby that I had promised him that if he went out for you in that hurricane, you would see that he was properly taken care of?"

Humphrey cocked his head slightly and dug his hands into his trouser pockets. "Of course, I remember, but I can't be bound by your promises."

Even James, accustomed as he was to Humphrey's selfish, pampered ways, found this surprising. "The man risked his life to save you. I'm sure you remember that when we returned to the bungalow after the storm, it had washed away. I have little doubt that you would have perished with it had this man not rescued you. His boat was ruined, and all you can say is that you can't be bound by my promises?"

"Very well." Humphrey dug his wallet out of his pocket, opened it, and handed a fifty-dollar bill to the chauffeur. "Give him this, and tell him he has my thanks."

"How can fifty dollars possibly compensate this man?"

"It isn't my fault his boat was damaged."

"Fault is hardly the issue here."

"Look, do as I say. Give this money to Mr. Stokely or Captain Stokely, or whatever, and get rid of him."

James folded his arms across his chest. "I am a chauffeur, not a butler. I answered the door as you requested. If you wish to send this man off with a measly fifty dollars, then you can do it yourself. Furthermore, I can only imagine the shame and disgrace your parents would feel if they were here to…"

"Aha!" Humphrey rose from his seat and wagged his index finger at James. "Aha! How many times have I told you that you aren't my nanny? I don't need you to tell me what my parents would or would not think! I'll give this money to Stokely myself." Red-faced, the young man stalked off to the front door of the mansion.

"Please take this money with my thanks," said Humphrey, trying to keep the heat out of his voice.

The wrinkles of the old seaman's face twitched into a faint smile. "Surely you're joking. My boat alone required nearly five thousand dollars of repairs and the insurance only covered…"

"I'm afraid that your insurance troubles are not of my making."

The smile vanished from the old man's face. "Very well," he said calmly, "then I'll see you in court."

James stood in the dining room just as Humphrey had left him — his arms folded over his chest. "Well?" he said.

"He threatened to sue me," snapped Humphrey angrily.

"I think I'll finish my lunch in the kitchen."

"You do that!"

James took his plate and glass and made for the kitchen door. "I don't know what's going to become of you, Master Humphrey. When you were stranded in that bungalow, I doubt the thought even crossed your mind that you should have listened to me."

Humphrey threw himself into his chair, furious in the

knowledge that what James said was precisely so. "Just go! And tell Louise to serve my duck with an extra helping of gravy — unless you find it too much to carry out that request as well!"

Judge Myra Horowitz finished reading the material that Humphrey Hamilton Cromwell, III's attorney had handed her. She removed her reading glasses and set them down on her desk. Then she addressed Captain William Stokely. "The facts presented in Court today are undisputed. You risked your life to rescue Mr. Cromwell, and he certainly owes you a debt of gratitude. Nevertheless, the law in this matter is clear. Mr. Cromwell never agreed to reimburse you for any particular loss that might occur as a result of your undertaking to save him. Both parties testified that Mr. Cromwell said that Mr. Stokely could 'name his price,' or words to that effect, but that was *after* the rescue and cannot constitute a legally binding contract. I don't mind saying that I find Mr. Cromwell's attitude in this matter somewhat reprehensible and his ethics questionable, but I am required to decide this case strictly according to the law, without regard for my personal opinion of his behavior. Accordingly, I must enter judgment in favor of Mr. Cromwell."

Outside the Courthouse, Humphrey swept smugly into the limousine, a triumphant grin lighting his face. James put down the newspaper he had been reading and said, "Where to, sir?"

"Take me to the *Tre Bon* Restaurant to celebrate. Now it's my turn to say, 'I told you so.' The Judge ruled in my favor."

James glanced in the rearview mirror at his employer. "Hardly surprising."

"What? You're not surprised? I told you he should have taken the fifty dollars."

James shook his head, only with the greatest effort managing to mask his disgust as he muttered under his breath, "It's incredible that anyone can be this way."

When people are faced with serious problems, they often promise a great deal to whoever will help them. Later, when the problems are resolved, they tend to forget about those commitments or think that they should not be held to their promises. Often, the same fellow who is full of thanks and praise when desperately in need of a loan feels resentment when the time comes to repay it. A popular American saying is that the surest way to make an enemy is to lend money to a friend.

When King David declared in the *Hallel*, "My vows to *Hashem* I will fulfill before all His people,"[315] he meant that he had an attitude diametrically opposite to that of those who are ungrateful.

When facing the dangers of battle, King David swore to offer sacrifices. Not only would he fulfill those obligations as required by *Halachah*, but he would do so with the proper thankful frame of mind — not merely as one who, having forgotten the dire circumstances in which he made the commitment, grudgingly forces himself to keep his word.

This outlook plays a special role in the recitation of the *Haggadah*. We must not view the story of the departure from Egypt as ancient history, entombed and forgotten with the Pharaohs. The story must be alive and real, as though it recently happened, so that we enthusiastically express our thanks to *Hashem*. That is what true gratitude is all about.

---

[315] Psalms 116:12-14.

לְשָׁנָה הַבָּאָה בִּירוּשָׁלָיִם
WHEN WILL THE FUTURE
REDEMPTION TAKE PLACE?

The *Talmud* records a dispute between Rabbi Eliezer and Rabbi Yehoshua about the date when the world was created. Rabbi Eliezer held that God created the world on *Rosh Hashannah*, the first day of the month of *Tishrei*. Rabbi Yehoshua, however, maintained that *Hashem* created the world during the month of *Nissan* when Passover falls.[316]

The *Shem Mishmuel* holds that both opinions are correct. *Hashem* created the physical world at the time of *Rosh Hashannah*. There is also a supernatural world — a spiritual realm which makes miraculous events possible. That was created during the month of *Nissan*.[317]

Rabbi Eliezer and Rabbi Yehoshua also disagree when it comes to pinpointing the time of the future redemption. Rabbi Eliezer holds that it will occur during the month of *Tishrei*, while Rabbi Yehoshua holds that it will occur during *Nissan*.[318] In this case, there is an additional reason why both opinions may be right.

◈ ◈ ◈ ◈ ◈ ◈ ◈

Mr. Fried had to honk his car horn several times before his two sons emerged from the house. Avi, an older boy in his teens, opened the rear door to let his six-year old brother, Yankie, scramble inside.

"What took you boys so long?" asked Mr. Fried, looking at

---

[316] B.T. *Rosh Hashannah* 10B-11A.
[317] *Bee'urei Hachassiduth Leshas*, p. 230.
[318] B.T. *Rosh HaShannah* 11A-B.

them in the rear-view mirror as they fastened their seatbelts.

"*Imma* wanted us to take some extra towels," explained Yankie.

"We won't take a long time in the changing room," said Avi. "We've got our swimsuits on under our clothes."

Mr. Fried started driving to the Jewish Community Center pool. "I'm not really being impatient. It's just that the last time we went, you two complained you didn't have enough time to swim."

As Mr. Fried made a left-hand turn down Elmont Street, he turned on the CD player.

"Are you going off the high dive again, Avi?" asked Yankie.

"Sure thing! I'm used to it now," answered Avi confidently. "Last time I dove off, I made it across the whole length of the pool holding my breath under the water."

"Yeah, I know. How do you manage to hold your breath so long?"

"It's easy once you get used to it." Avi leaned forward and whispered to his father. "Did you tell Yankie about what you want him to do today, *Abba*?"

"Not yet, but I will now. How about swimming all the way across the adult pool today, Yankie? I think you can do it."

Yankie frowned. "I've never tried that before."

"Aw, there's nothing to it," said Avi. "I've watched you practicing with *Abba* in the kiddie pool. You're doing great!"

Yankie bit his lip. "I don't think I want to."

"Don't you remember how I told you that it's a *Mitzvah* for a father to teach his sons how to swim?" asked Mr. Fried.

"Yeah."

"Don't you want to help me do a *Mitzvah?*"

"I guess." Yankie sounded doubtful.

"I promise you that you'll make it across. Don't worry about holding your breath or which stroke you use."

When Mr. Fried and his boys came out of the changing room, Avi went straight to the diving board. He made a smooth dive and swam clear across the length of the pool underwater. A big smile lit up his face when he popped up at the far end gasping for air.

"That was great!" yelled Yankie, clapping his hands.

Avi grabbed hold of the cement edge of the pool, swung himself out and pointed a finger at his little brother. "Now it's your turn, Yankie."

Although they had talked about it in the car, Yankie still looked stunned. "Me?" he said.

Mr. Fried slipped into the pool and swam to the opposite side from where Yankie stood. Although the water was way over Yankie's head, it only came up to his father's shoulders. "Just take your time and remember everything we practiced last week. Go ahead and get into the pool."

Avi came around and stood at the side of the pool behind his father. He bent over and rested his hands on his knees. "It's so easy that you'll wonder why you thought you couldn't do it," he called to his brother.

Yankie slipped gingerly into the pool, carefully holding the side with both hands. Slowly, he released one hand and turned towards his father. "Are you sure…?"

"Don't worry about anything," said Mr. Fried, trying to bolster the boy's confidence. "I promise that you'll get across the pool." Mr. Fried winked at Avi when he said this, but Yankie did not notice.

Yankie let go of his other hand and started to swim towards his father. With each stroke, he looked towards his smiling father and took courage.

Everything went well until Yankie reached the middle of the pool and some water accidentally went up his nose. The startled boy panicked and stopped kicking his feet, which suddenly felt like lead. Flailing his arms and gasping, he started to sink.

With a few quick strokes, Mr. Fried reached Yankie, lifted him up, and carried him the rest of the way across the pool.

Avi crouched down next to the side of the pool where his father held his panting brother. "See, you made it across!"

"But that doesn't count," sputtered Yankie. "I messed up in the middle."

Avi put his hand on his brother's shoulder and laughed. "Sure it counts! Don't you get it? Abba promised that you would make it across the pool. If you had managed to swim all by yourself, that would have been fine, but since you couldn't do it, he helped you, and you still made it across."

If the Jews repent and perform good deeds, they will merit redemption on their own, and it will come during the month of *Tishrei*, which features holidays of repentance and good deeds. If the Jews do not merit salvation, *Hashem* will redeem them just as He did during Passover when they did not fully merit it on their own. If the redemption occurs in that fashion, it will take place during *Nissan*.[319]

REDEMPTION

Two high school students, Yitzi and Shuie, sat in the *Beith Medrash* concentrating on a difficult section of the *Gemara*.

"How can Rabbi Yochanan say this?" asked Yitzi. "On the previous page he said just the opposite!"

Shuie ran his index finger back over the words. "You're

---

[319] Based on *Iyun Yaakov* on B.T. *Rosh Hashannah* 11A; see also B.T. *Sanhedrin* 98A.

right. It sounds like a complete contradiction."

Yitzi rubbed his forehead. "Maybe that word we weren't sure about translating didn't mean what we thought it meant."

Shuie picked up the thick dictionary at his elbow and started leafing through it. "Okay. I'll double check." After a few moments, he flipped the book around and showed it to his friend. "Sure looks like we got it right."

Yitzi frowned. "Yeah, that word has to mean 'going backwards' just like we thought."

Yitzi was rubbing his forehead harder now. He ran his index finger back over the text as he mumbled the words to himself. "I still don't get it," he said at last.

"Me either," said Shuie, who had also been rereading the *Gemara*, "and I don't see anything in *Tosafoth* that even talks about this part of the *Gemara*. Let's take a look at the *Maharsha*."

The young men flipped to the end of the volume. "He doesn't seem to say anything," muttered Yitzi. Shuie unbuttoned his sleeves and rolled them up as he always did when trying to concentrate. The two boys then proceeded to examine every commentator available in the back of their *Gemaras*.

"I don't understand," repeated Yitzi in a sing-song voice. "I don't understand. We've looked through all the commentaries, but no one even mentions our question, let alone offers an answer."

"I always said you were a great *Chavrutha*," said Shuie. "It's probably a question nobody every thought of. I'll bet we make history."

Yitzi shook his head. "Come on, Shuie. The question is obvious. Anyone who reads this *Gemara* has to see that Rabbi Yochanan said just the opposite on the previous page, but how come no one talks about it?"

The young students spent another half hour searching through books in the *Beth Medrash*, but still could not find any material to shed light on their question.

"This is really frustrating," said Yitzi at last. "We've hit some kind of dead-end here."

"Yeah, it's difficult, but don't worry. My father says the more effort you put into learning the more you get out of it. After having thought about the question so much, we'll really appreciate the answer when we find it."

"Hey, look!" Yitzi pointed. "*Rebbe* just walked into the room. Let's go ask him."

"*Rebbe*," exclaimed Shuie after the boys greeted their teacher, "you won't believe the great question Yitzi came up with! Look how Rabbi Yochanan says one thing on this page and just opposite on the next page. We couldn't even find anyone who discusses this question."

"Does *Rebbe* really think I've come onto something?" Yitzi sounded doubtful.

The *Rebbe* smiled at his young students and asked them to sit down with him. He then explained the answer to Yitzi's question. "You see," he concluded, "the *Gemara* itself asks this question a bit further on and gives the answer. If you had continued reading, you would have seen that."

Yitzi shook his head. "I feel like such a dummy!"

The *Rebbe* patted Yitzi's back. "Quite the opposite, Yitzi. The fact that you raised a question that the *Gemara* itself asks shows you're really using your head. Of course, since the *Gemara* also answers the question, there's no need for any commentator to do so."

This story illustrates an important point about redemption. Many times, the situation of the Jewish people looks desperate. In fact, matters sometimes look so bad that there is not even a glimmer of hope. It is just like Yitzi and Shuie struggling over a difficulty in the *Gemara* so perplexing that they could not even

find a commentator who discussed it. They searched everywhere to find a solution except right in the *Gemara* itself. At the end, however, the answer proved simple, even obvious. The *Mishnah* teaches that just before the arrival of the *Mashiach*, matters will appear more hopeless than they ever have.[320] It will be precisely at that moment that the final redemption will arrive.

THE ROMAN SOLDIER

Yochai and Augustus made an unusual pair. Yochai was a dark-haired, wiry Jewish shepherd. Augustus was a broad-shouldered Roman soldier, with a light complexion and bright red hair. Now in their late teens, the young men had been friends since childhood.

"Do you like it?" asked Augustus as he showed his new armor to Yochai. "I made the covering for the breastplate myself."

Yochai ran his calloused fingers along the leather pieces. Augustus had used thick sinews to sew them together over a bronze plate. Then he had etched the likeness of two warriors bearing spears into the taut leather. Another Roman might have given any Jew who touched his armor a sound drubbing, but not Augustus. Nor was he in any way offended by his friend's Jewish practices. "I don't understand Hebrew, but your prayers have a special ring," he used to say. "Like the melodious sound of the birds and crickets, or like a trickling brook." Yochai would laugh when he heard such talk and reply, "What kind of soldier are you? You sound more like a poet!"

Augustus enjoyed camping out and often joined Yochai when he herded his flocks high in the Judean mountains. There they would build themselves a campfire at night. At times,

---

[320] *Sotah* 9:15.

Yochai would entertain his friend with music from his flute. At other times, Augustus would teach Yochai how to play dice. And what a dice player Augustus was! He could fling the dice so high into the air that they were lost in the darkness of the night where the firelight did not reach, but when they came down, he never failed to catch them. He could throw them up with one hand and catch them behind his back with the other. There was hardly a time when Yochai did not return from the mountains with new dice tricks to teach to the younger boys of his village, though his elders frowned upon such activities.

Occasionally, the friends discussed religion. "You know," said Augustus one time, "I once met a man who studied the works of the Greek philosophers. He told me that the gods were really just heroes who lived many years ago. As time went on, the stories about them grew until people came to believe that they were gods."

Yochai smiled. "Do you believe that too?"

"It makes sense to me. And I can prove it from your *Torah*!"

"How?"

"I once heard a Jew say that *Hashem* never revealed the location of Moses' grave so that people would not worship him as a god. So you see that it's possible for people to make heroes into gods."

Yochai found the revelation of Augustus's familiarity with part of the *Torah* both surprising and pleasing. He knew that he really should not pursue this conversation any further, but curiosity got the better of him. "But didn't the Greek philosophers also believe in idols as you do?" he inquired.

"I guess so, but I heard that Aristotle taught that there is a Being who is the first cause of everything. It sounds just like the God of the Jews."

"Why do you spend so much time with primitive Jews?" asked Augustus's father, Gaius, as he reclined upon a couch eating grapes.

"Why do you say that, father?" Augustus stood straight before his father, his hands clasped respectfully behind his back. "You know I've been friends with Yochai for years."

Just then, Augustus's mother, Junia, entered the room with a servant, who carried a tray of fine cakes. "I heard what you were talking about as I came in," she said. "Your father is right. It was one thing to play with Jewish boys when you were little, but now you must prepare to assume the role of an adult Roman citizen."

Augustus bit his lip. Of course, his father was right. Every young Roman knew that it was a solemn duty never to disobey one's father. A father had a right to beat — even kill — a disobedient son, and rightfully so, thought Augustus.

"You said I deserved a few days off from my military training because I did so well in the sword practice with Romulus," he said weakly. "You didn't tell me not to go where I please."

Gaius helped himself to a cake. "Of course, you can go wherever you please in your free time." His voice was not angry, just firm. "I simply can't understand why you would want to be around Jews, though."

Junia's servant set the tray on a thick wooden table of simple design. Gaius dismissed the servant with a wave of his hand and munched absent-mindedly on the cake.

"But our ancestors were Greeks." Augustus tried to be tactful, for he could not contradict his father. "You have taught me so many wonderful stories about Alexander the Great. You told me that he admired Jews."

Gaius flicked some stray crumbs from the table. "Don't twist things around. It's true that Alexander the Great admired the Jewish sages, but the boys with whom you keep company are

shepherds. What could be lower than that? Besides, when the Romans conquered this land, we adopted Roman citizenship. We are not really Greeks anymore."

"I know these boys are not people to model myself after, father. I would never forsake our great heritage or my own glorious future." Augustus hung his head. "Still, they are fun to be with and they know a lot. Just today, Yochai showed me how to tell the age of a sheep by looking at its teeth and…"

Gaius burst out laughing. "Of course, a shepherd knows about sheep! Do you think you are being trained to fight sheep? You must focus on learning how to fight so that you can have a glorious career with the mightiest army on earth and become a captain like me."

"I do wish to be like you, father."

Gaius rose from his couch, came around the table and gave his son a hearty clap on his shoulder. "Of course you do, son. If it pleases you to make camp with these shepherds during your spare time, I suppose there isn't too much harm. Hiking through the mountains certainly helps keep you fit. Just don't get too friendly with them. Remember, even their own people look down on shepherds. Your real friends should be people like Romulus. He's a perfect model of Roman youth: tough, persevering, and willing to risk anything for the sake of the Empire."

"I'll do as you say, father." Augustus saluted his father smartly, pushing back the wild red curls of his hair as he did so. Gaius gazed fondly at his son as he gave him another pat on the shoulder and returned to the table. Augustus smiled confidently as he strode from the room.

"That boy worries me," said Junia after her son left.

"Nonsense!" Gaius waved his hand dismissively. "He has a good spirit and talk about strength! I've never seen a young man his age throw a discus so far."

"He seems willing enough and certainly his military training is excellent. Still, all he ever talks about is that filthy

Yochai. You never hear him utter a word about the Roman boys he knows."

Gaius shrugged carelessly. "You heard our conversation. He knows where his duty lies. He'll soon outgrow his boyish friendship with those shepherds. Keep in mind that he'll be joining a new cohort of young soldiers in a few weeks. I've never seen men more closely knit than those in one of my cohorts. Augustus will soon forget about those Jews."

Yochai sat playing his shepherd's pipe in the cramped mud hut that his grandmother rented from another villager. The hut was just a single room, with a dirt floor packed hard and smooth by many years of use. It was snug enough in any type of weather provided that Yochai remembered to plaster the roof regularly. Unfortunately, he rarely remembered. Then, when the roof sprung a leak during the rainy winter, Yochai would apologize profusely to his grandmother for his neglect, using so many self-deprecating expressions such as "lazy and worthless grandson" and "undeserving and unappreciative" that she hardly had a chance to offer any criticism of her own. He would then rearrange things in their tiny abode so that he slept nearest the leak with an earthenware pitcher next to him to catch whatever dripped from the roof. Even if the pitcher overflowed and soaked him, he would simply continue sleeping. As he used to put it, "Someone who can sleep out in the open with sheep can sleep with anything."

On this particular occasion, the weather being dry, Yochai sat upon the dirt floor feeling as much comfort and dignity as a wealthy nobleman, while he concentrated deeply upon the tune that flowed from his pipe. Even the violent entry of his partner, Shlomo, failed to disturb the young shepherd's focus.

Impatient at Yochai's lapse in the duty of greeting a guest,

Shlomo banged his staff against the wall, producing an ear-shattering crack. "What lovely music," he said sarcastically.

"What's wrong with it?" Yochai looked up.

"Nothing, I suppose. Except, perhaps, that you should spend more time taking things seriously."

"Music clears my mind for *Torah* study," was the innocent reply.

Shlomo laughed bitterly. "Hah! Come on, Yochai. Do you think you can fool me as easily as you fool Augustus? He may think you're some kind of a scholar, but I know the truth."

Still calm, Yochai tapped the mouthpiece of the pipe against the mud wall. He shrugged his shoulders. "Okay, so I'm not a scholar. I never said I was. I just try to learn *Torah* the same as..."

"Oh, sure you try!" Shlomo's face was hot and red. He shook his staff at Yochai, nearly striking him. "You try to learn whenever you aren't too busy playing your pipe or fooling around some other way!"

Yochai laid aside the pipe casually, wiped his mouth with the back of his hand in a deliberate fashion, and said, "What's wrong? Why are you so upset?"

"Have a look at this!" Shlomo thrust out his palm so that Yochai could observe the silver *Dinar* it held.

"Looks all right to me." Half a grin played across Yochai's face. He still did not bother rising from his place.

Shlomo snapped his hand shut and shook his fist. "That's all Mordechai the smith gave us for tending his sheep this month."

"But we agreed that the charge would be two *Dinarim*."

"That's right! But when I drove the sheep into the corral, he came out and yelled at me because they hadn't been trimmed properly."

"Trimmed properly?"

"Yes! Don't play your games with me! It's your job to

trim and comb the wool that's clotted with mud."

"I've been doing it."

"When? Last week?" Shlomo slammed the fist which held the *Dinar* so hard against the wall that the tiny hut shook. "Or maybe it was two weeks ago? Yochai, you're supposed to check them every day. That's your responsibility, but you're too busy playing with some Roman who, by the way, probably wouldn't think twice about slicing your head off. You never take anything seriously."

"I'll talk to Mordechai the smith." Yochai's voice was meek.

"You do that! In the meantime, I'll just hold onto this *Dinar*. We're lucky he didn't cancel his deal with us completely. Good luck getting the other *Dinar*."

Yochai smirked. "Do you think you scare me? I can live without that *Dinar*."

"Maybe so and while you're at it, I think I should look for a partner who takes his work a bit more seriously."

"Oh, it's always the same with you." Now it was Yochai's tone that grew sarcastic. "You're so responsible. Remember what happened last month when we sheared all the sheep. I know how to do it so that the fleece comes off all in one piece. How many complaints did we get when you did it and split each fleece into a dozen pieces?"

"I didn't say you're not good at what you do. The problem is getting you to do it."

At last Yochai rose to his feet indignantly. "I got home not too long ago after a hard day and just washed up. I don't want to dirty myself by wrestling with you, but perhaps you could use a little lesson."

"Sure!" Shlomo pounded his fist into the wall yet again. His face grew even redder. "Why not hit me? Is that another thing you learned from Augustus? To solve problems by fighting? Why don't you grow up already? Why not be a little respon-

sible?"

Suddenly, there was a knock at the door. "It's my grandmother. You'll have to go! I don't need you upsetting her. I'll
trim the sheep tomorrow, and I'll talk to Mordechai. I only agreed
to take responsibility to do all the trimming in the first place
because you didn't want to dirty your hands."

Yochai pulled the door open before Shlomo had a chance
to answer. "Grandmother, come in."

As flustered as Shlomo had become, Yochai had remained
composed throughout the argument. The calm, almost indifferent
expression on his face turned to one of deep concern, however, as
he observed the dazed expression on his grandmother's face.
Forgetting about their petty quarrel, Shlomo stepped forward as
he watched Yochai extend his hand to help support his grandmother.

"I... I have some news," murmured the old woman, her
voice trembling. "The Caesar is dead, assassinated by his own
bodyguards."

Yochai drew a breath of relief. "Oh, well, I don't think
that's anything to get too upset about. That's just Roman poli-
tics." Resuming his carefree attitude, he casually helped the old
lady walk to a narrow bed covered with rawhide. "That's certainly not the first or last time that sort of thing has happened." He
stared uncomprehendingly while his grandmother fumbled
about, positioning herself on the bed as though totally disoriented.

"Few of us will miss the old Caesar," she said, "but the
new one is much worse." She shook her head slowly. "He has
issued decrees against the Jewish religion making it illegal to wear
Tefillin, study *Torah*, or circumcise a baby." The shaken elder
grasped Yochai's hands so tightly that he too trembled.

"Don't worry grandmother." Yochai continued using a
matter-of-fact tone, though he found it harder to do so. "Doesn't
the *Torah* teach us that the wicked make all kinds of plans, but
Hashem stops them? Besides, who says the Roman army will

enforce the decrees?   Surely they know there will be strong resistance. I can ask my friend Augustus what's really going on. He may know…"

"Oh, sure," interrupted Shlomo, the expression of his face changed from anger to fearful astonishment. "He'll help you *if* he's still your friend, and *if* he tells the truth!"

Yochai looked hurt. As little as he cared about so many things, it bothered him that Shlomo distrusted his friend so much. His tone became emphatic. "I know for certain that he's different. Aren't there even descendants of the wicked Amalek who converted and became Jews? If that could happen, then how can you condemn Augustus just because …"

"I'm not saying there aren't any exceptions, but you have to be realistic, Yochai. How many Romans truly like Jews? I mean, besides just being polite. How many would take a risk to help us, stick by us even when things are difficult? The rabbis say that the best among snakes deserves to have his brains smashed. Snakes can't be trusted, and it's the same with Romans."

"It's not just that the Jews are different," Gaius explained to Augustus as they discussed the new decrees. "Greeks were different from Romans too, but when Rome became the dominant power, we changed. The Jews must change too."

"But they won't," insisted Augustus, his voice starting to tremble. "I know them. They will never agree to give up their *Torah*."

Gaius rubbed at his hair. "Some will, some won't." He sounded irritated. "My job is simply to enforce the law." Observing the troubled look on Augustus's face, he added, "Look son, I know you're friendly with some Jewish boys, but you're training to become a Roman soldier. You may even take my place some day. Being a soldier means doing many difficult things. You'll

get used to it."

Augustus did not respond.

"In fact," continued Gaius, "I don't want you to mention Jews around respectable people, and I don't want to find you associating with them anymore — especially shepherds. They are low people."

Augustus did not dare answer his father. He trembled visibly as he saluted and marched off to his barracks where it took him a long time to fall asleep.

In the dim light of dawn, the heavy snoring of a fellow soldier aroused Augustus. The ruckus emanated from his comrade, Romulus, who lay sprawled on the floor of the barracks. Augustus thought he could actually feel the vibrations of each snort. He certainly smelled the sickening stench that went with it.

"You foul pig!" Augustus whacked Romulus on the shoulder. "Stop that awful noise!" Romulus shifted heavily in his sleep, heedless of the rough ground upon which he lay. He grunted unintelligibly, then returned to snoring.

Augustus rolled over to distance himself from the noise, but it did little good. An officer arrived a few minutes later to awaken them.

"Good luck with that snoring pig," muttered Augustus as he wearily started to dress in his armor.

The other soldiers in the barracks also awakened. One stretched his arms and yawned while another rubbed and scratched at his hair, but Romulus continued to snore noisily.

The officer, who had been diverted by the others, now turned his attention to the persistent sleeper. No army cares much for etiquette, and the Roman army least of all. The officer delivered a rather rude kick to Romulus's thigh.

"Wah!" Romulus sat up abruptly.

"Good for you, you filthy mess!" exclaimed Augustus contemptuously, grimacing at the foul smell of Romulus's hair and clothing.

"You should have gone to the Bacchus wine celebration, Augie." Romulus staggered to a basin of water.

"What for? So that I could end up a filthy pig?"

Romulus gasped at the sensation of cold water upon his face. "I ate and drank and vomited. Then I ate and drank some more. I'm still shaky from it." A satisfied smirk played upon his face.

"Sounds lovely," said Augustus sarcastically.

Romulus patted at his dirty face with a ragged linen cloth, the water having done little to improve his appearance. "Don't play games with me! I've seen you drink more than your fill of good wine. What's up?"

Augustus stopped lacing his boots. "Nothing," he muttered in a sullen tone. To himself he half whispered, "Nothing you would understand."

Yochai and Shlomo sat beneath a shady cypress tree as they watched their flocks grazing among the coarse vegetation that covered a gently sloping hillside. From time to time, they heard the dogs barking at a sheep that had strayed too far from the others.

"Look what I have!" Yochai grinned as he displayed a silver *Dinar* to Shlomo. "I told you things would work out with Mordechai the smith."

Shlomo glanced at the *Dinar*, then turned to gaze out at the sheep. "So you were lucky this time," he said coolly. "But how many more mistakes will you make because you aren't careful?"

"Oh, stop being so moody! Money isn't so important!"

"You obviously think so." Shlomo picked up a stick and scraped idly at the ground.

"And so does our *Rebbe*," continued Yochai. "Didn't he teach us that one of the reasons we must give charity to the poor is

to train ourselves to understand that everything we have comes from *Hashem?*"

"Ha! You're a good one to be quoting *Rebbe*. You didn't even show up for the lesson this morning!"

"Well I can't help it if..."

"Do you know how serious it is to miss learning *Torah?* And when you don't show up, it's difficult for me because I have to learn on my own."

Yochai continued to shrug off the criticism. "I'll be there tomorrow."

Shlomo threw down the stick he had been holding and turned harshly on Yochai. "You'd better get a more serious attitude! You don't even have a regular bed or mattress to sleep on in your grandmother's hut — just a piece of rawhide thrown on the ground. It's typical of your laziness that you can't even gather some straw to make a mattress! Even so, when you have to get up in the morning, you cling to that rawhide as though it were a bed of goose down!"

Yochai rose and dusted himself off. "I won't deny anything you've said, but don't we often spend time learning while we tend the sheep?"

Shlomo rose too, his voice loud and passionate. "How can I ever get through to you? It's not the same. First of all, you missed *Rebbe's* lesson. Secondly, you can concentrate more on your learning when you're together with a group. Thirdly, if we have a question, the *Rebbe* is right there to answer it. Fourthly..."

"All right, all right," interrupted Yochai calmly. "I'll do better next time."

"You always say that!"

"Well, you know I want to learn. You agree with that don't you?"

"I suppose."

"So why don't you come and wake me up in the morning?"

"I have other things to do in the morning besides worrying about you! Grow up already!"

Yochai stared absently at his friend. It was this indifferent attitude — a lazy lack of concern about almost everything — that irritated Shlomo more than anything else. The more Yochai ignored his criticism, the more vehement Shlomo grew, finding himself unable to stop until he elicited some reaction — any reaction — from his partner.

Yochai often sensed this and obliged by becoming outwardly belligerent while inwardly laughing at his companion. Today, however, nothing seemed to stir Yochai. Perhaps the relentless hot weather that sapped the very life from every creature had made him too lethargic. Perhaps he had achieved a new peak of unabashed indifference.

"Sure," continued Shlomo, "stand there and stare at me dumbfounded like one of the sheep. Why should you care about a thing? You could probably go down to the deepest pit of *Gehinnom* and have no more reaction than to offer a half-witted stare!"

"Daniel!" shouted Yochai. Relieved not to have to respond to Shlomo, he pointed at the figure of Shlomo's younger brother climbing steadily towards them. The boy was panting heavily by the time he reached them.

"Father sent me," Daniel managed to gasp even though he was still a few meters away. "Soldiers....soldiers came to enforce the Caesar's decree!"

"Calm down," said Yochai. "Catch your breath, and tell us what happened."

Daniel crouched, placed his hands on his knees, and sucked in deep breaths of burning air. "Hundreds of them," he continued. "I never saw so many soldiers. They're going from house to house seizing holy scrolls. They beat up the rabbi in the village square — right in front of everybody! When a few Jews tried to stop them, they killed one!"

The boy's face streamed with tears. His body shook with terror. Yochai and Shlomo left their dogs to guard the flock as they raced back to the village.

Yochai awoke with a sudden start. The smell of smoke tainted the still night air, and he felt himself warmer than usual. He groped with his hands in the darkness of the cave until he made out the source of the warmth — Shlomo's goat-hair cloak covered him. Yochai sat up. He observed Shlomo sitting cross-legged and listless near the glowing embers of a dying fire. Yochai rose and approached his comrade.

"What's going on?" whispered Yochai. "Why are you up, and why do I suddenly find myself wrapped with your cloak?"

Shlomo did not stir. His eyes remaining transfixed on the dim coals, his only response a barely perceptible nod that acknowledged his friend's presence. Yochai sat down.

"Thanks for offering me the cloak," continued Yochai after a few minutes. "Especially now that winter is coming on, it really helps, but what about you? Wrap yourself with it and go to sleep. You know nothing bothers me when it comes to sleeping. You've said so yourself dozens of times." Yochai hoped that his mildly humorous self-deprecation would rouse his friend. Instead, he saw tiny tears, aglow from the firelight, glisten upon Shlomo's face. Yochai hugged his friend's shoulders. "You should be proud of your father and your whole family... I know they would be proud of you."

Shlomo shook his head slowly. He made a vain effort to wipe the tears with his hands, but they kept coming. "My father... When I got the news about my father last month... At least when the Romans murdered him and my little brother it was over quickly. But what about my mother and sisters?" He sobbed audibly now. "The report was that they were captured and...

who knows what happened to them?"

Yochai hugged his friend more tightly. Shlomo's head drooped in despair. "We're all like that now," said Yochai softly. "All of us boys who escaped to hide in this cave. We're twenty orphans with only our *Rebbe* as our father and mother. I'm like your brother now."

Shlomo pulled himself heedlessly from Yochai's grasp. "But how much longer can we continue like this?" He lifted the tattered sleeve of his tunic with bony fingers. "Look at my arm. Look at your own arms. Six months ago, either one of us could have lifted a full grown ram and carried it in one arm effortlessly. Now look at us!"

"But think about what *Rebbe* says. We have a chance to achieve a closeness to *Hashem* that few other Jews experience. I know I would never have learned *Torah* the way I do now if I had continued as a shepherd. It's true that we must hide all day, but we also learn *Torah* all day."

"Maybe so, but how much longer can we keep scurrying about at night foraging for food, scrambling through brambles, stubbing our feet on rocks, just in the hope of scrounging up a few berries or herbs to sustain ourselves?"

"Well, at least now that it's winter, there is plenty of rainwater."

"Sure! It gathers in smelly holes in the ground, more mud than water."

Yochai gave another firm shake to his friend's shoulders. "Perhaps we won't survive, Shlomo. Maybe we came to this cave to escape the Romans only to find death in a different form, but at least we have a place in the world to come. Some people struggle their whole lives to achieve what we've earned in a short time."

When Augustus entered the barracks, he found all the

other soldiers sound asleep, worn out from a tough day of drill-ing. Unbearably tired himself and eager to join them, he fumbled to untie the leather bands that fastened his boots and leggings.

"Great practice today," said Romulus cheerfully as he entered the room.

"Same as every day," muttered Augustus, incredulous that his friend could sound so eager while he and everyone else were so exhausted.

"Constant practice and drilling are what make good soldiers." Romulus repeated the watchword of their commander. "But today I really got into it."

It maddened Augustus that Romulus should show such blind enthusiasm. He tapped at a small lamp that flickered near a window. "Darned animal fat! It never burns properly. Always sputters so you have to adjust it a million times. I'll never under-stand why they can't give us oil to put in the lamps."

Romulus ignored this attempt to change the subject. "Ever since we got our armor, I've felt different about the army."

By this time, Augustus had changed into the light linen tunic in which he slept. "You can save your fanatical enthusiasm for tomorrow. I heard we're going on an all day march with fully loaded packs of equipment."

"I'm more than ready for it!"

Tired though he was, Augustus did not collapse into bed. Instead, he sat cross-legged on the dirt floor near the window with the flickering lamp. Producing his pair of dice, he tossed them against the wall. "Care for a game?"

"I thought you were tired?" Romulus's voice was tinged with a note of suspicion. "Shouldn't we rest for tomorrow's march?"

"Oh, come on. Just play a few rounds with me." The dice clattered as they struck the wall and floor. "You aren't afraid just because I beat Julius, are you?"

"Julius is a spearman. He outranks you."

"Not at playing dice. He lost a whole week's pay to me yesterday."

"By Jupiter, you're lucky!"

Augustus scooped up the dice for another toss at the wall. As he did so, Romulus spied a caterpillar crawling along the floor. Stooping down, he managed to convey it onto a piece of straw.

"What are you doing?" asked Augustus.

Romulus nodded at the sputtering lamp. "I get a thrill out of putting these little fellows into the fire and watching them squirm."

"But it's wrong to cause pain for no reason," protested Augustus with a tone of disgust.

Romulus ignored his comrade's fastidiousness as he edged closer to the lamp, balancing the caterpillar so that it would not fall from its straw perch. "You enjoy falconry, don't you? Falcons are hardly kind to their prey."

"It's different hunting for food."

Romulus did not take his eyes off of his quarry. "Sometimes your ideas are so silly, I think you should have been born a woman." Suddenly, Romulus took his eyes off the caterpillar and stared at Augustus. Then he abruptly flung the caterpillar and straw out the open window. "It's... it's the Jews, isn't it?" He whispered in an exceptionally low voice now. "Not hurting animals is some kind of custom of theirs, isn't it?"

Augustus shrugged his shoulders, still mindlessly tossing the dice against the wall. The rattling had become almost rhythmic.

Romulus sat himself down next to his friend. "I don't know what will become of you, Augie. I've seen how you maneuver with your sword when we practice." He made a deft motion in the air with an imaginary blade. "Swift, aggressive, and you don't tire easily. And I don't know anyone our age who can vault onto a galloping horse as skillfully as you can." He paused. "But this fascination with the Jews. I just don't understand..."

"Is it so strange that I miss my friends?"

"You may have had fun with them when you were little, but they are a lowly, accursed race."

"Even something lowly can have a use."

Romulus drew his lips into a disgusted grimace. "Nothing is as lowly as they are. The very word 'Jew' leaves a bad taste in my mouth. Anyway, our duty is to the Empire, and those people are its enemies. Think about that! And your family, Augustus. Doesn't your upbringing mean anything to you? A captain's son just shouldn't think the way you do. Don't you have a heart?"

"Sure I do, but it isn't made of marble like an idol's."

Romulus shuddered. "Don't blaspheme, and don't waste sentiment on those scum! Think of your family, your comrades, your duty!"

Shameful silence followed as Augustus put the dice away, his head hanging. He avoided meeting Romulus's staring eyes as he climbed into his bed.

Augustus sat sharpening his sword before the hearth in his father's command post. The sword was short yet sturdy, with a double-edged blade and a finely tipped point. Again and again he rubbed at it, tediously working over every millimeter.

"It is a great day for Rome," boasted Gaius as he entered the room. His gleeful voice fairly sang the words. "At last my men caught those Jewish pigs!"

Augustus, who had already heard the news, did not raise his eyes from his work. "I don't see what the great victory was," he responded matter-of-factly. "I heard that the Jews were unarmed and so weak from starvation that they hardly resisted."

"Even so, even so." Gaius sounded a bit annoyed that his son would question the greatness of his conquest. "They eluded us all those months, but we found their cave." He clasped his

hands like a child who has succeeded in catching a grasshopper after much effort.

Augustus set down the whetstone momentarily and ran his thumbnail along the edges of the sword blade. "Not quite perfect yet," he muttered to himself in a subdued voice. "Needs at least another half hour of work."

Gaius could not help beaming proudly at the powerful silhouette of his son against the flames of the hearth. The sight made it difficult for him to feel anger at how the boy ignored the importance of his great victory. He uncupped his hands.

"How did they find them?" Augustus deliberately kept his focus on the sword, picking up the whetstone and applying it yet again. He did not want his father to see the look of concern he knew his eyes betrayed.

"Two of my men caught one of them sneaking into the village. A wretched boy — a bag of bones really." Gaius approached the hearth, rubbing his hands in its warmth.

Augustus's heart skipped a beat. "What was his name?"

"Who knows and who cares?" answered Gaius with a disdainful wave of his hand.

Augustus rubbed more diligently with the whetstone. "How did they get him to reveal the location of the others?"

Gaius smirked. "You know that yourself, Augie. Only severe torture works on a stubborn Jew. My men knew just what to do."

"What happened to the boy after that?"

"Who knows? I have enough to do without worrying about filthy Jews. I told the men to entertain themselves with him as they pleased. They probably let the dogs finish him off."

Augustus uttered an unintelligible expletive. His father assumed that it was directed at the Jewish traitors, yet it gave him an uneasy feeling. Gaius shook his head solemnly as he continued to admire his son's image before the flames, the bright red hair blending with the fire. "The truth is, I haven't much taste for such sport myself, son, but who cares? The men did well. Let them enjoy their victory. By the way, I have some more interesting news for you. Among those captured was your so-called friend, Yochai."

Augustus abruptly laid down the sword. A sharp tightness settled into the pit of his stomach. Casting aside any further discretion, he blurted, "What will be done with him?"

Gaius shrugged his shoulders. "Same as the others, I suppose. Something has to be done to instill fear into the Jews. A gruesome death for these rebels will set an example for the

others."

"But they haven't really done anything…"

Gaius's eyes turned fierce. "Done anything? They hid for months studying the perverse teachings of their religion which Roman law has forbidden."

"But my friend…" Augustus's voice died off feebly.

"Stand up when you address me!" Gaius was furious. Augustus rose obediently. "Your so-called friend is a traitor," continued his father. "An enemy of Rome! How dare you even suggest any leniency!"

Augustus frowned awkwardly and bit his lips, his face reddening. "I apologize for my insolence father, and I am prepared to accept whatever punishment you see fit."

"That's better!" The edge in Gaius's voice softened. "You must understand that Yochai defied Roman authority. What he did was wrong, and any leniency would only encourage others to do the same."

"May I address you, father?" pleaded Augustus.

"Yes, if you are respectful about it."

Augustus swallowed hard. "Why kill him father? Banish him to some far-flung place. No one needs to know about it, and then it won't set a wrong example. The army has let Jews go free in the past for a handsome bribe. You could…"

"No son, not this time." Gaius's voice grew calm now, for he had anticipated such a plea. "Rome has brought civilization here. We've built roads, bridges, stadiums, and bathhouses. And do these worthless Jews appreciate any of it? Of course not! They cling to their awkward ways, despise our gods, and resent our very presence."

"But isn't there still some way…"

"No, Augustus. You are old enough to understand the way of the world by now. The strong flourish, and the weak perish. Look at how the Jews devote so much time to study instead of military training and exercise. The fools bring about

their own weakness. They deserve to die."

Augustus hung his head, but his father placed a hand under the boy's chin and lifted it. "In a hundred years there will be no more Jewish people. The wise ones will join the Roman Empire. The rest will be dead. You may not like it, but that's life."

Augustus felt a thick lump in his throat. He wanted to answer his father, but the words would not come. At last, he gasped, "I know you're right father, but still, isn't there some way…"

Gaius's eyes flickered with anger at the stubbornness of this boy, yet he restrained himself. "Augustus…" His voice grew thick. "I'm going to help you develop into the man I know you want to become. I'm going to order you to do something you will remember for the rest of your life and thank me for in future years. You personally must kill Yochai."

"Kill Yochai?" The words hung heavily in the air. Augustus could hardly believe he had uttered them. He tore away from his father, sank to his knees next to the hearth, and buried his face in his hands.

"You can do it, son," said Gaius firmly. "I understand that you think you like him, but if he were in your place, I can promise that he wouldn't hesitate to kill you. Think about that!"

Gaius approached his son. "Your so-called friend is an ungrateful traitor to the Roman Empire. He has violated the law and deserves death." Gaius lifted the sword Augustus had been polishing earlier and placed it resolutely into the trembling hands of the boy, who now gazed up at his father with glistening eyes. "Use this to do it! If you insist on showing mercy, then do so by striking through the heart so that the wretch may die quickly and not suffer!"

Augustus stared at the sword, its sharp blade glimmering brilliantly in the firelight. Several moments passed in silence. Then the boy gripped the handle of his weapon tightly, rose,

nodded resolutely to his father, and marched off to his barracks.

Augustus tossed on his coarse mattress in the barracks. Its roughness had seldom bothered Augustus in the past, yet he could not sleep soundly that night. Tough as he tried to act in front of his father, the unsettled feeling in his stomach would not leave him.

At last, Augustus got up and put on his clothing, except for his boots, which he hid beneath his tunic. Cautious not to awaken the other men in the barracks, he sneaked out in bare feet.

The bright full moon outside accentuated the blackness of the placid night sky as it bathed the world in gray. Augustus's pulse raced. The knot in his stomach tightened as he clumsily drew on his boots and groped through the grayness to the river-bank. There he sat down, watching the cool dark water glide gently by. The loneliness of the scene made him shiver.

Augustus gazed up at the moon. "You are beautiful yet cruel," he thought to himself. "You shine in glorious brightness while I suffer." When he turned again to view the river, the moon's reflection gazed steadily back at him, as though taunting him for trying to avoid its glare. He tossed a stone at the reflection, bursting it into infinite ripples of light. "That's how I'd like to destroy you," he muttered resentfully. He continued to stare as the ripples gradually subsided and the reflection recomposed itself, mocking him yet again.

That moon reminded Augustus of Yochai, who had told him once that the Jewish people are compared to the moon. Though their fortunes may wax and wane, they are never completely destroyed, just as the moon goes through phases of waxing and waning.

But it was not only the moon that reminded Augustus of Yochai. Everything did, even the river itself and the mountains

beyond where they had spent so much time playing, thinking, talking, sharing secrets and dreams together. An owl hooted. Augustus shuddered deeply as he remembered the haunting sound of Yochai's pipe.

The knot in Augustus's stomach tightened further. For a moment, he thought he could sense nothing else. 'How can I do what I have to do?' he thought. 'How can I do my duty?' Suddenly, anger welled up within him. He hated that moon and everything it stood for. He leaped from his place and splashed into the cold water, pounding fiercely with his fists at the silver reflection. Breathless, he dragged himself back to the bank where he sat down in a heap, his clothing thoroughly soaked, silvery droplets of water staining his curly red hair.

Then he saw it again. The moon. Still shining, still mocking. He buried his face in his hands and shut his eyes. He could not face that moonlight. 'My father loves me,' he thought. 'He knows what's best for me.' If only he could think of some reason to hate Yochai. That, at least, might make it easier. But it was no good. Each time he tried, he only remembered the fun they had enjoyed.

Dawn approached, yet the distraught young soldier sat at the riverside, his eyes still closed, his mind engulfed in darkness and confusion. When, at last, he found the courage to open his eyes, the moon had sunk low in the sky. He dragged himself back to the barracks, his head lowered to avoid catching sight of that moon.

Augustus did not bother to change his wet clothing or try to go back to sleep. The pain in his stomach would not let him. A hand placed on Augustus's shoulder gave him a start.

"You're thinking about your friend, aren't you?" said Romulus quietly.

There was no response.

No one else was up yet, but Romulus had already dressed. He laced the fingers of his hands together, placed them behind his

neck, and began to swing mindlessly from side to side in the rhythm of the endless exercises the soldiers practiced. "I know you have it in you to do your duty," he said after a while.

Augustus forced an odd half-smile to his lips. "Yes," he answered. "Today I will prove myself a man."

Romulus broke off his drilling, patted his buddy firmly on the shoulder and said, "I know you will."

Donning the armor of which he was so proud, Augustus marched to his father's quarters. There he stood at attention and presented himself to his father with a sharp salute.

"How fine you look in your uniform," said Gaius proudly. The bright red plume of the young man's helmet shining in the early daylight accentuated the redness of his freckled face.

"I've always practiced so hard to be a soldier," answered Augustus with resolve. "Now I have the chance to do the real thing."

"That's the spirit son. May Mars guide your footsteps to victory!"

Augustus forced a smile, but the pain in his stomach made it cold and empty. Gaius explained how to reach Yochai, who had been tied to a tree outside the village. "Go and face him alone. It will mean more to you that way."

Augustus saluted and turned from his father. As he marched, beads of sweat formed upon his brow. He touched his right hand to the scabbard that bore his sword. The cold metal made his hand shiver and turn clammy. The heavy, sour pain in his belly made him giddy. 'I must do what is right,' he whispered to himself over and over again.

The same brilliant moonlight that had shone upon Augustus at the riverside on that dreadful night also poured down upon Yochai. Roman soldiers had marched him along with his hands

tightly bound in coarse hemp rope. Faint from hunger and exhaustion, Yochai tripped and fell repeatedly only to be roused by the kicks and blows of the soldiers, who laughed merrily at his predicament. He stumbled so often that he wondered how they could still find amusement in it.

At last, the soldiers shoved Yochai against a tree and tied him fast. The boy had heard many stories about how the Romans killed their prisoners in the most painful ways possible. 'I don't mind dying,' he thought, 'if only they won't torture me.'

"The captain's son will be here in the morning to put an end to your miserable life," announced one of the soldiers.

'A typical Roman lie,' thought Yochai, knowing full well who the captain's son was. The soldier detected the disbelief in Yochai's sunken eyes.

"It's true!" The soldier laughed cruelly. "Your own so-called friend, the playmate of your boyhood, is now the very one who will kill you. That is, of course, provided that you make it through the rest of the night!"

The other soldiers joined the cruel laughter. As they disappeared into the night, Yochai thought their laughter sounded like so many chickens cackling, or perhaps demons. As for Augustus, he stoutly refused to believe it. The others might be wicked, but not his old friend, surely not Augustus. At least he kept trying to tell himself so. 'On the other hand,' he thought, 'A person's environment affects him. It's plain how much the Romans hate Jews. Can I really expect Augustus not to have felt their influence?'

The moonlight continued to stream down. Yochai's mind wandered to thinking about all the things he and Augustus had done together until his gaze fell upon his weary, thin hands bound before him. The gray moonlight made them appear ghostly, as though already dangling from a corpse. 'No use thinking about the past now. If Augustus doesn't kill me, I'm sure some other Roman will.' With that he resolved to spend his last

night on Earth reciting Psalms and pouring out his heart to his Creator. Difficult as it may be to believe that a young man who had gone through so much could still cry, Yochai's eyes produced an endless stream — the tears biting into his gaunt face, chilled by the night air.

Augustus marched along briskly, the giddiness from lack of sleep and his burning stomach contorted his face into a kind of perverse smile at times. At last, he reached the small cluster of trees where he found Yochai. For a moment the young soldier froze in his tracks, hesitating, unable to face his friend. He unsheathed his freshly sharpened sword and raised it in the dawning sunlight. 'Just do it and get it over with,' he thought.

The sunlight poured upon Augustus's face, flushing it bright red.

Yochai lifted his pale, tear-stained face at the sound of Augustus's footfalls. 'That is the redness of Edom, of Rome,' he thought. 'Perhaps Esau looked like that.'

As the blade of the sword caught the sunlight, it gleamed like a flash of lightning. Augustus marched steadily forward, now admiring the glowing sword, now glancing into the clear sky. Their eyes never met and neither boy said a word. 'Just do it and get it over with.' The same thought pounded over and over again in the soldier's brain. 'Today I will prove myself a man.'

Augustus shouted a bloodcurdling battle cry at the top of his lungs. Yochai closed his eyes. 'This is it,' he thought. He started to recite *Shema*, but he never had a chance to finish. Augustus had already lunged forward and cut him free.

Yochai was certain that his time to die had arrived. His

only wish was to get it over without any further suffering. Only at the end does it become clear what Augustus really meant when he promised his father that he would do the right thing and prove himself a man.

Divine redemption, too, is sudden, dramatic, and unexpected. The entire Jewish nation departed Egypt in less than eighteen minutes — the time it takes for dough to leaven. Why did it have to be this way?

The purpose of Creation is for people to recognize the existence and dominion of God. To create a lasting recognition sufficiently striking to make the Jews into a special people dedicated to *Hashem's* service and capable of receiving the *Torah* required an extraordinarily clear revelation.

It is one thing to speak theoretically about God creating and controlling the universe. It is another matter to experience it — to be subjected to the most degrading bondage and almost lose hope — and then to participate in sudden salvation through direct Divine intervention. This experience produced the deep and enduring impression necessary to create a Jewish people both worthy and capable of receiving the *Torah*.

The *Talmud* states that Isaac was born on Passover.[321] It seems peculiar, however, that he would have any connection with this holiday because he represents the trait of judgment.[322] How is redemption from slavery related to judgment?

Isaac's name, which God Himself selected, means "he will laugh."[323] People find things which are surprising to be humorous or amusing. Abraham and Sarah had been visited with a harsh judgment. After years of marriage, they had no children. Moreover, at their advanced age there was no longer any possibility of

---

[321] B.T. *Rosh Hashannah* 10B-11A.

[322] See, for example, *Zohar* I, 72A. The *Talmud* states that *Hashem* remembered Sarah, and she became pregnant with Isaac, on *Rosh Hashannah* — a time when the world is judged (B.T. *Rosh Hashannah* 10B-11A).

[323] Genesis 17:19.

having a child by natural means. Then the impossible happened, and all who heard about it laughed.[324] At birth, Isaac acquired the trait not merely of judgment, but of judgment followed by unexpected Divine salvation.

Later on, one special event in Isaac's life exemplified this trait. God's commandment to Abraham to sacrifice Isaac appeared to be a harsh judgment. It put Abraham in the terrible position of having to slaughter his own son. A horrifying proposition for any parent, it was especially appalling to Abraham, who epitomized the trait of kindness.

This was also a tremendous test for Isaac. Abraham had repeatedly stood up against the entire world for the sake of *Hashem*. Surely it offended Isaac's sense of justice for God to demand such a sacrifice from the one person loyal to Him. Moreover, *Hashem* had promised that Isaac would carry on Abraham's work — a promise which would not be fulfilled if Isaac were to die. Certainly, it must have appeared unjust for God to renege on His promise. Finally, Isaac himself had committed no offence which would have warranted his premature death.

However, *Hashem* never intended for Abraham to actually sacrifice Isaac. He only commanded him to do so as a way of causing them both to grow spiritually by displaying their willingness to transcend their own personalities to serve Him. Just when Abraham raised the knife to strike the fatal blow, God intervened.

This pattern of harsh judgment followed by sudden Divine intervention and rescue repeated itself when the Jews were enslaved in Egypt. God did not intend for the Jews to remain permanently enslaved. He only wanted them to grow spiritually, and it was the very horrors of Egyptian oppression followed by a sudden, miraculous rescue which caused that growth.[325]

---

[324] Genesis 21:6.

[325] This explains why *Rashi* states that the exile commenced with the birth of Isaac (*Rashi* on Genesis 15:13).

The Jews served as slaves for hundreds of years in Egypt, the most powerful civilization of its time. The last thing anyone would have expected was their abrupt departure.

The *Torah* emphasizes this aspect of the Exodus when it explains that we eat *Matzoth* because the speed and suddenness of the rescue was so great that there was no time for the dough to rise.[326] The very fact that it all happened so unexpectedly reinforced the lesson that God controls the universe and that anything is possible at any time. This is the "secret of faith" to which *Matzah* attests.[327]

The future liberation from exile will also be quick, dramatic, and unexpected. As the Psalmist says, "Then our mouths will be filled with laughter."[328] People will look back at the redemption and laugh at its surprising suddenness and the unexpected way in which it happened.

May this occur speedily and in our days!

---

[326] Exodus 12:39.

[327] See *Zohar* II, 41A.

[328] Psalms 126:2.

APPENDICES

GRACE ACCORDING TO *SEFARADI* CUSTOM:

קודם ברכת המזון אומרים :

לַמְנַצֵּחַ בִּנְגִינֹת מִזְמוֹר שִׁיר. אֱלֹהִים יְחָנֵּנוּ וִיבָרְכֵנוּ יָאֵר פָּנָיו אִתָּנוּ סֶלָה. לָדַעַת בָּאָרֶץ דַּרְכֶּךָ בְּכָל גּוֹיִם יְשׁוּעָתֶךָ. יוֹדוּךָ עַמִּים אֱלֹהִים יוֹדוּךָ עַמִּים כֻּלָּם. יִשְׂמְחוּ וִירַנְּנוּ לְאֻמִּים כִּי תִשְׁפֹּט עַמִּים מִישׁוֹר וּלְאֻמִּים בָּאָרֶץ תַּנְחֵם סֶלָה. יוֹדוּךָ עַמִּים אֱלֹהִים יוֹדוּךָ עַמִּים כֻּלָּם. אֶרֶץ נָתְנָה יְבוּלָהּ יְבָרְכֵנוּ אֱלֹהִים אֱלֹהֵינוּ. יְבָרְכֵנוּ אֱלֹהִים וְיִירְאוּ אֹתוֹ כָּל אַפְסֵי אָרֶץ.

אֲבָרְכָה אֶת יְהֹוָה בְּכָל עֵת תָּמִיד תְּהִלָּתוֹ בְּפִי. סוֹף דָּבָר הַכֹּל נִשְׁמָע אֶת הָאֱלֹהִים יְרָא וְאֶת מִצְוֹתָיו שְׁמוֹר כִּי זֶה כָּל הָאָדָם. תְּהִלַּת יְהֹוָה יְדַבֶּר פִּי וִיבָרֵךְ כָּל בָּשָׂר שֵׁם קָדְשׁוֹ לְעוֹלָם וָעֶד. וַאֲנַחְנוּ נְבָרֵךְ יָהּ מֵעַתָּה וְעַד עוֹלָם הַלְלוּיָהּ. וַיְדַבֵּר אֵלַי זֶה הַשֻּׁלְחָן אֲשֶׁר לִפְנֵי יְהֹוָה.

כשיש זימון המברך אומר :

הַב לָן וְנִבְרִיךְ לְמַלְכָּא עִלָּאָה קַדִּישָׁא.

הנוכחים עונים :

שָׁמַיִם.

ഇ 326 രൃ

The following is recited before Grace:

For the singer of melodies, a tuneful song. May God show us grace and bless us; may He show favor towards us forever. That it be known upon Earth Your ways, among all the nations Your salvation. Let the peoples acknowledge You, God; let all peoples acknowledge You. Nations shall rejoice and sing, for You judge peoples rightly and You guide nations upon the Earth forever. Let the peoples acknowledge You, God; let all peoples acknowledge You. For the land gave forth its produce; they shall bless God who is our God. May they bless God and revere Him all the ends of the Earth. [329]

I bless Hashem at all times, His praise is continually in my mouth.[330] When the last word of all is heard, fear God and keep His commandments for this is the entire [purpose of a] person.[331] My mouth shall speak the praise of *Hashem* and all flesh shall bless His holy Name forever and ever.[332] We shall bless God from now until eternity; Praise God![333] He said to me, "This is the table which is before *Hashem*."[334]

When at least three Jewish males are present, one of them should lead the recitation of Grace. The leader says:

Let us bless the holy, supernal King.

The others respond:

[With the permission of] Heaven.

---

[329] Psalm 67.

[330] Psalms 34:2.

[331] Ecclesiastes 12:13.

[332] Psalms 145:21.

[333] Psalms 115:18.

[334] Ezekiel 41:22. An angel said this to Ezekiel when showing him a vision of the Temple altar. This verse alludes to the fact that a person's table serves in place of the altar when there is no Temple (*Rashi*).

המברך ממשיך:

בִּרְשׁוּת מַלְכָּא עִלָּעָא קַדִּישָׁא וּבִרְשׁוּתְכֶם נְבָרֵךְ [במנין: אֱלֹהֵינוּ] שֶׁאָכַלְנוּ מִשֶּׁלּוֹ.

השומעים עונים:

בָּרוּךְ [במנין: אֱלֹהֵינוּ] שֶׁאָכַלְנוּ מִשֶּׁלּוֹ וּבְטוּבוֹ חָיִינוּ.

המברך חוזר ואומר:

בָּרוּךְ [במנין: אֱלֹהֵינוּ] שֶׁאָכַלְנוּ מִשֶּׁלּוֹ וּבְטוּבוֹ חָיִינוּ.

בָּרוּךְ אַתָּה יְהֹוָה אֱלֹהֵינוּ מֶלֶךְ הָעוֹלָם הָאֵל הַזָּן אוֹתָנוּ וְאֶת הָעוֹלָם כֻּלּוֹ בְּטוּבוֹ בְּחֵן בְּחֶסֶד בְּרֶוַח וּבְרַחֲמִים רַבִּים נוֹתֵן לֶחֶם לְכָל בָּשָׂר כִּי לְעוֹלָם חַסְדּוֹ וּבְטוּבוֹ הַגָּדוֹל תָּמִיד לֹא חָסַר לָנוּ וְאַל יֶחְסַר לָנוּ מָזוֹן תָּמִיד לְעוֹלָם וָעֶד כִּי הוּא אֵל זָן וּמְפַרְנֵס לַכֹּל וְשֻׁלְחָנוֹ עָרוּךְ לַכֹּל וְהִתְקִין מִחְיָה וּמָזוֹן לְכָל בְּרִיּוֹתָיו אֲשֶׁר בָּרָא בְּרַחֲמָיו וּבְרוֹב חֲסָדָיו כָּאָמוּר, "פּוֹתֵחַ אֶת יָדֶךָ וּמַשְׂבִּיעַ לְכָל חַי רָצוֹן." בָּרוּךְ אַתָּה יְהֹוָה הַזָּן אֶת הַכֹּל.

נוֹדֶה לְךָ יְהֹוָה אֱלֹהֵינוּ עַל שֶׁהִנְחַלְתָּ לַאֲבוֹתֵינוּ אֶרֶץ חֶמְדָּה טוֹבָה וּרְחָבָה בְּרִית וְתוֹרָה חַיִּים וּמָזוֹן עַל שֶׁהוֹצֵאתָנוּ מֵאֶרֶץ מִצְרַיִם וּפְדִיתָנוּ מִבֵּית עֲבָדִים וְעַל בְּרִיתְךָ שֶׁחָתַמְתָּ בִּבְשָׂרֵינוּ וְעַל תּוֹרָתְךָ שֶׁלִּמַּדְתָּנוּ וְעַל חֻקֵּי רְצוֹנֶךָ שֶׁהוֹדַעְתָּנוּ וְעַל חַיִּים וּמָזוֹן שֶׁאַתָּה זָן וּמְפַרְנֵס אוֹתָנוּ.

If ten or more Jewish males over age thirteen are present, substitute "Our God" for "Him" or "He" as the brackets indicate. The leader says:

With the permission of the Holy, Supernal King and with your permission, let us bless Him [our God] from whom we have eaten.

Those present respond:

Blessed is He [our God] from whom we have eaten and by whose goodness we live.

Blessed are You Hashem, our God, King of the Universe, the God who sustains us and the entire world with goodness, grace, kindness, generosity and great mercy, giving bread to all flesh for His kindness is eternal and in His great goodness we have constantly never lacked nor shall we ever lack food continually to all eternity, for He is a God who sustains and provides for all and His table is set for all and He has prepared sustenance and nourishment for all His creatures which He has created with mercy and with His abundant kindness, as is said, "You open Your hand and satisfy all life willingly."[335]   Blessed are you Hashem, Who sustains all.

We thank you Hashem, our God, because You bequeathed to our ancestors a desirable, good and spacious land, covenant and Torah, life and sustenance, and because You took us out from the Land of Egypt, redeemed us from the place of servitude, sealed Your covenant in our flesh, taught us Your Torah, informed us of the laws of Your will, and because of the life and sustenance which you furnish and provide us.

---

[335] Psalms 145:16.

עַל הַכֹּל יְהֹוָה אֱלֹהֵינוּ אֲנַחְנוּ מוֹדִים לָךְ וּמְבָרְכִים אֶת שְׁמָךְ
כָּאָמוּר, "וְאָכַלְתָּ וְשָׂבָעְתָּ וּבֵרַכְתָּ אֶת יְהֹוָה אֱלֹהֶיךָ עַל הָאָרֶץ הַטֹּבָה
אֲשֶׁר נָתַן לָךְ." בָּרוּךְ אַתָּה יְהֹוָה עַל הָאָרֶץ וְעַל הַמָּזוֹן.

רַחֵם יְהֹוָה אֱלֹהֵינוּ עָלֵינוּ וְעַל יִשְׂרָאֵל עַמָּךְ וְעַל יְרוּשָׁלַיִם
עִירָךְ וְעַל הַר צִיּוֹן מִשְׁכַּן כְּבוֹדָךְ וְעַל הֵיכָלָךְ וְעַל מְעוֹנָךְ וְעַל דְּבִירָךְ
וְעַל הַבַּיִת הַגָּדוֹל וְהַקָּדוֹשׁ שֶׁנִּקְרָא שִׁמְךָ עָלָיו. אָבִינוּ רְעֵנוּ זוּנֵנוּ
פַּרְנְסֵנוּ כַּלְכְּלֵנוּ הַרְוִיחֵנוּ הַרְוַח לָנוּ מְהֵרָה מִכָּל צָרוֹתֵנוּ וְנָא אַל
תַּצְרִיכֵנוּ יְהֹוָה אֱלֹהֵינוּ לִידֵי מַתְּנוֹת בָּשָׂר וָדָם וְלֹא לִידֵי הַלְוָאָתָם
אֶלָּא לְיָדְךָ הַמְּלֵאָה וְהָרְחָבָה הָעֲשִׁירָה וְהַפְּתוּחָה. יְהִי רָצוֹן שֶׁלֹּא
נֵבוֹשׁ בָּעוֹלָם הַזֶּה וְלֹא נִכָּלֵם לְעוֹלָם הַבָּא. וּמַלְכוּת בֵּית דָּוִד מְשִׁיחָךְ
תַּחֲזִירֶנָּה לִמְקוֹמָהּ בִּמְהֵרָה בְיָמֵינוּ.

[בשבת אומרים:] רְצֵה וְהַחֲלִיצֵנוּ יְהֹוָה אֱלֹהֵינוּ בְּמִצְוֹתֶיךָ
וּבְמִצְוַת יוֹם הַשְּׁבִיעִי הַשַּׁבָּת הַגָּדוֹל וְהַקָּדוֹשׁ הַזֶּה כִּי יוֹם גָּדוֹל
וְקָדוֹשׁ הוּא מִלְּפָנֶיךָ. נִשְׁבּוֹת בּוֹ וְנָנוּחַ בּוֹ וְנִתְעַנֵּג בּוֹ כְּמִצְוַת חֻקֵּי
רְצוֹנָךְ וְאַל תְּהִי צָרָה וְיָגוֹן בְּיוֹם מְנוּחָתֵנוּ וְהַרְאֵנוּ בְּנֶחָמַת צִיּוֹן
בִּמְהֵרָה בְיָמֵינוּ כִּי אַתָּה הוּא בַּעַל הַנֶּחָמוֹת וְהֲגַם שֶׁאֲכַלְנוּ וְשָׁתִינוּ
חָרְבַּן בֵּיתְךָ הַגָּדוֹל וְהַקָּדוֹשׁ לֹא שָׁכַחְנוּ. אַל תִּשְׁכָּחֵנוּ לָנֶצַח וְאַל
תִּזְנָחֵנוּ לָעַד כִּי אֵל מֶלֶךְ גָּדוֹל וְקָדוֹשׁ אָתָּה.

For everything, *Hashem*, our God, we thank You and bless Your Name, as is said, "You shall eat and be satisfied and bless *Hashem*, your God, for the good land which He gave you."[336] Blessed are You, God, for the Land and for the sustenance.

Have mercy, *Hashem*, our God, upon us and upon Israel Your people, upon Jerusalem Your city, upon Mount Zion the seat of Your glory, upon Your shrine, upon Your dwelling, upon Your sanctuary, and upon the great and holy House upon which Your Name is called. Our Father, shepherd us, nourish us, sustain us, provide for us, grant us relief, deliver us speedily from all our troubles, and please do not cause us *Hashem*, our God, to rely upon gifts from flesh and blood or their loans, but rather Your full, generous, rich and open hand. May it be Your will that we not be ashamed in this world nor humiliated in the world to come. Restore the kingdom of the House of David, Your anointed, to its place speedily and in our days.

[*On the Sabbath add the following*:] Take pleasure and grant us relief *Hashem*, our God, through Your commandments and the commandment of the seventh day, this great and holy Sabbath; for this day is great and holy before You. Let us rest and relax upon it and take delight in it according to the commandment of the laws of Your will. Let there not be trouble or grief on the day of our rest and show us the consolation of Zion speedily, in our days, for You are the Master of consolations. Though we have eaten and drunk, the destruction of Your great and holy House we have not forgotten. Do not ever forget or neglect us ever, for You are a God who is a great and holy King.

---

[336] Deuteronomy 8:10.

אֱלֹהֵינוּ וֵאלֹהֵי אֲבוֹתֵינוּ יַעֲלֶה וְיָבֹא וְיַגִּיעַ וְיֵרָאֶה וְיֵרָצֶה
וְיִשָּׁמַע וְיִפָּקֵד וְיִזָּכֵר זִכְרוֹנֵנוּ וְזִכְרוֹן אֲבוֹתֵינוּ זִכְרוֹן יְרוּשָׁלַיִם עִירָךְ
וְזִכְרוֹן מָשִׁיחַ בֶּן דָּוִד עַבְדָּךְ וְזִכְרוֹן כָּל עַמְּךָ בֵּית יִשְׂרָאֵל לְפָנֶיךָ
לִפְלֵיטָה לְטוֹבָה לְחֵן לְחֶסֶד וּלְרַחֲמִים לְחַיִּים טוֹבִים וּלְשָׁלוֹם בְּיוֹם
חַג הַמַּצּוֹת הַזֶּה בְּיוֹם מִקְרָא קֹדֶשׁ הַזֶּה לְרַחֵם בּוֹ עָלֵינוּ וּלְהוֹשִׁיעֵנוּ.
זָכְרֵנוּ יְהֹוָה אֱלֹהֵינוּ בּוֹ לְטוֹבָה וּפָקְדֵנוּ בוֹ לִבְרָכָה וְהוֹשִׁיעֵנוּ בוֹ
לְחַיִּים טוֹבִים בִּדְבַר יְשׁוּעָה וְרַחֲמִים חוּס וְחָנֵּנוּ וְחֲמוֹל וְרַחֵם עָלֵינוּ
וְהוֹשִׁיעֵנוּ כִּי אֵלֶיךָ עֵינֵינוּ כִּי אֵל מֶלֶךְ חַנּוּן וְרַחוּם אָתָּה.

וְתִבְנֶה יְרוּשָׁלַיִם עִירְךָ בִּמְהֵרָה בְיָמֵינוּ. בָּרוּךְ אַתָּה יְהֹוָה
בּוֹנֵה יְרוּשָׁלָיִם. (בלחש: אָמֵן).

בָּרוּךְ אַתָּה יְהֹוָה אֱלֹהֵינוּ מֶלֶךְ הָעוֹלָם הָאֵל אָבִינוּ מַלְכֵּנוּ
אַדִּירֵנוּ בּוֹרְאֵנוּ גּוֹאֲלֵנוּ קְדוֹשֵׁנוּ קְדוֹשׁ יַעֲקֹב רוֹעֵנוּ רוֹעֵה יִשְׂרָאֵל
הַמֶּלֶךְ הַטּוֹב וְהַמֵּטִיב לַכֹּל שֶׁבְּכָל יוֹם וָיוֹם הוּא הֵטִיב לָנוּ הוּא
מֵטִיב לָנוּ הוּא יֵיטִיב לָנוּ הוּא גְמָלָנוּ הוּא גוֹמְלֵנוּ הוּא יִגְמְלֵנוּ לָעַד
חֵן וָחֶסֶד וְרַחֲמִים וְרֶיַח וְהַצָּלָה וְכָל טוֹב. אָמֵן.

הָרַחֲמָן הוּא יִשְׁתַּבַּח עַל כִּסֵּא כְבוֹדוֹ.

הָרַחֲמָן הוּא יִשְׁתַּבַּח בַּשָּׁמַיִם וּבָאָרֶץ.

הָרַחֲמָן הוּא יִשְׁתַּבַּח בָּנוּ לְדוֹר דוֹרִים.

הָרַחֲמָן הוּא יִמְלוֹךְ עָלֵינוּ לְעוֹלָם וָעֶד.

Our God and God of our ancestors, may it rise, come, reach, be seen, be pleasing, be heard, be recalled and be memorialized our remembrance and the remembrance of our ancestors, the remembrance of Jerusalem Your city, the remembrance of the *Mashiach*, son of David, Your servant, and the remembrance of Your entire people the House of Israel before You for deliverance, good, grace, kindness, mercy, a good life and peace on this day of the Festival of *Matzoth*, on this day of holy gathering, to show mercy upon us on it and to save us. Remember us upon it *Hashem*, our God, for good, and recall us upon it for blessing, and save us upon it for a good life with a word of salvation and mercy. Take pity and be gracious to us, and be compassionate and merciful to us and save us, for our eyes are to You, for You are a God who is a merciful and gracious King.

Rebuild Jerusalem Your city speedily in our days. Blessed are You, God who rebuilds Jerusalem. *Amen.*

Blessed are You *Hashem*, our God, King of the Universe, the God who is our Father, our King, our Champion, our Creator, our Redeemer, our Holy One, the Holy One of Jacob, our Shepherd, the Shepherd of Israel, the good King, the One who does good to all, for each and every day He has done good for us, does good for us, and will do good for us; He has supplied us, supplies us, and will supply us forever with grace, kindness, mercy, relief, saving and all good. *Amen.*

May the Merciful One be praised upon His holy throne.

May the Merciful One be blessed in Heaven and on Earth.

May the Merciful One be blessed through us to all generations.

May the Merciful One reign over us forever and ever.

הָרַחֲמָן הוּא קֶרֶן לְעַמּוֹ יָרִים.

הָרַחֲמָן הוּא יִתְפָּאֵר בָּנוּ לָנֶצַח נְצָחִים.

הָרַחֲמָן הוּא יְפַרְנְסֵנוּ בְּכָבוֹד וְלֹא בְבִזּוּי בְּהֶתֵּר וְלֹא בְאִסּוּר בְּנַחַת וְלֹא בְצַעַר.

הָרַחֲמָן הוּא יִתֵּן שָׁלוֹם בֵּינֵינוּ.

הָרַחֲמָן הוּא יִשְׁלַח בְּרָכָה רְוָחָה וְהַצְלָחָה בְּכָל מַעֲשֵׂה יָדֵינוּ.

הָרַחֲמָן הוּא יַצְלִיחַ אֶת דְּרָכֵינוּ.

הָרַחֲמָן הוּא יִשְׁבּוֹר עוֹל גָּלוּת מְהֵרָה מֵעַל צַוָּארֵנוּ.

הָרַחֲמָן הוּא יוֹלִיכֵנוּ מְהֵרָה קוֹמְמִיּוּת לְאַרְצֵנוּ.

הָרַחֲמָן הוּא יִרְפָּאֵנוּ רְפוּאָה שְׁלֵמָה רְפוּאַת הַנֶּפֶשׁ וּרְפוּאַת הַגּוּף.

הָרַחֲמָן הוּא יִפְתַּח לָנוּ אֶת יָדוֹ הָרְחָבָה.

הָרַחֲמָן הוּא יְבָרֵךְ כָּל אֶחָד וְאֶחָד מִמֶּנּוּ בִּשְׁמוֹ הַגָּדוֹל כְּמוֹ שֶׁנִּתְבָּרְכוּ אֲבוֹתֵינוּ אַבְרָהָם יִצְחָק וְיַעֲקֹב בַּכֹּל מִכֹּל כֹּל כֵּן יְבָרֵךְ אוֹתָנוּ יַחַד בִּבְרָכָה שְׁלֵמָה וְכֵן יְהִי רָצוֹן וְנֹאמַר אָמֵן.

May the Merciful One raise the honor of His people.

May the Merciful One glory in us to all eternity.

May the Merciful One sustain us with honor and not with disgrace, through permitted means and not through forbidden ones, with ease and not with difficulty.

May the Merciful One place peace among us.

May the Merciful One send blessing, relief, and success to all the work of our hands.

May the Merciful One cause our path to succeed.

May the Merciful One speedily break the yoke of exile from our necks.

May the Merciful One speedily cause us to walk upright to our land.

May the Merciful One grant us a complete healing — healing of the soul and healing of the body.

May the Merciful One open His generous hand for us.

May the Merciful One bless each and every one of us through His great Name as our ancestors, Abraham, Isaac, and Jacob were blessed "with all," "from all," and "all."[337] So may He bless us [all] together with a complete blessing, and so may it be His will, and let us say, *Amen.*

---

[337] The *Torah* tells how God blessed each of the Patriarchs with "all." "*Hashem* blessed Abraham *with all*" (Genesis 24:1). Isaac told Esau that, "I ate *from all*" (Genesis 27:33). Jacob urged Esau to take the generous gifts he presented him "because I possess *all*" (Genesis 33:11).

הָרַחֲמָן הוּא יִפְרוֹשׁ עָלֵינוּ סֻכַּת שְׁלוֹמוֹ.

[בשבת:] הָרַחֲמָן הוּא יַנְחִילֵנוּ עוֹלָם שֶׁכֻּלּוֹ שַׁבָּת וּמְנוּחָה לְחַיֵּי הָעוֹלָמִים.

הָרַחֲמָן הוּא יַנְחִילֵנוּ יוֹם שֶׁכֻּלּוֹ טוֹב.

הָרַחֲמָן הוּא יִטַּע תּוֹרָתוֹ וְאַהֲבָתוֹ בְּלִבֵּנוּ וְתִהְיֶה יִרְאָתוֹ עַל פָּנֵינוּ לְבִלְתִּי נֶחֱטָא וְיִהְיוּ כָל מַעֲשֵׂינוּ לְשֵׁם שָׁמַיִם.

[אורח מוסיף:]

הָרַחֲמָן הוּא יְבָרֵךְ אֶת הַשֻּׁלְחָן הַזֶּה שֶׁאָכַלְנוּ עָלָיו וִיסַדֵּר בּוֹ כָּל מַעֲדַנֵּי עוֹלָם וְיִהְיֶה כְּשֻׁלְחָנוֹ שֶׁל אַבְרָהָם אָבִינוּ כָּל רָעֵב מִמֶּנּוּ יֹאכַל וְכָל צָמֵא מִמֶּנּוּ יִשְׁתֶּה וְאַל יֶחְסַר מִמֶּנּוּ כָּל טוֹב לָעַד וּלְעוֹלְמֵי עוֹלָמִים.

הָרַחֲמָן הוּא יְבָרֵךְ אֶת בַּעַל הַבַּיִת הַזֶּה וּבַעַל הַסְּעֻדָּה הַזֹּאת הוּא וּבָנָיו וְאִשְׁתּוֹ וְכָל אֲשֶׁר לוֹ בְּבָנִים שֶׁיִּחְיוּ וּבִנְכָסִים שֶׁיִּרְבּוּ. בָּרֵךְ יְהֹוָה חֵילוֹ וּפֹעַל יָדָיו תִּרְצֶה. וְיִהְיוּ נְכָסָיו וּנְכָסֵינוּ מֻצְלָחִים וּקְרוֹבִים לָעִיר וְאַל יִזְדַּקֵּק לְפָנָיו וְלֹא לְפָנֵינוּ שׁוּם דְּבַר חֵטְא וְהִרְהוּר עָוֹן שָׁשׂ וְשָׂמֵחַ כָּל הַיָּמִים בְּעֹשֶׁר וְכָבוֹד מֵעַתָּה וְעַד עוֹלָם. לֹא יֵבוֹשׁ בָּעוֹלָם הַזֶּה וְלֹא יִכָּלֵם לְעוֹלָם הַבָּא. אָמֵן כֵּן יְהִי רָצוֹן.

May the Merciful One spread His tent of peace upon us.

[On the Sabbath add:] May the Merciful One bequeath us a world which is completely Sabbath and rest for eternal life.[338]

May the Merciful One bequeath us a day which is completely good.

May the Merciful One plant His *Torah* and His love in our hearts, and may His fear be upon our faces so that we not sin, and may all our deeds be for the sake of Heaven.

[A guest should add:]

May the Merciful One bless this table upon which we have eaten and arrange upon it all the delicacies of the world and may it be like the table of Abraham, our father, in that all who hunger eat from it and all who thirst drink from it, and let no goodness be lacking from it forever and to all eternity.

May the Merciful One bless the master of this house and master of this meal, he, his children, his wife, and all that is his, with children who live and property which increases. "May *Hashem* bless his property and be pleased with the work of his hands."[339] May his property and our property be successful and close to the city,[340] and may no sinful matter or iniquitous thought meet up with him or with us. May he be happy and joyous all the days, with wealth and honor from now until eternity. May he not be embarrassed in this world nor humiliated in the world to come. *Amen* and so may it be pleasing.

---

[338] The Sabbath experience is one-sixtieth of the world to come (B.T. *Berachoth* 57B).

[339] Deuteronomy 33:11.

[340] Since most people used to be farmers, it was important for their landholdings to be located where the owner could easily supervise them. Today, this blessing implies that a person should be able to manage his or her business conveniently and effectively.

הָרַחֲמָן הוּא יְחַיֵּינוּ וִיזַכֵּנוּ וִיקָרְבֵנוּ לִימוֹת הַמָּשִׁיחַ וּלְבִנְיַן בֵּית הַמִּקְדָּשׁ וּלְחַיֵּי הָעוֹלָם הַבָּא. מַגְדִּיל יְשׁוּעוֹת מַלְכּוֹ וְעֹשֶׂה חֶסֶד לִמְשִׁיחוֹ לְדָוִד וּלְזַרְעוֹ עַד עוֹלָם. כְּפִירִים רָשׁוּ וְרָעֵבוּ וְדֹרְשֵׁי יְהוָה לֹא יַחְסְרוּ כָל טוֹב. נַעַר הָיִיתִי גַּם זָקַנְתִּי וְלֹא רָאִיתִי צַדִּיק נֶעֱזָב וְזַרְעוֹ מְבַקֶּשׁ לָחֶם. כָּל הַיּוֹם חוֹנֵן וּמַלְוֶה וְזַרְעוֹ לִבְרָכָה. מַה שֶּׁאָכַלְנוּ יִהְיֶה לְשָׂבְעָה וּמַה שֶּׁשָּׁתִינוּ יִהְיֶה לִרְפוּאָה וּמַה שֶּׁהוֹתַרְנוּ יִהְיֶה לִבְרָכָה כְּדִכְתִיב, "וַיִּתֵּן לִפְנֵיהֶם וַיֹּאכְלוּ וַיּוֹתִרוּ כִּדְבַר יְהוָה." בְּרוּכִים אַתֶּם לַיהוָה עֹשֵׂה שָׁמַיִם וָאָרֶץ. בָּרוּךְ הַגֶּבֶר אֲשֶׁר יִבְטַח בַּיהוָה וְהָיָה יְהוָה מִבְטַחוֹ. יְהוָה עֹז לְעַמּוֹ יִתֵּן יְהוָה יְבָרֵךְ אֶת עַמּוֹ בַשָּׁלוֹם. עֹשֶׂה שָׁלוֹם בִּמְרוֹמָיו הוּא יַעֲשֶׂה שָׁלוֹם עָלֵינוּ וְעַל כָּל יִשְׂרָאֵל וְאִמְרוּ אָמֵן.

ממשיכים עם הברכה על הכוס השלישית בדף 99.

May the Merciful One cause us to live, merit, and draw close to the days of the *Mashiach*, the restoration of the Temple, and life in the world to come. "[God is] a great worker of salvations for His king and does kindness for his anointed one, for David and his offspring forever."[341] "Young lions want and hunger, but those who seek *Hashem* do not miss any good."[342] "I was a youth and also grew old, yet I never saw a righteous person abandoned nor his offspring scrounging for bread. All the day he is gracious and lends and his offspring is blessed."[343] May that which we have eaten be satisfying, and that which we have drunk be healing, and that which we have left over be a blessing, as is written, "He put [food] before them, and they ate and left over according to the word of *Hashem*."[344] "Blessed are you to *Hashem*, Maker of Heaven and Earth."[345] "Blessed is the man who trusts in *Hashem*; *Hashem* shall be his shelter."[346] "May *Hashem* give strength to His people; may *Hashem* bless His people with peace."[347] May He who makes peace in His heights make peace for us and for all Israel, and let us say *Amen*.[348]

The *Seder* continues with the blessing for the Third Cup at the top of page 100.

---

[341] Psalms 22:51.

[342] Psalms 34:10-11.

[343] Psalms 37:25-26.

[344] II Kings 4:44. Elisha had prophesied that a small quantity of food would be more than enough for a large company of men, and so it was.

[345] Psalms 115:15.

[346] Jeremiah 17:7.

[347] Psalms 29:11.

[348] Although there are many opposing spiritual forces in Heaven, God's Presence is readily manifest to them, and they are aware that they all emanate from Him. Therefore, they do not fight. Instead, they work together to serve *Hashem*. When the *Mashiach* comes and God's Presence is revealed on Earth, all people will come to understand the same principle so that all conflict will disappear.

NISHMATH ACCORDING TO *SEFARADI* CUSTOM:

נִשְׁמַת כָּל חַי תְּבָרֵךְ אֶת שִׁמְךָ יְהֹוָה אֱלֹהֵינוּ וְרוּחַ כָּל בָּשָׂר
תְּפָאֵר וּתְרוֹמֵם זִכְרְךָ מַלְכֵּנוּ תָּמִיד. מִן הָעוֹלָם וְעַד הָעוֹלָם אַתָּה אֵל
וּמִבַּלְעָדֶיךָ אֵין לָנוּ מֶלֶךְ גּוֹאֵל וּמוֹשִׁיעַ פּוֹדֶה וּמַצִּיל וְעוֹנֶה וּמְרַחֵם
בְּכָל עֵת צָרָה וְצוּקָה אֵין לָנוּ מֶלֶךְ עוֹזֵר וְסוֹמֵךְ אֶלָּא אַתָּה אֱלֹהֵי
הָרִאשׁוֹנִים וְהָאַחֲרוֹנִים אֱלוֹהַּ כָּל בְּרִיּוֹת אֲדוֹן כָּל תּוֹלָדוֹת הַמְהֻלָּל
בְּכָל הַתִּשְׁבָּחוֹת הַמְנַהֵג עוֹלָמוֹ בְּחֶסֶד וּבְרִיּוֹתָיו בְּרַחֲמִים וַיהֹוָה
אֱלֹהִים אֱמֶת לֹא יָנוּם וְלֹא יִישָׁן. הַמְּעוֹרֵר יְשֵׁנִים וְהַמֵּקִיץ נִרְדָּמִים
מְחַיֶּה מֵתִים וְרוֹפֵא חוֹלִים פּוֹקֵחַ עִוְרִים וְזוֹקֵף כְּפוּפִים הַמֵּשִׂיחַ
אִלְּמִים וְהַמַּפְעֲנֵחַ נֶעֱלָמִים וּלְךָ לְבַדְּךָ אֲנַחְנוּ מוֹדִים. וְאִלּוּ פִינוּ מָלֵא
שִׁירָה כַּיָּם וּלְשׁוֹנֵנוּ רִנָּה כַּהֲמוֹן גַּלָּיו וְשִׂפְתוֹתֵינוּ שֶׁבַח כְּמֶרְחֲבֵי
רָקִיעַ וְעֵינֵינוּ מְאִירוֹת כַּשֶּׁמֶשׁ וְכַיָּרֵחַ וְיָדֵינוּ פְרוּשׂוֹת כְּנִשְׁרֵי שָׁמַיִם
וְרַגְלֵינוּ קַלּוֹת כָּאַיָּלוֹת, אֵין אָנוּ מַסְפִּיקִין לְהוֹדוֹת לְךָ יְהֹוָה אֱלֹהֵינוּ
וֵאלֹהֵי אֲבוֹתֵינוּ וּלְבָרֵךְ אֶת שִׁמְךָ מַלְכֵּנוּ עַל אַחַת מֵאֶלֶף אַלְפֵי
אֲלָפִים וְרוֹב רִבֵּי רְבָבוֹת פְּעָמִים הַטּוֹבוֹת נִסִּים וְנִפְלָאוֹת שֶׁעָשִׂיתָ
עִמָּנוּ וְעִם אֲבוֹתֵינוּ. מִלְּפָנִים מִמִּצְרַיִם גְּאַלְתָּנוּ יְהֹוָה אֱלֹהֵינוּ וּמִבֵּית
עֲבָדִים פְּדִיתָנוּ. בְּרָעָב זַנְתָּנוּ וּבְשָׂבָע כִּלְכַּלְתָּנוּ מֵחֶרֶב הִצַּלְתָּנוּ
מִדֶּבֶר מִלַּטְתָּנוּ וּמֵחֳלָיִם רָעִים וְרַבִּים דִּלִּיתָנוּ. עַד הֵנָּה עֲזָרוּנוּ
רַחֲמֶיךָ וְלֹא עֲזָבוּנוּ חֲסָדֶיךָ. עַל כֵּן אֵבָרִים שֶׁפִּלַּגְתָּ בָּנוּ וְרוּחַ וּנְשָׁמָה
שֶׁנָּפַחְתָּ בְּאַפֵּנוּ וְלָשׁוֹן אֲשֶׁר שַׂמְתָּ בְּפִינוּ. הֵן הֵם יוֹדוּ וִיבָרְכוּ
וִישַׁבְּחוּ וִיפָאֲרוּ אֶת שִׁמְךָ מַלְכֵּנוּ תָּמִיד כִּי כָל פֶּה לְךָ יוֹדֶה

May the soul of all the living bless Your Name *Hashem*, our God, and may the spirit of all flesh glorify and exalt Your memory, our King, constantly. From eternity to eternity, You are God, and except for You, we have no king, redeemer, or savior Who delivers, saves, answers, and shows mercy at all times of trouble and adversity. We have no king who helps and supports but You! God of the first ones and the last ones, God of all creatures, Master of all history, praised with all acclamations,[349] Who directs His universe with kindness and His creatures with mercy. *Hashem* is a true God who neither slumbers nor sleeps. He arouses the sleeping and awakens the slumbering, revives the dead, heals the sick, gives sight to the blind, makes upright those who are bent over, gives speech to the mute and resolves mysteries. You alone do we thank. If our mouths were full of song as the sea and our tongues of chant as the multitude of waves, our lips praise as the broad heavens, our eyes luminous as the sun and moon, our hands spread as the eagles of the heavens and our feet light as harts, we could not sufficiently thank you *Hashem*, our God, and God of our ancestors, and to bless Your Name, our King, for a millionth of the millions upon millions of favors, miracles, and wonders You performed for us and for our ancestors. In ancient times You redeemed us from Egypt *Hashem*, our God, and from the place of servitude You delivered us. In famine You sustained us and in plenty You provided for us. From the sword You saved us, from pestilence You rescued us, and from a multitude of severe illnesses You extricated us. Until now Your mercy has helped us, and Your kindness did not abandon us. Therefore, our limbs which You have fixed in us, the spirit and soul which You have blown into our nostrils, and the tongue which You placed in our mouths, they shall thank, bless, praise, and glorify Your Name, our King, constantly; for every mouth shall acknowledge You,

---

[349] *Ashkenazi* texts use "praised with **many** acclamations" since it is impossible for humans to express all the praise *Hashem* deserves. *Sefaradi*, and some *Chassidic* versions, read "praised with **all** acclamations" because that is how God **should** be praised even if humans cannot do so.

וְכָל לָשׁוֹן לְךָ תְשַׁבֵּחַ וְכָל עַיִן לְךָ תְּצַפֶּה וְכָל בֶּרֶךְ לְךָ תִכְרַע. וְכָל
קוֹמָה לְפָנֶיךָ תִשְׁתַּחֲוֶה. וְהַלְּבָבוֹת יִירָאוּךָ וְהַקֶּרֶב וְהַכְּלָיוֹת יְזַמְּרוּ
לִשְׁמֶךָ כַּדָּבָר שֶׁנֶּאֱמַר, "כָּל עַצְמֹתַי תֹּאמַרְנָה יְהֹוָה מִי כָמוֹךָ מַצִּיל
עָנִי מֵחָזָק מִמֶּנּוּ וְעָנִי וְאֶבְיוֹן מִגֹּזְלוֹ." שַׁוְעַת עֲנִיִּים אַתָּה תִשְׁמַע.
צַעֲקַת הַדַּל תַּקְשִׁיב וְתוֹשִׁיעַ. וְכָתוּב, "רַנְּנוּ צַדִּיקִים בַּיהֹוָה לַיְשָׁרִים
נָאוָה תְהִלָּה."

בְּפִי יְשָׁרִים תִּתְרוֹמָם
וּבְשִׂפְתֵי צַדִּיקִים תִּתְבָּרַךְ
וּבִלְשׁוֹן חֲסִידִים תִּתְקַדָּשׁ
וּבְקֶרֶב קְדוֹשִׁים תִּתְהַלָּל

בְּמַקְהֲלוֹת רִבְבוֹת עַמְּךָ בֵּית יִשְׂרָאֵל שֶׁכֵּן חוֹבַת כָּל
הַיְצוּרִים לְפָנֶיךָ יְהֹוָה אֱלֹהֵינוּ וֵאלֹהֵי אֲבוֹתֵינוּ לְהוֹדוֹת לְהַלֵּל לְשַׁבֵּחַ
לְפָאֵר לְרוֹמֵם לְהַדֵּר וּלְנַצֵּחַ עַל כָּל דִּבְרֵי שִׁירוֹת וְתִשְׁבָּחוֹת דָּוִד בֶּן
יִשַׁי עַבְדְּךָ מְשִׁיחֶךָ. וּבְכֵן

יִשְׁתַּבַּח שִׁמְךָ לָעַד מַלְכֵּנוּ הָאֵל הַמֶּלֶךְ הַגָּדוֹל וְהַקָּדוֹשׁ
בַּשָּׁמַיִם וּבָאָרֶץ כִּי לְךָ נָאֶה יְהֹוָה אֱלֹהֵינוּ וֵאלֹהֵי אֲבוֹתֵינוּ לְעוֹלָם
וָעֶד שִׁיר וּשְׁבָחָה הַלֵּל וְזִמְרָה עֹז וּמֶמְשָׁלָה נֶצַח גְּדֻלָּה גְבוּרָה תְּהִלָּה
וְתִפְאֶרֶת קְדֻשָּׁה וּמַלְכוּת בְּרָכוֹת וְהוֹדָאוֹת לְשִׁמְךָ הַגָּדוֹל וְהַקָּדוֹשׁ
וּמֵעוֹלָם וְעַד עוֹלָם אַתָּה אֵל.

every shall tongue praise You, every eye shall hope in You, every knee shall bend to You, every upright being shall prostrate itself before You, all hearts shall fear You, and all vital organs sing to Your Name, according to the word that is written, "All my bones shall say, 'Who is like You *Hashem*, Who saves the afflicted from one stronger than he and the poor and destitute from one who would rob him?'"[350] The outcry of the afflicted You hear! The complaint of the downtrodden You heed and save [him]. And it is written, "Sing, righteous ones, among [those who praise] *Hashem*; for the upright praise is desirable."[351]

In the mouth of the upright may You be exalted, by the lips of the righteous may You be blessed, by the tongue of the pious may You be sanctified and among the holy ones may You be praised...

among the myriad congregations of Your people, the House of Israel, for such is the obligation of all creatures before You *Hashem*, our God and God of our ancestors, to thank, praise, acclaim, glorify, exalt, adulate, and worship with all the words of song and praise of David, son of Jesse, Your anointed servant. And, therefore...

May Your Name be praised forever, our King, the God who is the great and holy King in Heaven and Earth, for to You is fitting *Hashem*, our God and God of our ancestors, forever and ever, song and praise, acclaim and hymn, strength and dominion, victory, greatness, might, adulation and glory, holiness and kingship, blessings and acknowledgement to Your great and holy Name, and from eternity unto eternity You are God.

---

[350] Psalms 35:10. Although people cannot physically perceive God now, after the dead are resurrected, the physical body will become refined so that it will be able to appreciate holiness (See *Ramban* in *Sha'ar Hagemul*).
[351] Psalms 33:1.

יְהַלְלוּךָ יְהֹוָה אֱלֹהֵינוּ כָּל מַעֲשֶׂיךָ וַחֲסִידֶיךָ צַדִּיקִים עוֹשֵׂי רְצוֹנֶךָ וְעַמְּךָ בֵּית יִשְׂרָאֵל כֻּלָּם בְּרִנָּה יוֹדוּ וִיבָרְכוּ וִישַׁבְּחוּ וִיפָאֲרוּ אֶת שֵׁם כְּבוֹדֶךָ כִּי לְךָ טוֹב לְהוֹדוֹת וּלְשִׁמְךָ נָעִים לְזַמֵּר וּמֵעוֹלָם וְעַד עוֹלָם אַתָּה אֵל. בָּרוּךְ אַתָּה יְהֹוָה מֶלֶךְ מְהֻלָּל בַּתִּשְׁבָּחוֹת.

שותים את הכוס הרביעית בהסבה בלי ברכה ראשונה ואחרי השתיה מברכים:

בָּרוּךְ אַתָּה יְהֹוָה אֱלֹהֵינוּ מֶלֶךְ הָעוֹלָם עַל הַגֶּפֶן וְעַל פְּרִי הַגֶּפֶן וְעַל תְּנוּבַת הַשָּׂדֶה וְעַל אֶרֶץ חֶמְדָּה טוֹבָה וּרְחָבָה שֶׁרָצִיתָ וְהִנְחַלְתָּ לַאֲבוֹתֵינוּ לֶאֱכוֹל מִפִּרְיָהּ וְלִשְׂבּוֹעַ מִטּוּבָהּ. רַחֶם יְהֹוָה אֱלֹהֵינוּ עָלֵינוּ וְעַל יִשְׂרָאֵל עַמֶּךָ וְעַל יְרוּשָׁלַיִם עִירֶךָ וְעַל הַר צִיּוֹן מִשְׁכַּן כְּבוֹדֶךָ וְעַל מִזְבְּחֶךָ וְעַל הֵיכָלֶךָ. וּבְנֵה יְרוּשָׁלַיִם עִיר הַקֹּדֶשׁ בִּמְהֵרָה בְיָמֵינוּ וְהַעֲלֵנוּ לְתוֹכָהּ וְשַׂמְּחֵנוּ בְּבִנְיָנָהּ וּנְבָרֶכְךָ עָלֶיהָ בִּקְדֻשָּׁה וּבְטָהֳרָה [בשבת: וּרְצֵה וְהַחֲלִיצֵנוּ בְּיוֹם הַשַּׁבָּת הַזֶּה] וְשַׂמְּחֵנוּ בְּיוֹם חַג הַמַּצּוֹת הַזֶּה בְּיוֹם טוֹב מִקְרָא קֹדֶשׁ הַזֶּה כִּי אַתָּה טוֹב וּמֵטִיב לַכֹּל וְנוֹדֶה לְּךָ יְהֹוָה אֱלֹהֵינוּ עַל הָאָרֶץ וְעַל פְּרִי הַגֶּפֶן [בארץ ישראל אומרים "גַפְנָהּ" במקום "הַגֶּפֶן"]. בָּרוּךְ אַתָּה יְהֹוָה עַל הָאָרֶץ וְעַל פְּרִי הַגֶּפֶן. [בארץ ישראל מסיימים "גַפְנָהּ" במקום "הַגֶּפֶן"]

 נִרְצָה

מצוה להמשיך לספר אודות יציאת מצרים אפילו אחרי סיום הסדר. לכן מנהג להמשיך עם אמירת "אֶחָד מִי יוֹדֵעַ" הנמצא בדף 137.

May all Your works praise You *Hashem*, our God, and Your pious and righteous ones who perform Your will, and Your people, the House of Israel, in their entirety, with song shall thank, bless, praise, and glorify Your honored Name, for You it is fitting to acknowledge, and to Your Name it is pleasant to sing, and from eternity to eternity You are God. Blessed are You, God, King Who is praised with acclamations.

The Fourth Cup should be drunk while reclining on the left side without first reciting a blessing. After finishing the wine, say:

Blessed are You *Hashem*, our God, King of the Universe, for the vine, for the fruit of the vine, for the produce of the field, and for the good, desirable, and spacious land which You desired and bequeathed to our ancestors to eat from its fruit and to be satisfied from its goodness. Have mercy *Hashem*, our God, upon us and upon Israel Your people, on Jerusalem Your city, on Mount Zion, the habitation of Your glory, on Your altar, and on Your Sanctuary. Rebuild the holy city of Jerusalem speedily in our days, bring us up to it, gladden us with its restoration, and we will bless You upon it in holiness and purity. [*On the Sabbath add*: Take pleasure and grant us relief on this Sabbath day.] Gladden us on this day of the festival of *Matzoth*, on this holiday of holy gathering, for You are good and do good to all, and we thank You *Hashem*, our God, for the Land and for the fruit of the vine [in the Land of Israel, substitute "for the fruit of its vine"]. Blessed are You *Hashem* for the Land and for the fruit of the vine. [In the Land of Israel, this blessing concludes "for the fruit of its vine" instead of "for the fruit of the vine."]

CONCLUSION

It is a *Mitzvah* to continue discussing the Exodus even after the conclusion of the *Seder*, so it is customary to continue with "Who knows one?" (אֶחָד מִי יוֹדֵעַ) on page 138.

Some have the custom to recite the Song of Songs after the *Seder*:

א א שִׁיר הַשִּׁירִים אֲשֶׁר לִשְׁלֹמֹה: ב יִשָּׁקֵנִי מִנְּשִׁיקוֹת פִּיהוּ כִּי טוֹבִים דֹּדֶיךָ
מִיָּיִן: ג לְרֵיחַ שְׁמָנֶיךָ טוֹבִים שֶׁמֶן תּוּרַק שְׁמֶךָ עַל כֵּן עֲלָמוֹת אֲהֵבוּךָ: ד מָשְׁכֵנִי אַחֲרֶיךָ
נָּרוּצָה הֱבִיאַנִי הַמֶּלֶךְ חֲדָרָיו נָגִילָה וְנִשְׂמְחָה בָּךְ נַזְכִּירָה דֹּדֶיךָ מִיַּיִן מֵישָׁרִים אֲהֵבוּךָ: ה
שְׁחוֹרָה אֲנִי וְנָאוָה בְּנוֹת יְרוּשָׁלִָם כְּאָהֳלֵי קֵדָר כִּירִיעוֹת שְׁלֹמֹה: ו אַל תִּרְאוּנִי שֶׁאֲנִי
שְׁחַרְחֹרֶת שֶׁשְּׁזָפַתְנִי הַשָּׁמֶשׁ בְּנֵי אִמִּי נִחֲרוּ בִי שָׂמֻנִי נֹטֵרָה אֶת הַכְּרָמִים כַּרְמִי שֶׁלִּי לֹא
נָטָרְתִּי: ז הַגִּידָה לִּי שֶׁאָהֲבָה נַפְשִׁי אֵיכָה תִרְעֶה אֵיכָה תַּרְבִּיץ בַּצָּהֳרָיִם שַׁלָּמָה אֶהְיֶה
כְּעֹטְיָה עַל עֶדְרֵי חֲבֵרֶיךָ: ח אִם לֹא תֵדְעִי לָךְ הַיָּפָה בַּנָּשִׁים צְאִי לָךְ בְּעִקְבֵי הַצֹּאן וּרְעִי אֶת
גְּדִיֹּתַיִךְ עַל מִשְׁכְּנוֹת הָרֹעִים: ט לְסֻסָתִי בְּרִכְבֵי פַרְעֹה דִּמִּיתִיךְ רַעְיָתִי: י נָאווּ לְחָיַיִךְ
בַּתֹּרִים צַוָּארֵךְ בַּחֲרוּזִים: יא תּוֹרֵי זָהָב נַעֲשֶׂה לָּךְ עִם נְקֻדּוֹת הַכָּסֶף: יב עַד שֶׁהַמֶּלֶךְ
בִּמְסִבּוֹ נִרְדִּי נָתַן רֵיחוֹ: יג צְרוֹר הַמֹּר דּוֹדִי לִי בֵּין שָׁדַי יָלִין: יד אֶשְׁכֹּל הַכֹּפֶר דּוֹדִי לִי
בְּכַרְמֵי עֵין גֶּדִי: טו הִנָּךְ יָפָה רַעְיָתִי הִנָּךְ יָפָה עֵינַיִךְ יוֹנִים: טז הִנְּךָ יָפֶה דוֹדִי אַף נָעִים אַף
עַרְשֵׂנוּ רַעֲנָנָה: יז קֹרוֹת בָּתֵּינוּ אֲרָזִים רָהִיטֵנוּ [רחיטנו כתיב] בְּרוֹתִים:

ב א אֲנִי חֲבַצֶּלֶת הַשָּׁרוֹן שׁוֹשַׁנַּת הָעֲמָקִים: ב כְּשׁוֹשַׁנָּה בֵּין הַחוֹחִים כֵּן רַעְיָתִי
בֵּין הַבָּנוֹת: ג כְּתַפּוּחַ בַּעֲצֵי הַיַּעַר כֵּן דּוֹדִי בֵּין הַבָּנִים בְּצִלּוֹ חִמַּדְתִּי וְיָשַׁבְתִּי וּפִרְיוֹ מָתוֹק
לְחִכִּי: ד הֱבִיאַנִי אֶל בֵּית הַיַּיִן וְדִגְלוֹ עָלַי אַהֲבָה: ה סַמְּכוּנִי בָּאֲשִׁישׁוֹת רַפְּדוּנִי בַּתַּפּוּחִים
כִּי חוֹלַת אַהֲבָה אָנִי: ו שְׂמֹאלוֹ תַּחַת לְרֹאשִׁי וִימִינוֹ תְּחַבְּקֵנִי: ז הִשְׁבַּעְתִּי אֶתְכֶם בְּנוֹת
יְרוּשָׁלִַם בִּצְבָאוֹת אוֹ בְּאַיְלוֹת הַשָּׂדֶה אִם תָּעִירוּ וְאִם תְּעוֹרְרוּ אֶת הָאַהֲבָה עַד שֶׁתֶּחְפָּץ: ח
קוֹל דּוֹדִי הִנֵּה זֶה בָּא מְדַלֵּג עַל הֶהָרִים מְקַפֵּץ עַל הַגְּבָעוֹת: ט דּוֹמֶה דוֹדִי לִצְבִי אוֹ לְעֹפֶר
הָאַיָּלִים הִנֵּה זֶה עוֹמֵד אַחַר כָּתְלֵנוּ מַשְׁגִּיחַ מִן הַחַלֹּנוֹת מֵצִיץ מִן הַחֲרַכִּים: י עָנָה דוֹדִי
וְאָמַר לִי קוּמִי לָךְ רַעְיָתִי יָפָתִי וּלְכִי לָךְ: יא כִּי הִנֵּה הַסְּתָיו [הסתו כתיב] עָבָר הַגֶּשֶׁם חָלַף
הָלַךְ לוֹ: יב הַנִּצָּנִים נִרְאוּ בָאָרֶץ עֵת הַזָּמִיר הִגִּיעַ וְקוֹל הַתּוֹר נִשְׁמַע בְּאַרְצֵנוּ: יג הַתְּאֵנָה
חָנְטָה פַגֶּיהָ וְהַגְּפָנִים סְמָדַר נָתְנוּ רֵיחַ קוּמִי לָךְ [לכי כתיב] רַעְיָתִי יָפָתִי וּלְכִי לָךְ: יד יוֹנָתִי
בְּחַגְוֵי הַסֶּלַע בְּסֵתֶר הַמַּדְרֵגָה הַרְאִינִי אֶת מַרְאַיִךְ הַשְׁמִיעִנִי אֶת קוֹלֵךְ כִּי קוֹלֵךְ עָרֵב וּמַרְאֵיךְ
נָאוֶה: טו אֶחֱזוּ לָנוּ שׁוּעָלִים שׁוּעָלִים קְטַנִּים מְחַבְּלִים כְּרָמִים וּכְרָמֵינוּ סְמָדַר: טז דּוֹדִי לִי
וַאֲנִי לוֹ הָרֹעֶה בַּשּׁוֹשַׁנִּים: יז עַד שֶׁיָּפוּחַ הַיּוֹם וְנָסוּ הַצְּלָלִים סֹב דְּמֵה לְךָ דוֹדִי לִצְבִי אוֹ
לְעֹפֶר הָאַיָּלִים עַל הָרֵי בָתֶר:

ג א עַל מִשְׁכָּבִי בַּלֵּילוֹת בִּקַּשְׁתִּי אֵת שֶׁאָהֲבָה נַפְשִׁי בִּקַּשְׁתִּיו וְלֹא מְצָאתִיו: ב
אָקוּמָה נָּא וַאֲסוֹבְבָה בָעִיר בַּשְּׁוָקִים וּבָרְחֹבוֹת אֲבַקְשָׁה אֵת שֶׁאָהֲבָה נַפְשִׁי בִּקַּשְׁתִּיו וְלֹא
מְצָאתִיו: ג מְצָאוּנִי הַשֹּׁמְרִים הַסֹּבְבִים בָּעִיר אֵת שֶׁאָהֲבָה נַפְשִׁי רְאִיתֶם: ד כִּמְעַט
שֶׁעָבַרְתִּי מֵהֶם עַד שֶׁמָּצָאתִי אֵת שֶׁאָהֲבָה נַפְשִׁי אֲחַזְתִּיו וְלֹא אַרְפֶּנּוּ עַד שֶׁהֲבֵיאתִיו אֶל בֵּית
אִמִּי וְאֶל חֶדֶר הוֹרָתִי: ה הִשְׁבַּעְתִּי אֶתְכֶם בְּנוֹת יְרוּשָׁלִַם בִּצְבָאוֹת אוֹ בְּאַיְלוֹת הַשָּׂדֶה אִם
תָּעִירוּ וְאִם תְּעוֹרְרוּ אֶת הָאַהֲבָה עַד שֶׁתֶּחְפָּץ: ו מִי זֹאת עֹלָה מִן הַמִּדְבָּר כְּתִימֲרוֹת עָשָׁן

מְקֻטֶּרֶת מוֹר וּלְבוֹנָה מִכֹּל אַבְקַת רוֹכֵל : ז הִנֵּה מִטָּתוֹ שֶׁלִּשְׁלֹמֹה שִׁשִּׁים גִּבֹּרִים סָבִיב לָהּ
מִגִּבֹּרֵי יִשְׂרָאֵל : ח כֻּלָּם אֲחֻזֵי חֶרֶב מְלֻמְּדֵי מִלְחָמָה אִישׁ חַרְבּוֹ עַל יְרֵכוֹ מִפַּחַד בַּלֵּילוֹת : ט
אַפִּרְיוֹן עָשָׂה לוֹ הַמֶּלֶךְ שְׁלֹמֹה מֵעֲצֵי הַלְּבָנוֹן : י עַמּוּדָיו עָשָׂה כֶסֶף רְפִידָתוֹ זָהָב מֶרְכָּבוֹ
אַרְגָּמָן תּוֹכוֹ רָצוּף אַהֲבָה מִבְּנוֹת יְרוּשָׁלָם : יא צְאֶינָה וּרְאֶינָה בְּנוֹת צִיּוֹן בַּמֶּלֶךְ שְׁלֹמֹה
בָּעֲטָרָה שֶׁעִטְּרָה לּוֹ אִמּוֹ בְּיוֹם חֲתֻנָּתוֹ וּבְיוֹם שִׂמְחַת לִבּוֹ :

ד א הִנָּךְ יָפָה רַעְיָתִי הִנָּךְ יָפָה עֵינַיִךְ יוֹנִים מִבַּעַד לְצַמָּתֵךְ שַׂעְרֵךְ כְּעֵדֶר הָעִזִּים
שֶׁגָּלְשׁוּ מֵהַר גִּלְעָד : ב שִׁנַּיִךְ כְּעֵדֶר הַקְּצוּבוֹת שֶׁעָלוּ מִן הָרַחְצָה שֶׁכֻּלָּם מַתְאִימוֹת וְשַׁכֻּלָה
אֵין בָּהֶם : ג כְּחוּט הַשָּׁנִי שִׂפְתוֹתַיִךְ וּמִדְבָּרֵיךְ נָאוֶה כְּפֶלַח הָרִמּוֹן רַקָּתֵךְ מִבַּעַד לְצַמָּתֵךְ : ד
כְּמִגְדַּל דָּוִיד צַוָּארֵךְ בָּנוּי לְתַלְפִּיּוֹת אֶלֶף הַמָּגֵן תָּלוּי עָלָיו כֹּל שִׁלְטֵי הַגִּבֹּרִים : ה שְׁנֵי
שָׁדַיִךְ כִּשְׁנֵי עֳפָרִים תְּאוֹמֵי צְבִיָּה הָרוֹעִים בַּשּׁוֹשַׁנִּים : ו עַד שֶׁיָּפוּחַ הַיּוֹם וְנָסוּ הַצְּלָלִים אֵלֶךְ
לִי אֶל הַר הַמּוֹר וְאֶל גִּבְעַת הַלְּבוֹנָה : ז כֻּלָּךְ יָפָה רַעְיָתִי וּמוּם אֵין בָּךְ : ח אִתִּי מִלְּבָנוֹן כַּלָּה
אִתִּי מִלְּבָנוֹן תָּבוֹאִי תָּשׁוּרִי מֵרֹאשׁ אֲמָנָה מֵרֹאשׁ שְׂנִיר וְחֶרְמוֹן מִמְּעֹנוֹת אֲרָיוֹת מֵהַרְרֵי
נְמֵרִים : ט לִבַּבְתִּנִי אֲחֹתִי כַלָּה לִבַּבְתִּינִי בְּאַחַת [בְּאַחַד כתיב] מֵעֵינַיִךְ בְּאַחַד עֲנָק מִצַּוְּרֹנָיִךְ :
י מַה יָּפוּ דֹדַיִךְ אֲחֹתִי כַלָּה מַה טֹּבוּ דֹדַיִךְ מִיַּיִן וְרֵיחַ שְׁמָנַיִךְ מִכָּל בְּשָׂמִים : יא נֹפֶת
תִּטֹּפְנָה שִׂפְתוֹתַיִךְ כַּלָּה דְּבַשׁ וְחָלָב תַּחַת לְשׁוֹנֵךְ וְרֵיחַ שַׂלְמֹתַיִךְ כְּרֵיחַ לְבָנוֹן : יב גַּן נָעוּל
אֲחֹתִי כַלָּה גַּל נָעוּל מַעְיָן חָתוּם : יג שְׁלָחַיִךְ פַּרְדֵּס רִמּוֹנִים עִם פְּרִי מְגָדִים כְּפָרִים עִם
נְרָדִים : יד נֵרְדְּ וְכַרְכֹּם קָנֶה וְקִנָּמוֹן עִם כָּל עֲצֵי לְבוֹנָה מֹר וַאֲהָלוֹת עִם כָּל רָאשֵׁי בְשָׂמִים :
טו מַעְיַן גַּנִּים בְּאֵר מַיִם חַיִּים וְנֹזְלִים מִן לְבָנוֹן : טז עוּרִי צָפוֹן וּבוֹאִי תֵימָן הָפִיחִי גַנִּי יִזְּלוּ
בְשָׂמָיו יָבֹא דוֹדִי לְגַנּוֹ וְיֹאכַל פְּרִי מְגָדָיו :

ה א בָּאתִי לְגַנִּי אֲחֹתִי כַלָּה אָרִיתִי מוֹרִי עִם בְּשָׂמִי אָכַלְתִּי יַעְרִי עִם דִּבְשִׁי
שָׁתִיתִי יֵינִי עִם חֲלָבִי אִכְלוּ רֵעִים שְׁתוּ וְשִׁכְרוּ דּוֹדִים : ב אֲנִי יְשֵׁנָה וְלִבִּי עֵר קוֹל דּוֹדִי דוֹפֵק
פִּתְחִי לִי אֲחֹתִי רַעְיָתִי יוֹנָתִי תַמָּתִי שֶׁרֹּאשִׁי נִמְלָא טָל קְוֻצּוֹתַי רְסִיסֵי לָיְלָה : ג פָּשַׁטְתִּי אֶת
כֻּתָּנְתִּי אֵיכָכָה אֶלְבָּשֶׁנָּה רָחַצְתִּי אֶת רַגְלַי אֵיכָכָה אֲטַנְּפֵם : ד דּוֹדִי שָׁלַח יָדוֹ מִן הַחֹר וּמֵעַי
הָמוּ עָלָיו : ה קַמְתִּי אֲנִי לִפְתֹּחַ לְדוֹדִי וְיָדַי נָטְפוּ מוֹר וְאֶצְבְּעֹתַי מוֹר עֹבֵר עַל כַּפּוֹת
הַמַּנְעוּל : ו פָּתַחְתִּי אֲנִי לְדוֹדִי וְדוֹדִי חָמַק עָבָר נַפְשִׁי יָצְאָה בְדַבְּרוֹ בִּקַּשְׁתִּיהוּ וְלֹא
מְצָאתִיהוּ קְרָאתִיו וְלֹא עָנָנִי : ז מְצָאֻנִי הַשֹּׁמְרִים הַסֹּבְבִים בָּעִיר הִכּוּנִי פְצָעוּנִי נָשְׂאוּ אֶת
רְדִידִי מֵעָלַי שֹׁמְרֵי הַחֹמוֹת : ח הִשְׁבַּעְתִּי אֶתְכֶם בְּנוֹת יְרוּשָׁלָם אִם תִּמְצְאוּ אֶת דּוֹדִי מַה
תַּגִּידוּ לוֹ שֶׁחוֹלַת אַהֲבָה אָנִי : ט מַה דּוֹדֵךְ מִדּוֹד הַיָּפָה בַּנָּשִׁים מַה דּוֹדֵךְ מִדּוֹד שֶׁכָּכָה
הִשְׁבַּעְתָּנוּ : י דּוֹדִי צַח וְאָדוֹם דָּגוּל מֵרְבָבָה : יא רֹאשׁוֹ כֶּתֶם פָּז קְוֻצּוֹתָיו תַּלְתַּלִּים שְׁחֹרוֹת
כָּעוֹרֵב : יב עֵינָיו כְּיוֹנִים עַל אֲפִיקֵי מָיִם רֹחֲצוֹת בֶּחָלָב יֹשְׁבוֹת עַל מִלֵּאת : יג לְחָיָו
כַּעֲרוּגַת הַבֹּשֶׂם מִגְדְּלוֹת מֶרְקָחִים שִׂפְתוֹתָיו שׁוֹשַׁנִּים נֹטְפוֹת מוֹר עֹבֵר : יד יָדָיו גְּלִילֵי זָהָב
מְמֻלָּאִים בַּתַּרְשִׁישׁ מֵעָיו עֶשֶׁת שֵׁן מְעֻלֶּפֶת סַפִּירִים : טו שׁוֹקָיו עַמּוּדֵי שֵׁשׁ מְיֻסָּדִים עַל
אַדְנֵי פָז מַרְאֵהוּ כַּלְּבָנוֹן בָּחוּר כָּאֲרָזִים : טז חִכּוֹ מַמְתַקִּים וְכֻלּוֹ מַחֲמַדִּים זֶה דוֹדִי וְזֶה רֵעִי
בְּנוֹת יְרוּשָׁלָם :

ו א אָנָה הָלַךְ דּוֹדֵךְ הַיָּפָה בַּנָּשִׁים אָנָה פָּנָה דוֹדֵךְ וּנְבַקְשֶׁנּוּ עִמָּךְ: ב דּוֹדִי יָרַד
לְגַנּוֹ לַעֲרוּגוֹת הַבֹּשֶׂם לִרְעוֹת בַּגַּנִּים וְלִלְקֹט שׁוֹשַׁנִּים: ג אֲנִי לְדוֹדִי וְדוֹדִי לִי הָרֹעֶה
בַּשּׁוֹשַׁנִּים: ד יָפָה אַתְּ רַעְיָתִי כְּתִרְצָה נָאוָה כִּירוּשָׁלָ͏ִם אֲיֻמָּה כַּנִּדְגָּלוֹת: ה הָסֵבִּי עֵינַיִךְ
מִנֶּגְדִּי שֶׁהֵם הִרְהִיבֻנִי שַׂעְרֵךְ כְּעֵדֶר הָעִזִּים שֶׁגָּלְשׁוּ מִן הַגִּלְעָד: ו שִׁנַּיִךְ כְּעֵדֶר הָרְחֵלִים
שֶׁעָלוּ מִן הָרַחְצָה שֶׁכֻּלָּם מַתְאִימוֹת וְשַׁכֻּלָה אֵין בָּהֶם: ז כְּפֶלַח הָרִמּוֹן רַקָּתֵךְ מִבַּעַד
לְצַמָּתֵךְ: ח שִׁשִּׁים הֵמָּה מְלָכוֹת וּשְׁמֹנִים פִּילַגְשִׁים וַעֲלָמוֹת אֵין מִסְפָּר: ט אַחַת הִיא יוֹנָתִי
תַמָּתִי אַחַת הִיא לְאִמָּהּ בָּרָה הִיא לְיוֹלַדְתָּהּ רָאוּהָ בָנוֹת וַיְאַשְּׁרוּהָ מְלָכוֹת וּפִילַגְשִׁים
וַיְהַלְלוּהָ: י מִי זֹאת הַנִּשְׁקָפָה כְּמוֹ שָׁחַר יָפָה כַלְּבָנָה בָּרָה כַּחַמָּה אֲיֻמָּה כַּנִּדְגָּלוֹת: יא אֶל
גִּנַּת אֱגוֹז יָרַדְתִּי לִרְאוֹת בְּאִבֵּי הַנָּחַל לִרְאוֹת הֲפָרְחָה הַגֶּפֶן הֵנֵצוּ הָרִמֹּנִים: יב לֹא יָדַעְתִּי
נַפְשִׁי שָׂמַתְנִי מַרְכְּבוֹת עַמִּי נָדִיב:

ז א שׁוּבִי שׁוּבִי הַשּׁוּלַמִּית שׁוּבִי שׁוּבִי וְנֶחֱזֶה בָּךְ מַה תֶּחֱזוּ בַּשּׁוּלַמִּית כִּמְחֹלַת
הַמַּחֲנָיִם: ב מַה יָּפוּ פְעָמַיִךְ בַּנְּעָלִים בַּת נָדִיב חַמּוּקֵי יְרֵכַיִךְ כְּמוֹ חֲלָאִים מַעֲשֵׂה יְדֵי אָמָּן:
ג שָׁרְרֵךְ אַגַּן הַסַּהַר אַל יֶחְסַר הַמָּזֶג בִּטְנֵךְ עֲרֵמַת חִטִּים סוּגָה בַּשּׁוֹשַׁנִּים: ד שְׁנֵי שָׁדַיִךְ כִּשְׁנֵי
עֳפָרִים תָּאֳמֵי צְבִיָּה: ה צַוָּארֵךְ כְּמִגְדַּל הַשֵּׁן עֵינַיִךְ בְּרֵכוֹת בְּחֶשְׁבּוֹן עַל שַׁעַר בַּת רַבִּים אַפֵּךְ
כְּמִגְדַּל הַלְּבָנוֹן צוֹפֶה פְּנֵי דַמָּשֶׂק: ו רֹאשֵׁךְ עָלַיִךְ כַּכַּרְמֶל וְדַלַּת רֹאשֵׁךְ כָּאַרְגָּמָן מֶלֶךְ אָסוּר
בָּרְהָטִים: ז מַה יָּפִית וּמַה נָּעַמְתְּ אַהֲבָה בַּתַּעֲנוּגִים: ח זֹאת קוֹמָתֵךְ דָּמְתָה לְתָמָר וְשָׁדַיִךְ
לְאַשְׁכֹּלוֹת: ט אָמַרְתִּי אֶעֱלֶה בְתָמָר אֹחֲזָה בְּסַנְסִנָּיו וְיִהְיוּ נָא שָׁדַיִךְ כְּאֶשְׁכְּלוֹת הַגֶּפֶן וְרֵיחַ
אַפֵּךְ כַּתַּפּוּחִים: י וְחִכֵּךְ כְּיֵין הַטּוֹב הוֹלֵךְ לְדוֹדִי לְמֵישָׁרִים דּוֹבֵב שִׂפְתֵי יְשֵׁנִים: יא אֲנִי
לְדוֹדִי וְעָלַי תְּשׁוּקָתוֹ: יב לְכָה דוֹדִי נֵצֵא הַשָּׂדֶה נָלִינָה בַּכְּפָרִים: יג נַשְׁכִּימָה לַכְּרָמִים
נִרְאֶה אִם פָּרְחָה הַגֶּפֶן פִּתַּח הַסְּמָדַר הֵנֵצוּ הָרִמּוֹנִים שָׁם אֶתֵּן אֶת דֹּדַי לָךְ: יד הַדּוּדָאִים
נָתְנוּ רֵיחַ וְעַל פְּתָחֵינוּ כָּל מְגָדִים חֲדָשִׁים גַּם יְשָׁנִים דּוֹדִי צָפַנְתִּי לָךְ:

ח א מִי יִתֶּנְךָ כְּאָח לִי יוֹנֵק שְׁדֵי אִמִּי אֶמְצָאֲךָ בַחוּץ אֶשָּׁקְךָ גַּם לֹא יָבֻזוּ לִי: ב
אֶנְהָגֲךָ אֲבִיאֲךָ אֶל בֵּית אִמִּי תְּלַמְּדֵנִי אַשְׁקְךָ מִיַּיִן הָרֶקַח מֵעֲסִיס רִמֹּנִי: ג שְׂמֹאלוֹ תַּחַת
רֹאשִׁי וִימִינוֹ תְּחַבְּקֵנִי: ד הִשְׁבַּעְתִּי אֶתְכֶם בְּנוֹת יְרוּשָׁלָ͏ִם מַה תָּעִירוּ וּמַה תְּעֹרְרוּ אֶת
הָאַהֲבָה עַד שֶׁתֶּחְפָּץ: ה מִי זֹאת עֹלָה מִן הַמִּדְבָּר מִתְרַפֶּקֶת עַל דּוֹדָהּ תַּחַת הַתַּפּוּחַ
עוֹרַרְתִּיךָ שָׁמָּה חִבְּלַתְךָ אִמֶּךָ שָׁמָּה חִבְּלָה יְלָדַתְךָ: ו שִׂימֵנִי כַחוֹתָם עַל לִבֶּךָ כַּחוֹתָם עַל
זְרוֹעֶךָ כִּי עַזָּה כַמָּוֶת אַהֲבָה קָשָׁה כִשְׁאוֹל קִנְאָה רְשָׁפֶיהָ רִשְׁפֵּי אֵשׁ שַׁלְהֶבֶתְיָה: ז מַיִם רַבִּים
לֹא יוּכְלוּ לְכַבּוֹת אֶת הָאַהֲבָה וּנְהָרוֹת לֹא יִשְׁטְפוּהָ אִם יִתֵּן אִישׁ אֶת כָּל הוֹן בֵּיתוֹ בָּאַהֲבָה
בּוֹז יָבוּזוּ לוֹ: ח אָחוֹת לָנוּ קְטַנָּה וְשָׁדַיִם אֵין לָהּ מַה נַּעֲשֶׂה לַאֲחֹתֵנוּ בַּיּוֹם שֶׁיְּדֻבַּר בָּהּ: ט
אִם חוֹמָה הִיא נִבְנֶה עָלֶיהָ טִירַת כָּסֶף וְאִם דֶּלֶת הִיא נָצוּר עָלֶיהָ לוּחַ אָרֶז: י אֲנִי חוֹמָה
וְשָׁדַי כַּמִּגְדָּלוֹת אָז הָיִיתִי בְעֵינָיו כְּמוֹצְאֵת שָׁלוֹם: יא כֶּרֶם הָיָה לִשְׁלֹמֹה בְּבַעַל הָמוֹן נָתַן
אֶת הַכֶּרֶם לַנֹּטְרִים אִישׁ יָבִא בְּפִרְיוֹ אֶלֶף כָּסֶף: יב כַּרְמִי שֶׁלִּי לְפָנָי הָאֶלֶף לְךָ שְׁלֹמֹה
וּמָאתַיִם לְנֹטְרִים אֶת פִּרְיוֹ: יג הַיּוֹשֶׁבֶת בַּגַּנִּים חֲבֵרִים מַקְשִׁיבִים לְקוֹלֵךְ הַשְׁמִיעִנִי: יד
בְּרַח דּוֹדִי וּדְמֵה לְךָ לִצְבִי אוֹ לְעֹפֶר הָאַיָּלִים עַל הָרֵי בְשָׂמִים:

This page is dedicated in honor of our long-time supporters and benefactors —

THE GHERMEZIAN FAMILY
AND
THE DANESH FAMILY

May they enjoy נחת and success in all their endeavors.

Rabbi Reuben Khaver
and the members of
Ohr Nissan Talmud Center

לעלוי נשמות

שלמה בן אהרון ז״ל

עובדיה בן אהרון ז״ל

דוד בן אהרון ז״ל

דולת בת אהרון ז״ל

אפת בת עזיז ז״ל

תהי נשמתם צרורה בצרור החיים

לעלוי נשמות

גאדל אהרון בן נחום ז״ל

שלומית יהודית בת בנימין ז״ל

לאה בת חיים ז״ל

פייגע דוואשע בת חיים ז״ל

תהי נשמתם צרורה בצרור החיים

לעלוי נשמת

עליזה חיה ז״ל

בת

יחיאל יהודה ליב שיחיה

תהי נשמתה צרורה בצרור החיים

לעלוי נשמות

In loving memory of

DR. JUDAH KATZNELSON

יהודה בן הרב מאיר זביל ז"ל

and

MR. FRED STERBA

נח בן יהודה אריה ז"ל

Beloved Husband and Father of
Eva Katzenlson

תהי נשמתם צרורה בצרור החיים